Fair Share

Index

Fair Share

Senior Activism, Tiny Publics, and the Culture of Resistance

GARY ALAN FINE

The University of Chicago Press
Chicago and London

The University of Chicago Press, Chicago 60637
The University of Chicago Press, Ltd., London
© 2023 by The University of Chicago
Published 2023
Printed in the United States of America

32 31 30 29 28 27 26 25 24 23   1 2 3 4 5

ISBN-13: 978-0-226-82381-2 (cloth)
ISBN-13: 978-0-226-82383-6 (paper)
ISBN-13: 978-0-226-82382-9 (e-book)
DOI: https://doi.org/10.7208/chicago/9780226823829.001.0001

Library of Congress Cataloging-in-Publication Data

Names: Fine, Gary Alan, author.
Title: Fair share : senior activism, tiny publics, and the culture of resistance /
    Gary Alan Fine.
Other titles: Senior activism, tiny publics, and the culture of resistance
Description: Chicago : University of Chicago Press, 2023. | Includes bibliographical
    references and index.
Identifiers: LCCN 2022017563 | ISBN 9780226823812 (cloth) | ISBN 9780226823836
    (paperback) | ISBN 9780226823829 (ebook)
Subjects: LCSH: Older people—Political activity—Illinois—Chicago. | Senior
    power—Illinois—Chicago. | Political activists—Illinois—Chicago. | Community
    organization—Illinois—Chicago. | Social movements—Illinois—Chicago.|
    Progressivism (United States politics) | Chicago (Ill.)—Politics and government. |
    United States—Politics and government—2017–2021.
Classification: LCC HQ1064.U6 1324 2023 | DDC 305.2609773/11—dc23/eng/20220425
LC record available at https://lccn.loc.gov/2022017563

♾ This paper meets the requirements of ANSI/NISO Z39.48-1992
(Permanence of Paper).

To my late friends, above or below, who demand that angels provide all a fair share and demons confront infernal warming

Contents

Prologue

A Snowy Day in Racine

What a difference a day makes! With the inauguration of Donald J. Trump as the forty-fifth president of the United States on January 20, 2017, after a bitter campaign, a surprising election night, and for some a dismaying outcome, progressive political activists were galvanized into action. The day after his swearing in, as many as five million Americans participated in women's marches in cities throughout the United States, one of the largest single-day protests in American history. Some 250,000 protesters gathered in Chicago's Grant Park.

As the winter progressed, protests were held weekly in Chicago on what were termed Resist Trump Tuesdays (known more pungently as FU Trump Tuesdays). Although the energy began strong, it waned and demonstrations were less well attended, eventually ending in April. Often the spirit was willing but the flesh was weak. Still, it was remarkable that these gatherings continued through a frigid Chicago winter. Living in a windy, icy city can be a struggle for anyone,[1] but it is especially hard for seniors with mobility challenges. Although seniors may be marginalized in social movements and in civic life generally because of their vulnerability and because of dismissive beliefs toward the elderly, they provide powerful images of the necessity for social justice. Their vulnerability becomes a symbolic resource that gives a movement moral authority, and their numbers give the movement strength.

I depict the movement culture and political activism of senior citizens through an account of one yeasty group: a tiny public. I begin by describing a demonstration held during that first season of the nascent Trump administration. Despite the weather—or because of it—the event became a central focus of the group's collective memory and both reflected the way activists produce a public performance and revealed its limits.

In Chicago, a coalition of progressive groups organized these Resist Trump Tuesdays, rotating responsibility for planning weekly events, each with a different theme. I attended several protests, including one fronted by the group I call Chicago Seniors Together, my ethnographic site. On this Tuesday in March, the organization decided to send busloads of seniors and other supporters to the Racine, Wisconsin, office of Congressman Paul Ryan, the Republican Speaker of the House of Representatives, to protest feared cuts to Social Security and Medicare.

This was a matter of impassioned concern for many seniors, even if the cuts were unlikely to be enacted. These seniors suggested, perhaps with justice, that it was because of the energy of protesters that the Republican majorities preserved this sacred social compact. As Dina, one of the elderly protesters, pointed out, "We brought the message that health care is a human right." Her friend Lisa remarked, "We're going with the message that we want health care for all." She added, echoing the 1960s, the origin of her activist career, "We're going to take the streets" (field notes). Today we hear this demand in the calls among progressives for "Medicare for All."

The organization hoped this demonstration would be a major gathering bringing allies together, even if it was unlikely that the Speaker would be present in his local constituency office. They were more hopeful that they would receive favorable media attention. Counting members of the organization and allies from Chicago and southeastern Wisconsin, we numbered approximately 125 souls, mostly older women. As the weather darkened, these intrepid seniors and their staff organizers got their wish for drama. A snowstorm moved into Racine County, and some seventeen inches, much of it lake effect snow, fell on the small city, at times producing whiteout conditions. (Approximately five inches fell in Chicago during this same period.) Although staffers considered canceling the rally, they chose to proceed, while fretting that few would brave the elements. Some seniors did cancel, but the decision to go ahead was wise.

Perhaps because this was in the early glow of the Trump Resistance when opposition to the new administration seemed thrilling, perhaps because it was an adventure, or perhaps because Chicago was not blanketed so deep, the two buses were filled with excited, chattering seniors.

We joked about the worsening weather as we drove north for seventy-five miles. The snow grew deeper and thicker and the winds got harsher. The storm was routinely described as a blizzard, although this label was inaccurate in strictly meteorological terms. Finally we arrived at the Olympia Brown Unitarian Church in downtown Racine, two blocks from Congressman Ryan's local office, to discover that the chair lift on one of the buses didn't work

FIGURE 1. A snowy day in Racine, Wisconsin

properly. By late morning, snowdrifts in downtown Racine reached three feet and sidewalks were slick. Walking on these streets challenged even those with perfect balance. After trooping into the church to get warm, to get caffeinated, and to take a potty break (toilets are essential for senior activism), over one hundred numb demonstrators trudged out into the slashing snow, snaking a line on the nearly deserted pavements of this small midwestern city. Organizers asked seatmates to look out for each other in case someone got lost, and they selected gregarious individuals to be chant leaders and marshals to keep the march orderly.

We must have been a strange sight as demonstrators, some using canes, walkers, and motorized chairs, negotiated the nearly impassable sidewalks, walking slowly and unsteadily over the growing mounds of snow. We marched by Congressman Ryan's office twice, chanting, then gathered on a nearby plaza where the outdoor portion of the program had been planned. We didn't notice whether Ryan's staffers peered out, and the demonstrators didn't try to enter the building. Whether workers were aware of the demonstration or whether they cared couldn't be determined. Several Racine police officers were present in case of disruptions or medical emergencies, no doubt vexed at being stationed outdoors.

Later, the coalition eagerly noted the press attention that the demonstration received in Wisconsin, in the Chicago media market, and—mostly—on the network of progressive websites. Elderly activists demonstrating in a snowstorm provide a powerful visual, their fear framed by the chill weather. However, it's difficult to determine if the effort had any effect in shaping public opinion in the Badger State or beyond. It didn't alter the stance of the Speaker of the House. If demonstrators march on an empty street, does anyone hear their tread?

In truth this assessment might be too dismissive, and not only because a mere handful of viewers or readers might have had their opinions changed or strengthened. More to the point, the demonstration increased the protesters' commitment as they shared a moment and an experience. The blustery weather enhanced collective memory and generated narratives demonstrating that, despite their infirmities, these elderly Americans cared enough to persevere in demanding what they considered justice.

Although one staff organizer claimed that "we didn't luck out with the snow," this might have been precisely wrong. Lacking snow, it would have been just a road trip, not a source of heroic stories. Recognizing this history and the friendships that emerged proved powerful in creating a group culture. If not sufficient in itself to motivate future protests, such attachments are a necessary feature of movement work. The combination of memory and commitment characterizes successful social movements.[2] A movement is a community; robust narratives cement this affiliation. On the bus, demonstrators gaily shared cookies and other treats with old and new friends. Returning, seniors proudly recounted how they overcame the opposition from the skies, reveling in their willingness to transform values into action despite discomfort.

The march was dramatic, but the speeches made protesters' demands explicit and powerful. The march had to be leavened by group talk, making clear the significance of our shared experience. Two places were set aside for talk: the platform at the outdoor square and the church where we reassembled for our box lunches. Perhaps talk isn't as dramatic as action in long-term recall, but it shapes memories by highlighting salient actions and provides a language for recollection and sharing. Further, the speeches revealed that the demonstration grew from the experiences of the everyday participants and not the strategies of the professional staff.

None could doubt the speakers' ardent feelings of injustice, even if this was only talk. On the stage were a Racine councilwoman, a local minister, and several African American community leaders. But this wasn't all. Members of Chicago Seniors Together recounted the harrowing medical conditions they and their family members suffered—in one case including renal failure—

requiring government support. One passionately described her daughter's epilepsy. Their audience received these personal stories as a powerful indictment of a coldhearted politician and an uncaring bureaucracy and pressed the need for involvement.[3] The cases were treated not as anecdotal, but as representative. As the stories personalized the problem, pointing to malign structural forces, they provided emotional jolts that made the demonstration a demand for moral clarity.[4] Each brief talk was filled with details that conveyed the personal stakes of the protesters.

Inside the warm, comfortable church, storytelling continued, each tale building a case against Republicans' unconcern. One older activist who'd had a double organ transplant shared his fear, saying, "I can't afford life without health insurance. My insurance has literally saved my life. Millions of people will lose their insurance in Paul Ryan's plan." As a staffer explained, "We want to continue to tell these stories. . . . Keep your stories [coming] because that keeps our movement going." Making narratives personal and having them spoken makes them harder to challenge and easier to accept. Of course, the audience was primed to embrace these premises, even if they omitted specific policy prescriptions.

These chilly examples were matched by heated rhetoric: "We'll have to eat dog food. That ain't right. It's a death plan. We'll resist!" or "Mr. Trump, where's the truth? . . . This is mean and shameful" (field notes). Although the tenor of the event was joyful, the emotions were often raw. The pain expressed in talk led to a communal consciousness of why their gathering mattered. The postcards that organizers asked marchers to send Speaker Ryan were filled with demands and invective. One woman shared her tough message with pride: she got plaudits for her "sassy" comments. Whether or not her comments impressed the congressman, they allowed us to *joke in anger*.

Given the mix of severe weather and the lack of any immediate effect, I was moved by my friends' enthusiasm and by their eagerness to chant slogans, capturing shared fears in pithy form: "Ryan keeps lying, people keep dying"; "We want health care, not Ryan's wealth care"; and, most curiously, "Ryan and Trump, sitting in a tree, / taking all the health care they can see. / First comes kids, then comes seniors, / then comes all but the one percenters." If this reflected a certain adolescent rebellion—a merging of angst and jouissance—so did the colorful posters ("Repeal and Replace Paul Ryan"; "Ryan, Have You No Mercy?") that, except for their political wrath, might have adorned a high school prom. Senior protest can smell like teen spirit.

Heading home, riders were asked to give a feeling word that described their experience (a common strategy after meetings and demonstrations). Many claimed to be "energized" or some equivalent positive synonym—

far outnumbering those who claimed to be "cold." These emotions justified the travail.

Most relevant to my argument is the claim made by the executive director of a Wisconsin progressive organization after we had retired to the church to warm up with coffee or tea. He declared, "Democracy is not just voting, it's what you did today. They frankly didn't expect you to brave the snow and be out there today.... We will go forward" (field notes). This remark spoke to the protesters' values, but it also addressed the intertwined concepts of a persistent and resistant group culture ("they frankly didn't expect you") and a duty to perform collective action ("it's what you did"). The combination permits social movements to "go forward."

As I describe in chapter 4, the demonstration in Racine reverberated in the collective memory of these senior activists. Despite its doubtful public effect, the event reflected a moment of intense commitment, mentioned whenever the group needed to reaffirm its members' willingness to sacrifice for justice.

The demonstration and its recall connect to issues that I address throughout the book: how ideology is structured, how national politics become local, how actions are organized and judged, how memories are narrated, what determines the relationship of an organization's staff and members, how group culture shapes forms of protest, and how networks support movement politics. Each of these themes addresses the activism that characterizes social movements in contemporary America, and each is shaped by the reality that these are seniors who have personal vulnerabilities but who care about the fate of their nation, their community, and their families as well as themselves. I do not claim these are the only people who care deeply about justice. Similar commitments, although different in content, are found among conservatives and libertarians, even perhaps among the proud boys and girls of the Boogaloo, Black Lives Matter, and Antifa movements. Members of each group lay on the line their bodies, their voices, and their wallets. They ask for fairness, justice, and civic virtue as they perceive these values, and they do this in the context of vibrant tiny publics, made up of marchers for justice who matter to each other, with whom they identify and share experience.

This modest demonstration on the empty, muffled, impassable streets of Racine provides my point of entry for considering what it means to join a social movement, a fight for justice, and a community of senior citizens. This action of the vulnerable and the committed presents the puzzle of how seniors as civic actors can be simultaneously marginalized and influential—in snow and in sun. A fair share is not just something demanded from the wealthy but a gift that seniors give each other as they willingly participate in a contentious democracy.

Introduction

Of Seniors, for Seniors

I was raised in a reliably progressive household, the oldest son of a Freudian psychoanalyst. Although I was not a red diaper baby, my nappies were light pink. My parents were liberal Democrats who contributed to the NAACP and the ACLU. My mother flirted briefly with the Communist Party in college—or, given the gender politics in that masculinist organization, perhaps they flirted with her.

I belong to the baby boom generation, a cohort now slowly being nudged off the civic stage. My first political memory was, as a ten-year-old in 1960, handing out literature for Adlai Stevenson as he attempted, unsuccessfully, to contest the candidacy of the more conservative John F. Kennedy. I attended the Democratic National Convention in 1968, for which I had cadged a press pass, and participated in a few demonstrations. In sum, I am an ethnographer who, as a senior citizen, belongs to the generation I describe and functions as an amiable spectator of the politics I encountered.

Seniors in Action

Seniors are a potent political force.[1] As a pressure group, seniors fight for their interests, but they also coalesce to press for changes that contribute to the common weal, hoping to better the lives of future generations of seniors. These Americans are found in movements on the left and on the right, and in some cases they dominate. How they do this and what their limitations are as a force for social change are my topics. With longer life expectancy and healthier seniors, elderly people's presence in politics is significant despite their infirmities. By analyzing the activities of members of this influential social category as they operate as a local social movement, I examine the intersection of their power and their constraints. Seniors demand and deserve a place in American politics, and they achieve this by acting together, relying on the resources, reputations, and relations their local involvement provides.

However, simply recounting occasions when seniors act and what they say is not sufficient. Description must be leavened with analysis. In this book I use the reality that seniors participate in an intense and close-knit group to consider what power can achieve and how that power is limited. I argue that seniors are not narrowly self-interested, that senior activism is distinctive, and that senior activism can tell us about activism and the politics of tiny publics more broadly.

The activist group I analyze—Chicago Seniors Together—constitutes a tiny public, a public that promotes change by working with colleagues who share a commitment to change. In this case the collaboration is shaped by the conditions of age, health, history, experience, and network ties. This is a study both of seniors and of a movement group. Analysis of civic action requires recognizing the influence of personal connections and the intensity of small communities.[2] Granular ethnographies of tiny publics, such as the one I present, reveal that social change depends on an activated interaction order. An organization of activist seniors, facing and overcoming obstacles, can be a force for reform or for revolt.

Despite their presence, seniors constitute a social category that often is dismissed, marginalized, and even oppressed. The empirical challenge is to explain those features of their culture, interaction, and relations that permit both power and powerlessness. As I propose, the answer is that through their relations with generational peers and younger ones, through their experiences and through the challenges posed by aging bodies, groups of seniors find opportunities for civic engagement.

To appreciate senior activism, we must recognize the effects of inequality in American society. This is especially evident for seniors who have health issues or lack networks of social support. Considered as a cohesive demographic group, American seniors are on average financially secure as the result of federal programs. Average wealth is highest for those aged seventy-five to seventy-nine, and median wealth is highest for those eighty-plus. This is supplemented by monthly Social Security payments and by Medicare benefits. Although some seniors live below the poverty line (approximately 14 percent), statistics reveal that few elderly people are deeply impoverished, being backstopped by government policy. These economic resources permit well-to-do seniors to support their political preferences.

Many government leaders, corporate CEOs, and professionals—even professors—have passed the once mandatory retirement age of sixty-five and then seventy.[3] Seniors vote at high rates and contribute to campaigns, charities, and churches they believe in. In addition, seniors have unstructured time if retired and are in better health than in the past. All this enables an extended career of public participation.

Of course this is not the whole picture. While seniors are healthier and more active than previously, they are still made vulnerable by encroaching bodily infirmities. As a demographic group, seniors are often not respected by younger people, perhaps because their presence suggests the inevitability of decline. Further, they may be portrayed as an interest group who selfishly hope to increase their entitlements or whose judgment is impaired by senility or other ailments. Yet, ironically, these vulnerabilities may benefit their activism, as I describe in chapter 3, as when being disrespected or injured by forces of control provides a marker of injustice. Infirmities make organizing demonstrations harder, yet such situations may produce compelling visuals.[4] As is true for many social movements—those linked to race, gender, sexuality, or disability—who the members are and how they are treated shapes the form of their demonstrations as well as public response.

These images both advance and detract from seniors' claims to shape public policy. Older Americans care about protecting and expanding Social Security and Medicare. They are passionate in protesting perceived threats to these programs—the third rail of American politics—considered by many the human rights agenda for the elderly.[5] As a result, seniors constitute both an interest group and a moral movement despite crucial divisions based on social class, identity politics, racial divides, and shifting party affiliations.[6] As in the feminist movement,[7] there is a cohort effect in senior politics, shaped by the historical conditions and experiences seniors have lived through.

While numerous public agencies and community centers cater to the needs of senior citizens,[8] few social movement groups have elder Americans as their primary participants. As a result, only a handful of studies have addressed the detailed context of seniors' activism.[9] In my multiyear ethnography, I describe one such organization that I call Chicago Seniors Together (CST), focusing on their group culture, their forms of interaction, and the practices that permit members—individually and collectively—to constitute a distinct tiny public within a larger progressive network. The name of the group is a pseudonym, as are all names of staffers and members.[10]

This book links the examination of this stable, ongoing social movement organization to the special challenges of senior citizens' civic participation. Even when discussing general processes of activism and agitation, I emphasize the capabilities and the limits senior activists have in their repertoires of contention. How does a group that engages in community organizing produce a recognizable culture, a set of shared local meanings and behavioral expectations that is comfortable for the senior members and for their relations with younger staff? How does senior activism matter as a force for change amid all the other pressure groups?

My tight focus on this single social movement group is rare in sociology.[11] To gain a purchase on broad processes, ethnographers often conduct less detailed studies of multiple organizations and their relations,[12] linkages,[13] commonalities,[14] or differences.[15] Although this is a valuable tradition, by ignoring the group context of activism they miss the importance of shared meanings. Even if activists try to think globally, they inevitably act locally. This stage is my domain. As a social psychologist, my ethnographies over nearly a half-century have focused on the group-based creation of local cultures through extended fieldwork. I befriend members, describe their culture, and depict their style of interaction. I term the detailed account that results "peopled ethnography,"[16] linking careful observation to the understanding of social processes. This extended fieldwork and set of in-depth interviews occurred over thirty months, examining lively progressive seniors using distinctive tactics in a contentious organization. Given the pandemic, I note that the research occurred before the COVID-19 lockdown. The CST now relies on Zoom calls, but it did not do so during my research.

Progressives often urge seniors to become more politically active in order to challenge the authority of technocratic elites, to incorporate diverse voices, to gain power for those who are vulnerable, and to wrest control of a market that permits inequality by appealing to the comfortable.[17] As a result, examining senior progressive politics has particular value in hearing voices that are often unheard. While militant groups sponsor disruptive actions, these must accord with seniors' capabilities. Because of the commitment to resisting perceived injustice as it is enforced by authorities, examining an activist group on the left has special value. Conservative senior politics exists as well and can be influential, but it typically demands less embodied involvement.

Chicago Seniors Together

As the Chicago humorist Finley Peter Dunne's "Mr. Dooley" memorably pointed out in 1895, "Politics ain't bean-bag."[18] In a democratic system, contentious politics is a valued form of civic commitment, and nowhere is that truer than in Dunne's hometown.

I chose a local, grassroots organization to understand the effects of social movement culture on forms of activism. This was not an iconic or highly influential group. Chicago Seniors Together is an organization without extensive power, media influence, or presence on social media, but it is respected among other modest-sized progressive organizations in their movement field.

Although cultures of interaction have been downplayed in social movement research,[19] my argument is grounded in the "cultural turn,"[20] seeing activists as a community. Political engagement emerges from sharing meanings and local practices, the basis of a tiny public that hopes for civic impact.[21] This engagement can be either, as in the present case, an independent group—although one in contact with other organizations—or a local chapter tied to a larger network but acting in a quasi-independent fashion.[22] Whereas other studies examine the complexities of institutional structures,[23] I focus on relational processes within a single organization.

Although seniors vote in high numbers, social movement organizations that older men and women participate in are rare. Best known are bureaucratic "movement" organizations, notably AARP, founded in 1958, an interest group but not an activist one, and the less well-known conservative Association of Mature American Citizens, founded in 2007. AARP was known as the American Association of Retired Persons until 1999, when, hoping to appeal to a larger population, especially those over fifty who had not retired, it changed the name to an acronym. Before AARP was founded, seniors were already actively engaged in fighting for government programs to support the elderly. This group included seniors who supported the Townsend Plan, helping to generate support for enacting Social Security in 1935.[24] More recently, the best-known senior group was the provocatively named Gray Panthers,[25] an outgrowth of 1960s mobilization. Maggie Kuhn, a radical activist with roots in religious-based organizing, founded the Panthers in 1970. The group borrowed its imagery from the Black Panther Party; it still exists, though only as a shell of its former self.

Within Chicago, a few activist groups have engaged seniors. Metro Seniors in Action was once a large and notable citywide activist organization,[26] but it collapsed amid financial scandal and operational inadequacy. Several influential members of Chicago Seniors Together migrated from that group after its demise. The Older Women's League (OWL), focusing on the needs of aging women, was a national organization founded in 1980 with local chapters, but it disbanded in 2017 and seems never to have been very active in Chicago.

Unlike many movement groups that appear and soon vanish, Chicago Seniors Together has a lengthy history and has promoted progressive politics in Chicago for over four decades, focusing on issues that matter to seniors, including affordable housing, nursing home reform, and a more secure system of health care. Although the group lacks extensive power, it has gained respect from progressives for commitment, ethics, and longevity.

Chicago Seniors Together was founded in the mid-1970s by a longtime community activist, a woman revered within the progressive community, with the support of colleagues. A building in Chicago that provides affordable senior citizen housing bears her name. This saga of organizational founding validates seniors' desire to fight for changes in the economy and politics that benefit vulnerable seniors, including subsidized housing, expanded Medicare and Social Security, and other government-sponsored initiatives. The organization is justly proud of its history of activism in Chicago, a city that gave birth to Jane Addams and Hull House, Saul Alinsky and the Industrial Areas Foundation, Mayor Harold Washington, and, most recently, Barack Obama.[27] Chicago has produced some highly progressive Democratic politicians, including the current mayor, Lori Lightfoot. Of course the city is not known only for progressive politics. "The Chicago way" refers to the power of machine politics in this once blue-collar city as reflected in the mayoralties of Richard J. Daley and his son Richard M. Daley. The police brutality at the 1968 Democratic National Convention and a continuing series of scandals reveal the political complexity of this City of the Big Shoulders. With a Republican governor, Bruce Rauner, during this research and a Democratic mayor, Rahm Emanuel—not considered progressive by many activists—as well as Republican political dominance on the national level, progressive activists understandably felt that challenges to meaningful "social justice" policies were substantial.

Every movement organization develops a cultural style that privileges ways of connecting past, present, and future in light of those forms of interaction that are considered appropriate.[28] For each, the action scenes are organized through a group culture. In this regard Chicago Seniors Together operates according to a modified Saul Alinsky model of community organizing,[29] an approach that emphasizes building strong relationships, recognizing shared values, and downplaying the spontaneous in favor of the carefully planned and systematically evaluated.[30] As a result, memories of past successes (and failures) are influential in shaping future actions. Alinsky's recognition of the importance of respecting tradition is central, as is emphasizing connections with religious and other civic organizations. Copies of Alinsky's works were available on the office bookshelf.

Despite this background, the Alinsky model is known primarily by the staff, who have been trained in influential theories of community organizing. Few seniors have a deep awareness of Saul Alinsky and his contributions to progressive activism, or if they are aware of the name, they know him as an important activist or as a hell-raiser. The careful planning of demonstrations and other movement activities is said to distinguish this style of organizing from organizing in the African American tradition. As one staff member noted, "There's some very White male things that I think come with the Alinsky model." In our racially sensitive age, the careful planning essential to the Alinsky model may be coded as racial or gendered privilege. Further, the lack of spontaneity that characterizes the group's actions distinguishes this group from the protests of younger progressives. Alinsky criticized the emotive—and sometimes violent—protests by antiwar students in the 1960s. Still, the Alinsky model emphasizes that social relations are vital in building a movement, and this makes it an apt site for my approach emphasizing that tiny publics depend on group cultures and interaction orders. As I describe in chapter 4, staff members emphasize the value of personal stories in motivating emotional affiliation. Still, full allegiance to Alinsky's 1940s style of organizing—such as training members in "power analysis," taught by an expert through what is called "popular education"—is questioned in the current environment, since some consider it too ideological and too top-down. While Chicago Seniors Together continues to use popular education on occasion, sometimes successfully, the approach is less central to community organizing now than it was during Alinsky's day. Proto-Marxist lectures hold little appeal even—or perhaps especially—to seniors. Saul Alinsky has been dead fifty years, and community organizing must address contemporary issues and forms of social relations.

The organization was headquartered several miles north of Chicago's downtown "Loop," in an area that has been gentrifying and is near elite neighborhoods such as the Gold Coast. Most members were residents of the North and Northwest Sides of Chicago, areas that are wealthier and Whiter than the South, Southwest, and West Sides.[31] Many members live in affordable senior housing despite once having middle-class professional or quasi-professional careers that still have led to straitened finances. A few members lived in the multiracial South Side neighborhood of Hyde Park, home to the University of Chicago. Although the organization aspired to diversity this was hard to attain, since the proportion of African American members (roughly 20 percent) was lower than their share of the city's population and, despite efforts described in chapter 6, the organization attracted few Latinx members. In this the CST was not so different from other activist organizations that are populated and supported by well-educated progressives with social and cultural capital.[32] More women than men participated in the organization, approximately two to one. As an organization of senior citizens, almost all members were between sixty and ninety-five; most were sixty to eighty, members of the midcentury American "baby boom" cohort born after World War II. The reality of physical mobility limitations—with some members relying on motorized chairs, walkers, or canes—required organizers to consider these conditions in planning events. This limited long marches, required restroom stops, and made seating essential.

I discuss the group structure more fully in chapter 5, where I analyze the relations between staff and members. Unlike some social movement organizations, Chicago Seniors Together hired staff, a process formally controlled by the ten-member Board of Directors, but with considerable input by the executive director. The staff consisted of five to seven full-time workers (the number fluctuated during the research). One organizer was male, but otherwise all staff members were women. Several focused on issues of health care or political engagement, while others were housing organizers. Except for the executive director, who was sixty, staff members were in their twenties and thirties. Four were Jewish, although with different levels of religious commitment. Over the course of the research there were several Latinx staffers and one who self-defined as gender fluid.

Chicago Seniors Together belonged to the People's Action coalition in the Chicago area (one of two broad local networks of progressive groups in the area). People's Action, a national network, holds an annual meeting in Washington, DC, that some members of the CST attended. The executive directors of the allied groups met at various sites during the year.

When I began my research in autumn 2015, Chicago Seniors Together numbered about 350 members; by 2017 the membership had climbed close to 650, although the number of active members increased more slowly. This increase was primarily due to the ferment brought to progressive activism by the election of President Donald Trump. Most of the leaders of the organization were White women, and this became more notable with the influx of new members after the 2016 election.

Social Movements and Tiny Publics

In this ethnography I apply the approach developed in my book *The Hinge: Civil Society, Group Cultures, and the Power of Local Commitments*. I argued there that *tiny publics*—outward-facing groups committed to engagement in the civic arena—are instigators of social change. I operate from a meso sociological level that draws on the importance of interaction orders, group cultures, and circuits of action. Together these concepts help to explain how senior activism constitutes a tiny public. Society depends on the activities of minute communities with understood rules of conduct, cultural traditions, and expected practices. This case of elderly progressives demonstrates how tiny publics, embedded in a commitment to a local culture, push for societal transformation. Despite their modest size, their provocations draw media attention and possibly even cause a change in perspective by viewers, politicians and publics alike. Vulnerable seniors marching, orating, and advocating for life-and-death causes can send a persuasive message. Group action can be powerful, especially when the group has a resonant story to tell. Before introducing a culturalist model of social movements, I will briefly present the conceptual touchstones leading to an analysis of tiny publics: the interaction order, group culture, and circuits of action.

THE INTERACTION ORDER

While an overemphasis on individual agency might suggest that interactional choices are highly idiosyncratic, sociologists know that this is never the case. Social life is impressively orderly, despite the prominence of agentic choices. People do not merely think and act as individuals; their performances are designed in light of the impressions of others. When seniors try to create events that all can participate in by allowing for disabilities, they are creating a style of protest. Performances are situated within a world of expectations, what Erving Goffman referred to as the interaction order.[33] While agency is essential, the interaction order asserts that people act in accord with well-understood expectations, even if they choose to violate those rules. By participating in an interaction order, group members recognize that their associations and their practices are stable, even while their collective action allows for challenges to broader structures. This stability does not simply emerge from the immediate encounter but results from *routines* embedded in ongoing social relations. The immediate encounter does not, by itself, establish fixed or scripted performances; rather, collective relations depend on the recognition of *eventful experience*. In treating our experience of past interaction as a model for the present, local communities are built through tacit agreement to transform action into order.

GROUP CULTURES

Interaction fields are never devoid of meaning. Behavior must be about *something*, especially in social movements where a community expresses a desire for change. The existence of group cultures—what I have termed "idiocultures"—suggests that culture consists of beliefs and practices held by those with ongoing relations. Recognizing that one's experiences and beliefs are shared contributes to collective identity, an important consequence of protest events. When we sang politicized carols outside the mayor's home, we not only briefly disrupted his neighbors' lives but reveled in our passionate joyfulness and our understanding of these missives. Meanings are embedded in a collective past, an immediate present, and a prospective future.

CIRCUITS OF ACTION

Social movements—and all social life—are spaces of orderly interaction operating through recurring practices. These routines constitute the group style.[34] Actions are repeated and become accepted through that repetition. Individuals must be able to foresee the likely responses of others and adjust accordingly. I refer to these stabilizing forces as *circuits of action*. While these assumptions about how others will respond are sometimes upended, to be useful, expectations must frequently be met. Nowhere is this more salient than in social movements, where coordination is crucial. Interaction is filtered through the collective awareness of what participants believe is appropriate. Offering feeling words after meetings—typically positive ones—served as a ritual that expressed both individual feelings and collective sentiment. Circuits of action incorporate the rules of the interaction order and the content of group cultures in practices that are anticipated and comforting. However, for interaction to be orderly within a collaborative group, negotiations and adjustments are essential, building relationships that are flexible but durable.

TINY PUBLICS

While all sites of interaction inform us of the structure of social life, we find this most clearly when individuals have a commitment to a civil consciousness. Tiny publics, grounded in interaction, combine group culture with attention to civic engagement. A *tiny public* is a group with a recognizable interaction order and a local culture that hopes to shape society. In other words tiny publics, such as Chicago Seniors Together, have both an internal order and a communal face that is outward-looking: they are Janus-faced and must negotiate the dilemmas of appealing to multiple audiences.[35] These communities may have small memberships, but they address a broader politics, and in their sociality they develop a collaborative commitment. One challenge faced by societies composed of tiny publics is that the desire for smooth interaction may make them conflict-averse, avoiding controversies that might productively be addressed, or may lead them to simply bow to the demands of the most powerful. As a result, tiny publics that hope to be adversarial are vital in bettering society precisely because of their challenge.

The Culture of Social Movements

Building on concepts that are integral to a meso-level, local sociology, I emphasize the culture of social movements as the basis for this research. Over the past century, researchers have examined the characteristics of participants, the effects of grievances, the relation of movements to the state and the political process, networking as a means of recruitment, the acquisition of resources, and the framing of movement goals. All of these topics are valuable.

My approach[36] focuses on the centrality of culture in tiny publics. Social movement organizations are, in several senses, cultural communities. They comprise a field of actors with shared emotion rules, common knowledge, and a preferred style of interaction.[37] Some movements depend on a leading group, whereas others are composed of a lattice of groups, ideally working in concert.

The concept of culture is bracingly broad, useful for both macro- and microanalyses of social movements. From a macro perspective, a movement not only is politically and socially situated but is also culturally situated within a recognizable societal order,[38] standing above local action scenes.[39] Norms, values, and traditions determine what claims, demands, and actions are permissible. Without this recognition, movements are likely to fail. Another approach emphasizes personal decisions. This micro perspective emphasizes individuals' choices to participate, often out of a set of grievances or a belief that their interests will be served. The social-psychological view treats activism as enacted by persons, with less attention to how they are shaped through their participation. Both approaches are valuable, but neither addresses the meso-level reality that movement groups are crucibles in which shared options of protest are developed and deployed. Relationships, emotions, and shared meanings transform a set of individuals into a tiny public in which participants commit to each other and to their project.

Focusing on the internal culture of the movement group does not deny its role in a larger political field, nor does it deny that individual preferences matter. Still, the close examination of interaction within a single organization provides a meso-level approach situated between personal preferences and societal structures. Every group provides a stage for performance.[40]

Treating social movements as local cultural domains permits us to investigate the processes through which commitment is generated.[41] A social movement consists of a *bundle of narratives* and a *set of traditions*, both tied to the reality of eventful experience.

Social movement groups, and by extension their networks, develop through interaction, and like all interaction they depend on members' recognition of meaningful references that produce collective identity.[42] These identities call out affective responses that follow rules of emotion.[43] As Deborah Gould argues in her study of ACT UP politics in the fight for government action to confront the AIDS epidemic, creating an emotive culture is central to sustaining social movements, both in motivating members and in challenging the sense of normalcy of their audiences and opponents. As a result, movements require a pedagogy of emotion.[44] Participants must learn to be agitators.

In cultural terms, we can conceive of a social movement as both a literal and a figurative space in which participants negotiate common identities through shared experiences. In this site, moving stories are embraced and demanding actions are taken as representing the organizational self.

However, identity must result in action. This creates what Edward Shils, speaking of the development of worldviews, labels an "ideological primary group."[45] Groups develop local cultures—idiocultures—that conjoin identities, structure activities, ritualize expectations, and promote routine practices.[46] That is especially true in circumstances—exemplified by social movement groups—where boundaries and opponents are salient: in other words, where alternatives are possible.

The group endorses topics and styles of interaction that might not be appropriate or meaningful elsewhere. In social movements, with their claims to better the world, this endorsement is frequently treated as a moral requirement. Legitimation operates through parallel processes of contextualization: cultural and interactional. First, through their reactions to the performances of others and through their own performances, participants reinforce the worth of those shared worldviews. Second, actors treat the movement as a space in which performing one's beliefs is legitimate and legitimated. Through enacted beliefs, participants affirm that they accept the demands of sociality. Ways of being politically engaged become evident within the tiny public. To belong to the group is to accept shared identification, ritual action, and the mobilizing of resources.

The enactment of culture involves activating symbolic and material resources to support an injustice frame.[47] For culture to have an effect, participants must believe that others feel the same or can be induced to do so. Merely recognizing the existence of a like-minded community is a necessary but not sufficient condition for mobilization. A communications network must be present to coordinate action; a consensual authority system permits social control and routinization. Finally, material resources enable public performances. This cultural approach to analyzing social movements from the meso level provides the basis for my account of Chicago Seniors Together.

Observing Activists

For decades I have taught students about social movements, but aside from brief ethnographic forays into the world of political party activists[48] and a group that supported families accused of child abuse,[49] I had not conducted a focused ethnography on a social movement group. As I neared age sixty-five, soon to receive my Medicare card though not ready to retire, I decided to observe a group of senior citizen activists. Finding the right site proved harder than I had anticipated, since the organizational field had few movement groups catering specifically to the elderly, although many social movements accept seniors as participants even if they do not adjust the culture to their needs. At last I found a suitable organization, and I was gratified that I was permitted to observe from bottom to top.

To understand how eventful experience is a resource for movement-based tiny publics, I draw on ethnographic research from a thirty-month observation of Chicago Seniors Together, conducted from fall 2015 until spring 2018. This group proved a particularly appropriate site to examine how narrative, history, and shared experience are resources for collective action. Because the project addresses well-publicized issues and events that are easily traceable, I specify that the organization is based in Chicago. However, some minor details have been altered to preserve the anonymity of informants, especially those who engaged in well-planned but unlawful civil disobedience. As I noted earlier, both the group name and the names of all participants are pseudonyms.

My research is based on long-term ethnographic field observations, supplemented by document analysis and in-depth interviews. I approached the project using the grounded theory methodology that involves looking for comparative cases and writing interpretive analyses, building on extensive field notes. My focus shifted at various points during the thirty months as different issues rose to prominence, as reflected in the organizational agenda.

In this extended ethnography, I observed numerous committees and public meetings and participated in demonstrations, marches, and other protests. Since I had not previously been involved with the organization, I began as an outsider; however, in the course of the research I engaged in actions and activities with fellow seniors although, like most members, I chose not to take part in civil disobedience. I attended board meetings, staff meetings, Finance Committee meetings, and meetings of issue-oriented committees. On each occasion I took notes, focusing on interactions that constituted the group culture, transcribing stories, anecdotes, and other narratives. I told participants I was there to do research. In dealing with the activist members I had the advantage of being a chronological peer. We had experienced the same range of historical events, even if my position as a professor of sociology gave me a different perspective. However, like any good ethnographer, I attempted to gain their trust so that they would share their stories, their concerns, and their world. Social seduction is necessary for gaining rapport and gathering data. I hope I have returned that trust with respect.

During the research, I developed friendships with staff and leaders and occasionally joined them for lunch. After a few months, members and leaders treated me as a full participant, although it took longer for the staff to accept my presence without suspicion. In the last months of the project I conducted thirty-five interviews: ten with staff and twenty-five with members. Interviews lasted one to three hours and were tape-recorded and transcribed. Having spent years with the group, I was able to ask questions about the events they and I had participated in, building on our relations, my local knowledge, and perhaps a decreased need to present socially desirable responses. Throughout the research, I contrasted their explanations and my observations with those from previous research projects and tested ideas against data that seemed to contradict them.

I joined the organization, paid dues, took part in phone banks, and contributed to fund-raising, but I was never considered a leader. I listened but did not direct. My role in meetings varied. In meetings of the board, the Finance Committee, the Leadership Committee, and staff meetings, I stayed quiet. There were two exceptions: at the start of the meeting in which the leader asked those present to introduce themselves (I announced my role as professor and researcher) and when we were asked to respond to a relational question or were posed a relational exercise. In these responses I attempted to be both honest and supportive of the group beliefs. Often at the end of the meeting leaders asked members for a feeling word to evaluate the meeting (my word was never negative but sometimes was neutral). I rarely spoke in larger committee meetings, but in smaller meetings planning actions, I participated more directly, and I talked when we divided into small discussion groups. As an ethnographer, I made an effort—one I judge to be largely successful—to befriend members who were part of my generation (or the one above) and the staff, younger but with several trained in the social sciences or in social work.

In the thirty months, a few moments of tension emerged, particularly in light of my level of involvement. Many seniors urged me to participate more actively, valuing my insights. Others, in contrast, particularly a few staff members, thought I should remain an observer and rarely be a participant. This was a balance I had to navigate, depending on circumstances. On one occasion staff chided me for offering to prepare an agenda for a future meeting after no one else had volunteered. I was told the task should have been assigned to a member to train for leadership roles. From the start of the research, I had hoped to attend staff meetings to watch how movement professionals directed members. Except for a pair of invitations in the first two years of research, my efforts were rebuffed, but with my continued presence and staff turnover, I was allowed to attend four consecutive staff meetings as I neared the end of the intensive research phase. Understandably the staff was concerned about what I might learn and, more particularly, what I might write, although my being a professor of sociology, with the politics this suggested, may have mitigated this concern.

This book is explicitly about older citizens who care about social justice, civic engagement, and political activism. In writing it I struggled with how much of my own perspectives to reveal. Like most Americans, I hold political beliefs. However, I also believe it is important in my pedagogic practice to bracket these beliefs in leading classroom discussion. I am delighted when students divulge that they are unsure of my politics, although many students made assumptions, not believing that any faculty member would be anything but a liberal or leftist. Still, the classroom should be a safe space for those who dissent from progressive orthodoxy, even if many conservative students perform liberalism quite well when they feel it is in their interest. I feel similarly about research. I believe I could write in a fair way about a conservative, radical, or libertarian organization, even Antifa or the Proud Boys, although one can never entirely jettison one's political perspective.

I am broadly sympathetic to the values of Chicago Seniors Together, although I do not agree on every issue or with every tactic. However, the book is about them, not about me. My specific areas of agreement and dissent, enthusiasm and skepticism, should not be central to the analysis. This is not an undercover exposé à la James O'Keefe's Breitbart-inspired Project Veritas, nor is it a bright and shiny advertisement for the virtues of community organizing. There are media subversives and academic advocates. I hope to be neither. In contrast, I intend to provide a nuanced sociological analysis of the culture of a social movement and a group of sincere seniors who through their collective commitment and shared histories make a claim for change. This is a case study, and it has the strengths and limits of that approach as I generalize from the case while recognizing that the granular details of this place and time are crucial to understanding how senior activism is formulated.

The Plan of the Book

To examine a culture of community activism, I have organized the book though seven thematic chapters, emphasizing the distinctive features of senior citizen participation in progressive protest while drawing on those broader concepts and themes that describe the culture of resistance more generally.

In chapter 1, "Causes, Commitment, and Culture," I begin where studies of political commitment should commence: with the ideals of the participants. Sociologists often marginalize the beliefs of movement actors as generating their involvement, replacing this insistent moral vision with the priority of resources, network pressures, political process, state involvement, or strategic framing. While each of these elements has a role, ignoring the *ideals* of participants is an error. I take seriously the convictions these activists publicly expressed as they gave of their time and energy through their social compacts. While features other than attitudes affect the likelihood of engagement, we must not ignore the impact of shared values on individual choices. Although real, these views are often amorphous and ambiguous, and this leads to my title, *Fair Share*, a powerful framing for the beliefs of these seniors. But what is a fair share? How much redistribution would constitute a just economy? Although tied to ideals, this phrase is made real only through policy choices presented in the context of the politics of the moment.

Chapter 2, "Coming of Age," is at the heart of my analysis, presenting the position of senior citizens in political activism. How do seniors choose to become active at the point when their physical vulnerabilities and threats to their mental acuity are increasing? In light of recruitment to activism, what are the careers of politically active seniors? The question extends beyond biography. As an ethnographer, I address how their physical limitations and social positions affected the forms of activism they participated in and how they were viewed by those they confronted. We see this, for instance, in the way police treated disruptive seniors. Performing civil disobedience created powerful images that police were well aware of.[50] Just as seniors may be marginalized as agitators, their vulnerability provides a source of strength that those younger and healthier cannot match.

The politics of age leads to chapter 3, "Where the Actions Are." What happens at a demonstration? How are actions organized to achieve desired ends with dedicated protesters? Social movements depend on the activation of skill sets. A key feature of all social movement activism is that participants must have the time and the desire to attend events that the group organizes and publicizes. Turnout is a marker of success but depends on many unpredictable factors. Organizers thus must aim high to reach their desired attendance. For seniors their temporal availability was both an advantage and a handicap. Once seniors have retired, their schedules became increasingly flexible, or at least they may lack insistent and scheduled demands. In contrast, the fragility of seniors made attendance unpredictable, a problem for an organization that depended on structured meetings and planned events.

Generational membership is tied to the extended memories of seniors, the topic of chapter 4: "Movement Memories and Eventful Experience." Shared memories shape relations among social movement participants. Scholars often ignore the way experience solidifies attachment. In contrast, I argue that all activism depends on how participants recall events, both privately and in public contexts. I integrate a social memory perspective with the examination of movements of resistance. Through narrative, participants build engagement by presenting the self-in-history as instigating collective action. I describe this as *eventful experience*, utilizing memorable moments as resources for generating commitment. Movements depend on members to communicate the critical moments of their lives, embedding personal timelines within group culture. Sharing personal experience through the memory of public events is a strategy by which individuals motivate collective action. The awareness of history builds a *culture of action*. Each movement group relies on the experiences of participants to cement its culture—what James Jasper refers to as *taste in tactics*[51]—incorporating past successes, present plans, and imagined future triumphs into a call for direct action.

The linkage between staff and members is the focus of chapter 5, "Staff Power and Senior Authority." I address the way the organization was internally organized with attention to the age structure of participants and the role of a culture of meetings as creating a belief in consensus and respect for seniors' schedules. Who determines the group culture? One feature of many established social movements is that they hire staff to plan activities, including those meetings that are so central. These staffers are compensated by the organization, so the movement must obtain grants, assess dues, or charge for events. Key to hiring staff is the need to raise money for their salaries, and this advantages groups with access to middle-class skills and resources. To obtain funding, the staff depended on a supportive membership and a favorable organizational ecology. For any action to succeed, enthusiastic participants are essential. They must accept the lead of staff, hoping that staff decisions accord with members' desires. In many movement organizations, and in Chicago

Seniors Together, leaders are groomed to assist the staff, recruit members, raise money, serve as liaisons with less involved members, and—crucially—become the face of the organization. However, in senior activism in particular the young staff confront a challenge in directing those who are older and more experienced, and in some cases troublesome.

Chapter 6, "Diversities," addresses the intersection of fundamental sociological categories that are potential points of a divided interaction order. Must a social movement be homogeneous to succeed? If not, which categories matter? Where and when is identity central? Chicago Seniors Together earnestly strove to avoid racism, sexism, class privilege, and homophobia. This effort was central to its identity as a progressive movement. However, these goals were more easily proclaimed than achieved. The organization was challenged in that its established base of support was among White communities on the North Side of Chicago. While the group included African Americans, recruiting on the non-White West and South Sides was both difficult and sporadic. This is a major topic of discussion, although with frustrating results. Beyond recruitment is the question of ideology. What does a "nonracist" organization look like in practice? While race was the central demographic concern, finding places for men in a movement in which women dominated can also be fraught. Were men to be marginalized because of their privilege, or did they bring needed diversity as well as material resources and organizational skills? How should class cultures be managed in an organization where most members have a middle-class background? Further, how should the organization treat LGBTQ members? Incorporating those who challenged traditional gender boundaries was a problem in a senior organization, given that members grew up when such issues were marginal.

In chapter 7, "The Nexus of Politics," I examine the effects of the political environment on movement activism and the role of a network of movement organizations. Each local movement is a hinge between the desires of its participants and the broader political environment. The 2016 American presidential election mattered, from broad policy changes to impelling individuals to become active in resisting those changes. When I began observing Chicago Seniors Together, Barack Obama was president, Illinois had a conservative Republican governor, and Chicago's mayor was a moderate, corporatist "New Democrat," disdained by progressive activists. As a result, the CST focused on city and state issues. November 2016 altered this political environment with the election of Donald Trump. (After the research was completed in 2018, Illinois elected a liberal Democratic governor, J. B. Pritzker, and in early 2019 Chicago elected a progressive mayor, Lori Lightfoot.) As a result of the 2016 election and the anger, dismay, and energy it provoked, membership nearly doubled and the focus turned to national issues such as the push for "Medicare for All" and a federal government housing policy. Social movements are inevitably shaped by an issue ecology and by pressures from allies (and foes) in their organizational field. This returns to the salience of ideas as embedded in social relations and group culture, here in the context of a wider network.

The conclusion, chapter 8 ("Our Fair Share"), provides an overview of my arguments, connecting senior activism to a theory of locally based collective action. I address the extent to which the CST should be treated as an organization *for* seniors, in which the particular interests of seniors are primary. In contrast, we may think of it as an organization *of* seniors in which members' political agenda is little different from that of other progressive organizations despite their demographic makeup. As a tiny public, group culture and an interaction order shape the possibilities of senior citizen engagement and their push for all to receive a fair share.

Causes, Commitment, and Culture

Democracy must begin at home, and its home is in the neighborly community.
JOHN DEWEY

What of social justice? Justice at its core must be social. Both the Tea Party and the MAGA world believe in justice and community. Yet they do not believe in "social justice" as the term is commonly applied in political discourse, nor, despite concern about a swampy "deep state," do they have what has been labeled "oppositional consciousness."[1] In the phrase of William Gamson, activists must establish an "injustice frame,"[2] rejecting status quo arrangements that produce inequity.

In all social movements, cultural frames develop through the creation of dramatic images and signature slogans that "belong" to ideological communities. Of course there are many injustices that activists can point to, leading to reforms and revolts, but if one can force an audience to focus on wrongs, the world can be righted.[3] Crucial are labels that become associated with communities of activity.

To embrace social justice—a term that might apply broadly—means to accept shared assumptions, perhaps ambiguous but readily differentiated from other conceptions of morality. Social justice is more than social, more than justice; it involves a fluid ideology linked to progressive politics and redistributive policies. Although the phrase has a lengthy history,[4] today it is used by those on the left, and it was a favorite phrase of Chicago Seniors Together, heard often when public events were scheduled, as detailed in chapter 3. When targeting Ken Griffin, at one point the wealthiest person in Illinois, on a Resist Trump Tuesday, we stood outside the downtown office of Citadel LLC, his hedge fund, loudly chanting in unison that he should pay his fair share. Although an amount was never specified, the emotion was raw and real.

The idea of a fair share demands a more equitable distribution of wealth through government-directed income transfers. Social justice suggests that each person deserves sufficient economic, political, and social opportunities to thrive. Yet what constitutes sufficient opportunities and how and at what cost they might be obtained must be specified. There is value in having the term vaguely defined, since it permits all to agree and its meaning to shift. This tension between clarity and ambiguity constitutes what James Jasper speaks of as "the articulation dilemma."[5] "Social justice" is part of a "democratic imagination"[6] that allows diverse citizens to imagine themselves as consensual communities with boundaries that differentiate them from imagined opponents.[7]

Belonging to a social movement organization involves accepting a set of beliefs linked to collective identity, orderly interaction, and local culture. Members share politics and sociality. In this chapter I begin with values and how they are framed, and with how members are recruited both through networks and through shared beliefs; then I turn to how movement organizations depend on friendships, emotions, and culture. While this applies to all activist organizations, it is especially salient for seniors, where the group provides a home base that protects them from isolation. Further, the desire to contribute to a better world is particularly evident in older citizens, whose vision for age-related justice is often broader than narrow self-interest.[8]

Ideologies and attitudes mobilize a desire for action, but this occurs in conjunction with the commitments an individual makes to others. Although recruitment occurs through activated networks,[9] individuals must believe that those in the political community they are joining share congenial beliefs, especially if participation involves potential reputational, temporal, or material costs. Further, those who choose activism adopt a participatory worldview. They are predisposed to believe that just and decent people must act to improve the world and are motivated by their values.[10] Values and relationships merge. As Paul Lichterman emphasizes, civic engagement must be more than internal beliefs or personal attitudes: it is a form of collective action.[11]

This connects to the *arc of participation* I discuss in chapter 2 in depicting seniors' activist careers. The translation of values into action is shaped by two mediating factors: opportunity and urgency,[12] both linked to structures in which action is facilitated. Chicago Seniors Together provided this access, regularly emphasizing that the members of the group must act jointly and continually to assert privileged values.

The values chosen reflect an expansive model of rights, more affirmative than the negative ones ("freedom from" rights) specified in the Bill of Rights. In a nation in which there has been a neoliberal challenge to the progressive policy goals of the Great Society agenda of Lyndon Johnson, enshrined in the Older Americans Act of 1965, senior activists hope to reassert the focus on positive rights to housing and health found in that legislation. Have the values of the so-called Gray Lobby failed? Will they rise again? As Luisa, a longtime staffer, argued, "We want to embrace those values that we hold dear. Health care is a right. Housing is a right. Education is a right. A living wage is a right, and a job is a right" (field notes). These are not values in the conventional sense of broad moral ordering principles, but these rights demand action. They emphasize that the ideas of the movement are not peripheral but central.

This approach places the articulation of values and beliefs in the center of social movement analysis but does so by recognizing that values become manifest through group practice and social relations. This accounts for the power of agency, a point often missed in discussing the politics of aging. The obligation to act permits us to see these elder citizens as heroes: if we endorse their politics. The reality is that many more elderly people share values and hold grievances than engage in activism,[13] so something else is needed to translate ideas into participation. This requires more than selves and persons; it takes local *worlds of commitment* that activate vulnerable bodies.[14] Members of Chicago Seniors Together insist that they are involved to support a cause they believe in, but this occurs within the context of powerful sociality.[15] Each social movement group is a tiny public, organized around common concerns and often linked to a network of similar groups.[16]

In this claim I address both the push and the pull features of senior activism.[17] Values, policies, and actions are connected. Desiring a common purpose leads the CST to focus its activism on senior issues rather than on the broader buffet of progressive preferences. Demanding senior rights allows participants to support their own interests, those of movement colleagues, and those of their demographic cohort. The push involves the desire to push institutions toward aging justice; the pull involves pulling members into a community of care and an emotional connection.

A perspective that emphasizes that beliefs matter differs from those that focus on apolitical network recruitment, such as to cultlike groups. These latter occur in a context where the recruit lacks strong beliefs but craves a place to belong at a particular life stage.[18] Pull has priority. As Doug McAdam points out, involvement depends on biographical availability.[19] Because of seniors' health and social constraints, this availability may be particularly salient for older progressives, who may find a pull to engage but also feel a push to support causes they are passionate about.

In considering a group with a clear political orientation, such as Chicago Seniors Together, it is unlikely that someone lacking beliefs consistent with those of the group would choose to join. One would have to bracket one's past, which—understandably—is rare. While recognizing this attitudinal linkage, it is equally true that individuals often are invited into a group by friends or relations who recognize a sympathetic ally. These recruiters feel that the new member belongs.

Recruitment and belief are connected, even if not inevitably overlapping. Before describing recruitment, I address some of the beliefs the group shared and how these beliefs bolstered participation. Framing depends on beliefs even while it solidifies those beliefs through a compelling label. As important as framing is in the creation of activism,[20] not all framing is successful. Effective framing must build on values, sometimes ambiguous but never absent. When effective, the framing must generate congenial imaginaries, consistent with local values and justice beliefs, must be persuasive in maintaining that the costs of social change are manageable, must separate those who accept the frame from those who reject it,[21] and must accord with the lived experiences of those recruited. Movements balance the desire to incorporate many participants with the recognition that becoming less exclusionary and more open may decrease the motivation to belong[22] and may lead to struggles over values and policies. Advocacy organizations frame the interpretation of senior politics in different ways: vibrant seniors, an uncaring government, demographic crisis, independent citizens, aging workers, wise mentors, or a throwaway generation. Each implies a distinct political stance and appeal to potential recruits.[23] I describe particular cases of recruitment in chapter 2 in analyzing alternative activist careers.

Fair Share

To consider the linkage between belief and framing, I begin with a mantra: "The rich should pay their fair share." Members of Chicago Seniors Together repeated this phrase often, such as when dozens protested at the offices of hedge fund owner Ken Griffin, as described above. The slogan is iconic and echoed widely in progressive communities. It articulates a master frame demanding the reduction of income inequality and the redistribution of wealth. Robert Benford and David Snow point to the power of slogans, such as "Power to the People" or "We Shall Overcome," as a form of frame amplification, highlighting collective beliefs through which events are interpreted.[24]

In an ethical society, everyone should pay a fair share and receive fair benefits. But what does this mean in a free market democracy? Its simultaneous specificity and ambiguity make it effective. At demonstrations, protesters chant that the rich, such as Mr. Griffin, must pay "their fair share."

Griffin, extremely wealthy, is simultaneously a major donor to civic causes, including the Obama Foundation, and a generous contributor to Republican campaigns. (Invariably it is a conservative man who is the target. I never heard calls for Bill Gates or George Soros to pay his fair share.) Fairness has rhetorical power, but does the label in itself have clear meaning? Yet it can be used as a marker—agreed on by participants—to justify policy proposals: taxes on inheritance, a tax on financial trades, a progressive income tax, user fees, and the like. The chanters apply the phrase to the demands of the moment, ultimatums that are continually shifting. In one sense the meaning is easily made applicable in particular cases, and perhaps that is sufficient. The wealthy, given their resources and their privileges, are said to be paying an insufficient portion of the American tax burden or an insufficient percentage of their income, justifying the claim, frequently made at CST rallies, that there is no spending problem, only a revenue problem. Conservatives point to the large proportion of taxes paid by the wealthy, but progressives point to the still larger proportion of wealth held by "millionaires and billionaires." This was posed dramatically by Warren Buffett, who asserted that he was being assessed at a lower tax rate than his secretary.[25] His sound bite was cited repeatedly.

The phrase I chose as my book title proclaims a general orientation but not a specific policy. Perhaps at times the phrase is overly vague, as in the way a Washington, DC, pressure group named Fair Share defines its mission: "Fair Share stands for an America where everyone gets their fair share, does their fair share, and pays their fair share; and where everyone plays by the same rules."[26] In practice, some form of resource transfer is central to participants' beliefs, linked to the demand that it is the proper role of government to protect the vulnerable by insisting on the responsibilities of the privileged. Social movements promote general orientations while legislators wrestle with the specifics. Activists see a meadow vista while policymakers labor in the weeds. Advocates discuss nutrition while politicians grind sausage.

I use "fair share" to explore how activism is generated through a desire to belong to a like-minded community. This phrase that might be taken as an economic prescription is transformed into a moral demand that, as used in group culture, is warmly malleable. Its penumbra of meaning can be expanded or contracted as needed. As several staffers pointed out,

> The rich should be paying the majority of the taxes, and corporations should
> be paying their fair share of taxes, and that we should be looking at structur-
> ing programs to benefit all people, and that they should be paid off the taxes
> of the people who are wealthy. There's lots of people who are not paying their

fair share of taxes. They may be paying a lot of taxes, but it's still not their fair share. (Interview)

I don't have an exact number or anything, obviously. I think that just the way that wealth is distributed in this country is terrible, and I think it's gotten a lot worse in the last twenty years. There's all those graphs where you can see the 1 percent shooting way, way up, way far off the graph, and I think there needs to be a redistribution of that. (Interview)

The phrase separates moral and immoral through boundary work: "us" and "them." "The rich," "the wealthy," or "the 1 percent" becomes shorthand for a category of persons with negative valance. "Corporations" and "big business" are treated as fundamentally immoral: "leeches . . . corporations hoard wealth and wealth could feed people." One staffer was explicit about capping wealth, "There's no need for anyone to have over a certain amount of money. And I don't know what that cap is. . . . No one needs a million dollars. I just don't think anybody needs that much money" (interview). This was brought home in an interview with a longtime member who referred to a friend who recruited her:

My friend who got me into [CST], her son-in-law is a . . . I don't know what venture capitalists do, but that's what he does. . . . He's a multibillionaire, lives out on the North Shore here somewhere, and she said, "No, they're not paying their fair share." The profits he makes, they're obscene. And she said that about him. She said, "I love my son-in-law. I love my daughter, but they are obscene." (Interview)

One member turned the tables on some colleagues, speaking of those who live comfortable lives but were unwilling to pay taxes on their retirement income, and scorning their desire to vacation in Florida. He reported that when he raised the issue, it was not well received:

I could easily pay more, but when I brought that up at a meeting, [saying] "We ought to take the higher end of the seniors' pensions," boy, cold water went onto that idea like nothing. Hey, don't even bring that up. . . . That went over like a lead balloon, you know. "I've gotta take care of my grandson," "I gotta go to Florida." (Interview)

His idea of a fair share pinched their privileges, however modest they might be compared with those of corporate elites. Assessments of wealthy people who were not personally known are harsher. These Americans were frequently labeled as greedy, desiring money for its own sake. A staffer suggested, "I feel like in this country, it's always been about if we cut the taxes of people who are wealthy and corporations that's gonna trickle down to poor people. It's been proven over and over that just doesn't happen" (interview).

Those interviewed were challenged to specify the basis on which fair share justice could be achieved. In practice, to avoid divisive disagreements and lengthy debates, the term was rarely defined. Participants assumed that everyone supported the values it was based on. For many this referred to a graduated income tax targeted at the rich or corporations. For others it involved eliminating hereditary wealth or demanding public ownership of corporations. And for still others it involved a flat tax without loopholes or deductions. On this last, consider the following assessment from a senior leader of the CST, seemingly referring to Warren Buffett and his secretary: "[The rich should pay] the same percentage that the poor are paying or that the middle-class is playing. Why should their percentage be any less than ours?" (interview).

This had been a controversial issue in Illinois, one of the few states with a flat income tax, and in 2020 voters defeated a constitutional change to permit a graduated tax. Many progressives see the flat tax as fundamentally unfair, as a staff member asserts:

> A billionaire should not be paying the same in taxes as a tenant in an affordable housing building, which is currently the case in Illinois. . . . I don't think that's how it should be. I think corporations and big companies and big real estate developers who've gotten rich on the backs of poor people should be paying a lot more money and be paying way more than their fair share. (Interview)

The slogan worked because it need not be specified in advance, as answers to my questions demonstrated. A social movement can gain adherents when it relies on frames of meaning that are recognizable, if ambiguous.

Civic Morality

The vision of everyone's contributing and receiving a fair share is one means by which social movement participants can express a shared moral compass. As I discuss in examining demonstrations in chapter 3, these frames must be expressed in a public space, with activists demonstrating that they willingly announce their beliefs.

Early in his career of agitation, in *Reveille for Radicals* Saul Alinsky suggested that "against social evil there are no rules of fair play."[27] One must fight evil with no holds barred. Alinsky's perspective—the ends justify the means—is evident when activists demonize their opponents' personhood. Those standing outside the group might demur, pointing to the structural context that channels individuals' choices. However, postulating a contentious model of Us versus Them increases motivation, separating one's opponents from a moral community. Evil is, to be sure, a strong word for disagreements in a democracy, but Alinsky believed that much moral reasoning was mere rationalizing, hiding self-interest.[28]

Ruth Braunstein, examining a progressive movement and a conservative movement, finds that both groups relied on moral rhetoric tied to religious values.[29] She writes, "Rather than speaking on behalf of any particular religious community, members of the two groups instead spoke in a broadly shared religious language that imbued active citizenship and American democracy itself with sacred significance." Politics was cemented to a moral order. Following from philosopher Charles Taylor's concept of social imaginaries,[30] participants imagine how society should be organized, grounding these imaginaries in symbols, discourses, and practices.[31] The issue is how to create a hopeful, uplifting vision while incorporating rhetorical attacks to generate the willingness to accept costs.

These moral framings—the uplifting vision and conflictual censure—are essential to group cultures in successful social movements. Each contributes to building power, central for any social movement that demands a "seat at the table." Much theory of community organizing connects to what is described as power analysis, explaining how a group that feels ineffective can conceptualize its role in order to bring about change, drawing on its sources of strength. As Rachel Ramirez points out,

> Community organizing's strengths in power analysis and looking at the "world as it is" can help leaders in organizations to engage with the terrain of the public sector in a more strategic way for greater success. One of the most important skills of an organizer is power analysis—that is, mapping the flow of power around a specific decision maker so that the organization can leverage power to pressure that decision maker.[32]

Organizations must build capacity in order to gain influence so that those they want to negotiate with will take their demands seriously. This is one reason organizations attempt to increase their size and resources: the number of participants (presumably voters) may sway politicians and policymakers. Movements hope for *entrance*, voice, and loyalty. As one member emphasized, "We want them to recognize our power as we recognize their power" (field notes). The CST attempted to train members in "what power looks like" through role-playing exercises in which participants were asked to make demands that were then denied by a colleague performing as an opposing politician. Despite limited material resources, groups of activists have embodied impact, labeled "people power." As one leader commented, "Because I care about people, I'm taking action for all." The challenge for the CST was that it

lacked sufficient numbers as well as resources to leverage the desired influence. This led one former staff organizer to express her frustration:

> In my tenure there I had zero actual policy wins. Very few. . . . We're just not
> big enough to wield enough power: we don't have enough money, we don't
> have enough people to wield the power it would take. . . . If we just had every
> senior in the city of Chicago . . . we would have a lot more clout and a lot more
> power at the table. That just wasn't the profile that the group had. (Interview)

She criticized the group's *imagined power*, the belief that its enthusiasm translated into the ability to shape events and pressure the powerful. A warm glow
is insufficient. In Charles Tilly's terms, groups require the ability to project
worthiness, unity, numbers, and commitment, the acronym WUNC,[33] along
with resources to make this meaningful.

Power is not easy to obtain; it is more possible to create a moral community, coupled with stigmatizing its rivals. The CST's executive director, Jane
Tate, speaking to an anti-Trump assembly, was passionate in declaring that
she has three grandchildren she advocates for:

> I envision a world that is different from here. I envision a world in which we
> elect a president who is not a rapist. . . . I do this work in honor of my sister
> who passed away this year. I do this work to stop people who are evil and who
> want to take away our health care. I want to work in solidarity with others.
> (Field notes)

A fellow staff member added, "If the very, very wealthy just put in their fair
share, there would be no problems." This perspective was evident when senior
leaders were required to share an issue that motivated them to become activists. The exercise was not hard. Richie Douglas talked about "the state's inability to continue the community care program." Jerry Hackworth called for
more inclusion in social life. And Tara Lamont admitted, "I'm very concerned
about living the golden life." Others spoke of economic justice or the demand
for diminished inequality, a demand made more intense as these seniors recognized an encroaching temporal horizon.

This emphasis on morality was evident in a brief essay composed by
Dr. Ben Golden, a wily and wiry member of the CST, writing on his ninetieth
birthday, having lived through generations of activism:

> We are under attack: Muslims, Jews, Christians, Buddhists, secularists, LGBTs.
> Many of us are demeaned as women, demonized as immigrants. We are de-
> nied the voting booth, forced into prison because of our color, refused basic
> rights as working and poor people. We refuse to be defined this way and we
> know we have to change this distorted framework and we know it has to be
> done now. . . . All of this takes solidarity. It is the formula for a life well worth

living so we can contribute our full potentials to our communities. (Typescript, 2017)

Ben's rhetoric articulated a set of moral constants. Sharing values allowed for making policy demands. At one gathering of the CST and its allies, attendees shared the following core values: equality, fairness, transparency, solidarity, compassion, dignity, community, real democracy, racial justice, humanity, and empathy. Should one believe that this includes all possible values, note the absence of freedom, liberty, tradition, and faith. Conservative groups would surely have included these.

Rhetoric includes not merely what is valued, but the boundaries that differentiate one's friends from one's opponents. In chapter 7 I describe emotional reactions to President Donald Trump. Much of the more colorful opprobrium treated his presidency as an "existential crisis," depicting him as "a monster," "vile," or "fascist." Few insults were off limits to describe a president who was seen as immoral and illegitimate. However, there were numerous other targets for the group's ire. As Jane Tate suggested after tax reform was passed in 2017, "We have an evil Congress, and we have the worst tax bill in history." A member groaned in agreement, "It is unconscionable. There is so much corporate and individual greed" (field notes). Said another about a health care bill, "I want to drive a stake into the heart of these people who keep bringing back this horrible bill." Another loudly condemned the Chicago Housing Authority (CHA) for forcing tenants to move out without support when a building was to be rehabilitated: "We're here to share the atrocities that have been perpetrated by the CHA. . . . They were basically treating us like lab rats" (field notes).

Through their heated rhetoric, movements motivate members.[34] Phrases and slogans frame social problems, as each of the policies promoted by the group and its allies had an appealing label ("The Fair Tax," "Keeping the Promise," "Fight for Fifteen," or "Medicare for All"). The rhetoric suggested a rosy picture of eventual harmony, the need for heroes to achieve desired change, and—using the rhetoric of complaint—images of dark forces and hostile villains that must be overcome to achieve a just society. Through these images this tiny public felt assured of the righteousness of its cause.

The Thorns of Community

To this point I have treated the organization as a hotbed of consensus. There is considerable truth to this picture. For the most part the activists worked harmoniously, with common beliefs and shared goals. However, not everyone agreed on every policy. In accounts of both the Raging Grannies and the Gray Panthers, significant disagreements were evident, strong enough to undercut the groups' success. The Grannies were so divided that some meetings ended in tears or anger. Eventually the group dissolved. This never happened with Chicago Seniors Together, thanks to the strong and admired staff who were influential in defining appropriate progressive goals; however, not all members accepted all policies, even if they often remained silent.

Despite the reality that the organization was explicitly progressive, unanimity did not exist on all issues. Apparent consensus resulted from a desire to conform to the positions of one's colleagues and of the staff. In addition, the specifics of policy were rarely discussed. Many members were less progressive than the staff. One member shared that he was skeptical of the power of unions; another supported the tactics of the Chicago Police Department; a third thought stopping gang violence was a priority; and still another wanted lower taxes. One leader explained to me that hiking taxes would drive corporations out of the state, damaging social support programs. On a dramatic occasion, I sat with three seniors—each a committed member—who disagreed with core issues like the fifteen-dollar minimum wage, college for all, and stopping all deportations. One of my informants confided, "I think I'm more of a Democrat," meaning she considered herself less of a radical. These seniors wished that Democrats and Republicans would collaborate to solve problems, a view that would have appalled some of the staff who saw Republicans as the enemy. In a similar vein, a member explained, "I believe in registering voters, and I don't care who they vote for." Others wished for an exclusive focus on senior issues, ignoring the wider progressive agenda, as did a refugee from the Soviet Union who explained, referring to racial justice, "I do not agree with everything you do. For me [what is important] is whatever happens with seniors. I can't be fighting for everything that I'm in doubt about" (field notes).

Still, the push for expansive agreement, supporting allies, was powerful and led to what the economist Timur Kuran described as "preference falsification"— proclaiming one's beliefs from a desire to conform while personally embracing a different view.[35] Members *privately* shared doubts about organizational policies. One leader explained, "There's been times when I didn't agree with some things. . . . Now that I'm co-chair [of the organization], if the majority agrees that we're going to do something, I think as chair I pretty much have to bite the bullet and do it unless it was really going against my grain" (interview). She prioritized loyalty to the community over her own instincts.

Perhaps the greatest policy disagreement was over single-payer health care, or what came to be called Medicare for All. At first many leaders were not interested in the issue, feeling that it was not a senior problem. Since Medicare covers the elderly, any expansion would not directly change senior health care and might even limit it. Beyond this, the policy seemed unwinnable in the short term. An Alinsky approach to organizing emphasizes that effective activism should focus on achievable victories. Idealism is nice, but power matters more. With a Republican Congress, Medicare for All would never be enacted. It was a dream, and in fact a dream that some members wished to defer. However, one member, Lauren Dornbush, pushed the organization on this matter, although for a time her concern was marginalized. Dr. Ben described her as his Joan of Arc, suggesting that he supported the goal but believed the effort was doomed to be a fiery failure.

In time organizational leaders, although not all members, came to support the issue as reflecting their values even if passage was unlikely. Organizing for a single-payer health care system inspired many members. This change occurred when progressive Democrats and Democratic Socialists around the nation embraced the same issue.

Not everyone in Chicago Seniors Together supported the plan. Some members, particularly those with adequate private health care, were skeptical of a government-run program. However, once the Health Care and Economic Justice Committee endorsed the proposal, these critics remained quiet, permitting the assumption that all agreed. Indeed, during my research there were few heated debates on any policy. Members assumed that the organization would have one position and that the staff would be influential in establishing these priorities. Those who were skeptical phrased their concern delicately. Esther Harvey, an influential member, explained,

> I don't see eye-to-eye on everything. . . . Not everything that the organization tends to believe in that I tend to agree with, but I don't really feel that my position is to speak up and counter that, because that's what the leadership of the organization feels is important. (Interview)

No one recognized Esther's concerns about a single-payer health care system:

> My fear about single payer is that you're going to have all these people that are vying to try to get into the doctor's [schedule]. What will happen is that some of the good doctors will leave and go to concierge practices, and so then it's going to be hard to get to some. . . . It's still very hard right now to be able to get in to see really good doctors. . . . I have a fair number of medical issues going on, [so] that's important to me to be able to access these good doctors, and also the delay in time that I know tends to happen in a single-payer system. . . . But I do see why, for many people, having that single payer would be helpful to them. (Interview)

Esther struggled with her class privilege as a retired professional. She admired the organization, worked hard, and contributed financially, but she believed some of the policies it promoted might erode her own quality of life.

Despite the disagreements that she and others had with organizational policies, her loyalty to the group overwhelmed her dissent and she chose to be silent rather than spark a debate that might be divisive and create ill will. The desire for community—and conformity—was sufficient to keep members in line, at least those who remained. Loyalty was prized, the exit of some seniors was accepted as inevitable, and voice became a form of deviance, even (or especially) in an organization that engages in agitation. Despite surface consensus, disagreement on some issues was evident, hidden by limited discussion and the desire for camaraderie. Rarely did any meeting allow extended debate, and when that happened it was considered an organizational failure as well as potentially stigmatizing to the critic. The organization remained strong because the progressive views of staff and selected leaders were treated as the group's defined positions. If secret ballots were held unanimity might be undercut, so none were held and few contested votes of any kind occurred. Votes were taken when unanimity was clear. The organization ensured consensus by erasing difference.

Coming and Staying

One influential member of the CST explained that the organization was a "community of ideas and needs." However, like all such movement groups, it required a continuing influx of recruits. As this member later noted, even though ideas motivated joining, people must be asked to join, and this ongoing recruitment was especially essential for an organization of seniors. He noted,

> It's a community that, as its members age, as it brings in newer, younger people, as members of it die and the survivors adjust, you have a deeper, richer community, because even if you're brand new and don't know anything, you're welcome for your energy, which we in the middle are starting to notice is declining, and the ones that have lost it are still grateful if you show up. (Interview)

The group needed to establish a *chain of commitment* that depended on cohort replacement.[36] The problem for a community is that when someone expresses a desire to belong, this engagement may not be lasting. The decision to join can produce exhaustion. As one leader vented about her early days, "I was burnt to a crisp." Another worried about giving a potential leader a major position: "I would be sad to see him burn out. He has a lot of good ideas for the future" (field notes). Several leaders said wistfully that they needed to learn to "say no." A leader who eventually quit the organization commented, "I said no as long as I could." Another well-respected leader, Richie Douglas, pointed out that commitment is a team sport: "You have to trust [those] who are in the fight with you to make this happen. I got a lot of energy from realizing that there are others who are doing the same thing" (field notes). Every tiny public places a premium on willingness to do the work, but this has costs in retaining participants.

The difficulty was to find the right level of involvement to nurture commitment without destroying it. This proved challenging in an activist organization whose members were continually exhorted to do more. Many participants preferred gabbing, planning, and complaining, avoiding the strains of public activism and mundane office work. Jane Tate, the executive director, distinguished between talkers and actors: "There are people who like to talk about things but not do anything. They are not the people you want in this organization. . . . People are going to be asked to do something, but they won't do it. They're not bad people, but this is not the right organization for them" (field notes).

Given that she made this comment at a meeting of the board, perhaps she was chiding those around the table who were happy to serve but were less active in the protests the organization sponsored. The trade-off was between recruiting a large organization and recruiting an active organization. As I describe in chapter 7, the outcome of the 2016 election brought in many new members, but relatively few wanted to participate other than in thrilling mega-events. Phone banking, stuffing envelopes, and knocking on doors were not pleasurable activist commitments.

The hope is that if members can be inspired (or pressured) to make public commitments, they will not back out of their promises. This is a strategy well known to social psychologists.[37] Promises in front of an audience count more than implicit agreements. Of course members frequently reneged and seniors had a wealth of excuses, many perhaps entirely justified. For some the embarrassment of having made commitments they did not keep impelled them to leave the organization or to stop attending meetings where commitments were solicited. Many meetings closed with the staff asking attendees what days they would they work for the organization or how many friends they would bring to events. Through these pressured promises, members felt trapped into organizational labor, no longer allowed to be free riders. At one meeting, staffers asked attendees to fill out "Action Alert" cards agreeing to attend several future events. These cards were then read aloud. It's easy to appreciate that participants may promise to attend events in a hazy future—events they subsequently must find excuses for avoiding. The dilemma of public commitments was evident at board meetings when those not attending had their excuses noted, although without explicit criticism. (One absent member, in Florida for the winter, was said to need "warm weather.") The comments signaled to those present that their absence would be remarked on.

In making personal commitments, the pressure was real, but members were also asked to commit to inviting friends or relatives, pushed for a "turnout number" that was then publicly noted. Jane encouraged board members to work toward a large gathering: "We want to push ourselves, but not to be unrealistic. What stretches us but is something we could achieve?" When they decided that eighty to one hundred attendees would be a good turnout, she asked, "What's the board's responsibility for turnout? Where is that base coming from? What's the role of the engagement of the board to involve people we want to get more engaged and more active?" Although she encouraged public commitments, and the organization would not have succeeded in powerful actions without this pressure, not everyone felt comfortable in having their promises recalled. This encouragement can be especially tricky when one doesn't want to impose on others. Still, such pressure was central to how the organization transformed commitment from a verbal announcement to a public action.

Recruitment to Justice

A long-standing truism of social movement research is that networks are the primary means of recruitment. There is much truth to this claim, and in my research with Chicago Seniors Together I found many instances of such recruitment. One member, Davey Gibbs, was renowned for his enthusiastic success in capturing members from his senior high-rise and his church. He had recruited some dozen members of the organization through his persuasive insistence. While Davey was the most diligent recruiter, he was by no means alone. Over time, I could trace skeins of relations. The *personal ask* was a powerful means of recruitment,[38] arguably the most powerful.

The personal ask is not, however, the only means of recruitment. This process downplays beliefs as advertisements for joining. Values and ideology matter in movement activism. Some of this might be due to the dramatic political heating in the aftermath of Donald Trump's election that impelled some Chicagoans to find a group in which to protest convivially. Still, they needed to become aware of Chicago Seniors Together. While this happened through networking, it also occurred at demonstrations, at neighborhood "listening sessions," and through online communities. One co-chair of the organization became involved because the CST held a listening session at her senior building. She agreed about the need to protect Social Security.

Potential members would not join the organization without believing that the politics of the CST largely matched their own views, at least their interests as senior citizens, but this attitudinal agreement was rarely sufficient. It is more effective when the potential joiner has already recognized the need for activism and the organization provides an easy entrance to a political community. For this reason, when engaging in telephone banking or knocking on doors, activists were told they must start with "values." A person who did not share the values of the organization (social justice, income redistribution, overcoming inequality, skepticism of elites) was unlikely to join. While members were routinely exhorted to reach out to friends and neighbors, the organization also grew from value connections. Although some found it appealing to persuade those who fundamentally disagreed with their core values, the staff insisted this was not a wise use of resources. The volunteer who commented to staff, "You're putting a wall between you and some people who like what Trump does" was told not to argue with those who doubted core beliefs. Doubters would not make good soldiers in the battle for the progressive transformation of society.

The 2016 election boosted the desire to reach out through shared values. In the words of one staff member, "We had the resistance thrust upon us." Suddenly there was an unexpected opportunity for organizational growth, and membership nearly doubled. Although that number did not last, it increased the possibilities of collective action. A similar linkage of ideological matching, group process, and network possibilities likewise applies to recruitment to the Tea Party and Occupy movements.

Alongside the power of networks and social relations as recruitment devices, beliefs matter for the growth of social movements. But beliefs must be supported by sociality. Relationships help define a moral compass by integrating values and connections.[39] Beliefs are insufficient when not supported by affiliations displayed within an interaction order. The potential complexity of this process was evident from an explanation by Davey Gibbs, a leader of the CST and a key informant. He shared his role in his Unitarian church and subsequently in the CST:

> When I got separated from my wife, I had just rejoined the church. I started to get active at various things. At my church, a lady gave a talk on Chicago Seniors Together. I thought, "Boy, that's good. I'll give them some money." But I didn't see myself as a senior until I retired [ten years later]. I went to a meet-

ing. I saw people from my church. I joined. At first not much happened, but in June of that year, that would be '99, Don Jones became the executive director. He moved the CST from a senior organization where they had meetings and talked about "Are your feet bothering you?" to community organizing. He went into that right away, and I was ripe for that. So I went into community organizing. I had done stuff as an individual and some Unitarian stuff, but that really turned me on. . . . I found a role in Chicago Seniors Together. . . . We were doing stuff I wanted to do [and that] I thought was important. I had the feeling that things weren't going good for people like me, left-wingers, and I moved into community organizing. (Interview)

Although less dramatic, the same elements were evident in the comments of a new member who joined after the 2016 election. Of the election aftermath she reported, "It's changed my life. I needed a project. It's done me a world of good. It's made me emboldened." A second said the election impelled her to act "so I would not just be sitting around." Said a third, "I'm tired of feeling frustrated" (field notes). These feelings, grounded in political beliefs, had power in motivating people to join. However, these emotions depend on a community to become activated, and this occurs through the shared feelings of colleagues.

The Feeling State

Every movement requires emotion work to create engagement, a justification for action.[40] As Deborah Gould points out, "In order to attract and retain participants and to pursue a movement's agenda, activists continually need to mobilize affective states and emotions that mesh with the movement's political objects and tactics."[41] Lacking a group culture and a supportive "emotional resonance," one's desire for engagement will dissipate.[42] In Erika Summers-Effler's dual ethnographies of anti-death penalty activists and members of the Catholic Workers,[43] she argues that emotional rhythms keep participants involved despite these groups' frequent failure to achieve their ends. Emotion work suffices to tie activists to their colleagues and their goals and to create a meaningful group culture. Affect is not just something that happens to individuals; it characterizes group life.

Inevitably, an emotional component is central to organizing.[44] Emotion makes values insistent. Movement groups provide a venue where a linkage between feeling and action is assumed. An interaction order not only presents demands for public behavior but includes pressure for revealed sentiments.[45] Movements succeed or crumble depending on whether they establish feeling rules and emotion work that lead to a desired consensus.[46]

Engagement would not last long were emotions not felt. The forms of feeling must be appropriate both for those experiencing them and for the onlookers. This was clear for Canada's Raging Grannies, a progressive group of older women who hoped to display both their rage and their empowerment in street theater performances that were alternately provocative and joyous.[47] Producing collective effervescence in an audience of strangers was the outcome they desired, as long as the emotional high provoked a moral shock that activated an injustice frame.[48] Demonstrations must avoid being tedious, but they also need to avoid hectoring or depressing those exposed. If they inconvenience the audience, the delay must be seen as the ultimate responsibility of the targeted villain. When successful, dramas of contention portray themes, images, and frames that capture the moment and characterize their movement and their hope to better the world.[49]

The importance of performed emotion was clear at Chicago Seniors Together. Whether felt internally or not, reference to emotion was a routine component of organizational culture. At the conclusion of meetings and in evaluations of political actions, participants were asked to share a "feeling word" describing their reaction to what had just taken place. One staff member emphasized that she didn't want to hear a "thought word." These feeling words include "confused," "excited," "confident," "exhilarated," "depressed," and "hopeful." This constituted a temperature gauge that permitted the staff to judge the event's success. Whether the exercise truly reflected an internal sensibility or was merely a form of impression management is an open question. Still, along with values, feelings were essential in establishing the CST as a moral domain.

Talking about one's emotions, while important, is insufficient. One does not experience feeling words as spoken, although one might have felt the emotion they referenced. A recognized grievance must move people from a tolerable status quo to devote precious time and scarce resources and to expose vulnerability in affiliating with a group that demands broad structural change. Participants must feel the wrongness—the burn—and, one hopes, feel it passionately.

But this emotional heating raises a question. One might wonder, as Rachel Ramirez speculates, whether it is ethical for organizers "to agitate their community leaders in a way that risks making them feel debased and dejected." Ramirez ponders whether, if people are content, they should be made to feel oppressed. Is contented oppression better than the righteous rage of justice warriors? These individuals, Ramirez notes, "already [have been] so kicked around in their lives."[50] Is it "nice" and ethical to force them to become agitated and to demand change that one hopes will benefit them as well as a population of free riders?

In Saul Alinsky–style agitation, generating anger and creating enemies are central to effective community organizing, establishing the willingness to bear costs to bring about change. Having a well-defined enemy that provokes negative emotions motivates the willingness to act.[51] Outrage is power. James Jasper points out that this involves creating a moral shock that occurs "when an unexpected event or piece of information makes such a sense of outrage in a person that she becomes inclined toward political action."[52] Rather than rousing a single individual, this rage motivates a group, leading to the collective embrace of a grievance frame.[53]

Provocation can produce moral anger, which was vital for the success of the tendentious ACT UP movement against AIDS.[54] Although anger has become seen as increasingly undesirable, even deviant, in contemporary American culture,[55] when molded, directed, and controlled it can be powerful, although some groups have more of a "right to anger" than others. We find this contrast of legitimate emotion in competing accounts of Black Lives Matter and the pro-life movement. As Jeffrey Stout points out,

> Anger is one of the most important traits [organizers] look for in potential leaders. Someone who professes love of justice, but is not angered by its violation, is not likely to stay with the struggle for justice through thick and thin, to display the passion that will motivate others to join in, or to have enough courage to stand up to the powers that be.[56]

One CST leader spoke of the need for "fire in the belly"—the basis, she felt, for effective organizational leadership.

This anger talk is evident in comments that Dan, the CST's male staffer, makes on our bus ride to Racine to protest Congressman Paul Ryan's plan to cripple the Affordable Care Act. Dan expresses what he defines as fury and says that the proposal, if enacted, will burden his family. His parents are supporting his grandparents, and an uncle is in drug treatment. "It will be hurting my family. I'm incredibly angry!" He asks, "Who's angry?" and we roar our support for Dan's family. Our chants, as I noted in the prologue, express this rage, whatever our private feelings: "Ryan keeps lying, people keep dying," and "The rich pay more, it's only fair." One speaker shared her sour belief, "We'll have to eat dog food. That ain't right. It's a death plan. We'll resist." While these might not have been the most elegant rhymes or the subtlest rhetoric, they were invigorating on this chilly day. At times it was unclear whether we were enraged or amused. On another occasion, after a frustrating and inconclusive Chicago City Council hearing, an organizer remarked, "No one made our anger and frustration known." From her perspective, we should have been more disruptive, using rage strategically.

During my observations I frequently heard anger referred to rhetorically, but it was hard to see in their behavior that people were actually "angry" in the moment, even when they used the label. This was particularly tricky given that seniors are cautious about displaying temper, since it can lead to questions about their cognitive or behavioral competence. Emotion work is always situated in light of how performers are viewed by authorities. Children, the elderly, and women do not have their anger taken seriously. They are seen as cute when they're mad. In their fury, racial minorities may be seen as dangerous and unpredictable rather than as committed. The interpretation of performed emotion is linked to one's place in the social order, a disadvantage for disfavored groups.

For seniors, expressing fear was considered more effective than showing anger, a concern for their future being something that they are legitimately entitled to express and that fits better into the culture of aging. Whether the fear was visceral or rhetorical was unclear,[57] as when one member said, "I'm scared to death about a Medicare voucher program" and another remarked, "I've never been so frightened for the future of my country as I am now" (field notes). Tears too, signaling a damp empathy, could provoke a positive response, promoting the desire to comfort through reform. As Henry Dowdall, a charismatic Black senior, explained after providing his personal heartfelt story, "Thank you for your tears. Tears are powerful. We can do anything through tears" (field notes).

The threat of the Trump agenda led many seniors to dread what might happen to those entitlement programs they relied on. Perhaps in retrospect that feared outcome was not likely, but the alarm was real. In generating support for knocking on doors or for telephone banking, emotion was a motivator, as when Dan noted, "I hope people will sign up if you feel anger or [are] frustrated or upset" (field notes). The mundane quality of the tasks often outweighed whatever emotion people were experiencing, since finding volunteers proved to be an organizational challenge.

If prospective volunteers did not experience meaningful and shared emotions, they were unlikely to participate. As I noted, fear motivated action, but so did joy, communion, empathy, and satisfaction. Negative emotions are only a part of the emotional palette. When Susan Locker left the Board of Directors after many years, she expressed how meaningful Chicago Seniors Together had been in her life: "I have had more joy, more commitment, and more friends" (field notes). Positive emotions are especially effective in building an organizational culture based on a politics of care that justifies civic welfare in contrast to negative expressions of agitation. This is evident among populations like seniors, in which anger's provocative claws are viewed negatively[58] but empathy's wings are better accepted. Like negative affect, communal good feeling can support challenges to an impassive status quo.

The difficulty with Alinsky-inspired community-based organizations is that the emotions generated are intentionally negative: resentment of injustice. Still, even here the anger and tension must be modulated so that participants feel comfortable: a happy senior is often taken as a healthy senior.[59] Perhaps for reasons of self-presentation, seniors are more likely than younger groups to report positive emotions and less likely to report negative emotions.[60] When young people riot in the streets it's understandable; it's more questionable for their grandparents. Acceptable emotional display is linked to the life cycle from temper tantrums on. In the CST, negative emotions were made more evident in banners, posters, speeches, and chants than in actions in the public square. Scripted remarks and formal talk can convey the rage that unscripted behavior cannot express.

The Activist Community

As the prominent American political theorist John Dewey remarked, democracy depends on neighbors.[61] Friends and confidants are essential to creating a just state. This is a claim not merely for the influence of social propinquity, but for the existence of powerful local cultures based on interests, commitment, and values. This need has two components. One desires something bigger than oneself—being able to make a difference—but along with this sense of consequence comes a desire for togetherness.[62] Both emphasize the rhetoric of We, not I in group communication (field notes). In this regard Ruth Braunstein properly speaks of the power of "situated intersubjectivity."[63]

Citizens' groups constitute key sites where this kind of *situated subjectivity* can be shared by providing opportunities for people to validate their experiences in light of others' and to develop more refined understandings of what kind of society they are living in, what it means to be a member of that society, and how they are connected to their fellow citizens and their government. In this way a group can develop *situated intersubjectivity*, as described by Braunstein, a collective sense of what kind of group it is, how it relates to other groups, and how (given the first two) it is prepared to act collectively.

Social movement organizations like Chicago Seniors Together demonstrate this process. To understand how a movement gains power, one must appreciate how it becomes a community. Civil rights leaders like Martin Luther King Jr. spoke of the "beloved community." Whether beloved or merely appreciated, community cements participants to activities with social or economic costs, and the sense of togetherness overcomes these obstacles.[64]

Civic involvement depends on the depth and extension of social relations.[65] The respected community organizer Ernesto Cortés Jr. made this argument effectively when he asserted that movements must develop political friendships and small gatherings that support them: "These small-group conversations, properly directed and aimed, then lead to research actions to explore the dynamics, dimensions, and complexities of an issue in order to prepare for action."[66]

Near the end of my research I attended what was labeled a "campaign leadership school." This two-day event was organized by Fair Economy Illinois, part of the activist network that Chicago Seniors Together belonged to. Attendees were trained in how to build their movements, emphasizing the importance of developing relationships with those who shared sympathetic values. One of the most compelling presentations was by a staffer at the CST. Luisa noted that politicians often use the image of community for their own ends, hosting luncheons or handing out turkeys at Thanksgiving. In contrast, she argued for a concept that she termed—with intended double meaning— "radical hospitality." Luisa described how the CST created a feeling of camaraderie that supported otherwise difficult actions: "When you go out on a winter's day with only a hand warmer or a granola bar, we can only do that if we build real community" (field notes). Many attendees supported her concept of radical hospitality, proclaiming, "Don't forget to say [to participants] how much I appreciate [your support]." This was posed in contrast to progressive campaigns in which workers were not appreciated ("radical inhospitality"). Luisa referred to a "crappy" experience in which undocumented workers who were paid for canvassing were trailed by the police but never were thanked by the organizers. In contrast, she asserted, the goal was to constitute the movement as a caring group.

This leadership school was a particularly dramatic moment when building community was treated as a necessary component of activist practice, but it was by no means the only occasion. Leaders of the CST were told that meetings should be "warm and welcoming," with greeters at the door hoping to incorporate new recruits. As Jane Tate explained, "We wanted to make sure that anyone who came felt that they [were] really welcome" (field notes). Some meetings opened with a sing-along, such as a collective rendition of "We Shall Overcome," sung with gusto if not always in tune. Food served as senior communion. As one member joked, "One sentence: 'If you feed them, they will come'" (field notes). Tasty snacks were often provided at meetings or for work groups. This was dramatically evident with a phone bank near Christmas that was advertised as a cookie exchange; most participants brought treats, and afterward several callers adjourned for a friendly lunch at a nearby sandwich shop. One staffer was known for bringing in honey cake, and a member was revered for her biscotti. The goal was not only to thank and to feed, as beneficial as those tactics might be, but "to get people talking with each other about their concerns."[67] As a result, leaders of larger meetings often divided the attendees into breakout groups for discussion, then brought them together to share ideas.

Community building was also evident in the CST's housing activism. Staffers wanted to recruit members from senior housing complexes, and once this was achieved each building was treated as a site for action. The organization could then establish "housing meetings," a powerful example of acting locally, however global the conception. For those without a powerful desire for activism, a local meeting was low-cost first involvement. The building was the site for organizing; each building had its own culture, its own demographics, and its own politics. The CST attempted to activate its network to find a person who could organize the building. The goal was to place supporters on residents' committees, with one staffer admitting candidly, "We need to infiltrate the senior board" (field notes). Once they identified this supporter, she could communicate with her neighbors. As a result, some buildings were known for a strong activist culture while others were passive. Those who organized their buildings, such as Philip, who not only organized his building but brought his neighbors to events, were esteemed.

Another feature of group life at Chicago Seniors Together proved central: the one-on-one or relational meeting. These meetings were frequently treated as crucial to building activism, deriving from the approach of Saul Alinsky and his colleagues at the Industrial Areas Foundation.[68] Such gatherings provided a "narrow compass" through which to build memory, imagination, and reflection. According to one leader, "We rely very heavily on one-on-ones. Two people. You're telling me about what brings you to the coalition. We get to know each other on a personal basis. It makes us like a family" (field notes). While central to organizational culture, these one-on-one meetings were not unique to CST but characterize many social movement organizations. As Jeffrey Stout points out, "Face-to-face meetings are now called one-on-ones or relational meetings, and they were essential components of each of the major democratic reform movements in U.S. history. . . . [Early feminist] 'parlor meetings' were precursors of what [Alinsky Industrial Area Foundation] groups call 'house meetings.'"[69] In the words of Ernesto Cortés Jr., "These small group meetings are about telling stories and developing narratives, but also about inquiring into the deep concerns affecting people's daily lives."[70] Such occasions provide opportunities for meaningful engagement by establishing frames of injustice through sharing experiences with sympathetic others.[71] While house meetings, consciousness-raising groups, or study circles[72] do not have the same dynamics as one-on-ones, given their larger size, they link group commitment into a sense of situated intersubjectivity through sociable connections and the education the group leaders provide. When effective, these are not merely bull sessions but involve socialization and sympathy. If I spend time in your parlor, enjoying your tea and sympathy, can I ever be truly hostile toward you? Such social forms tighten the network and create relational power. The meetings are particularly influential when they occur between members and staff. At the CST one-on-ones typically lasted about thirty minutes, with participants describing their diverse backgrounds and explaining their involvement in the movement. These are not spaces where the partners discuss political issues, but an opportunity to build relationships. While there might be some element of social control or surveillance in encouraging members to say the right things, this view may be overly skeptical. However, contentious conversations might reveal a person who should be frozen out of the organization.[73] In most cases one-on-ones build positive affect that ties people to the group and makes exit more difficult.

Sociality and Movement Politics

A strong movement depends on the linkage of community and sociability. Just as a political party must, on ritual occasions, be a party, a social movement must be social. Early research often depicted protesters as isolated and sometimes as irrational. Such was never the case, and this view is now discounted.[74] Socializing may be particularly salient for senior activists, for whom belonging to the group prevents social disengagement as well as defending against the public stigma of mental decline.

Friendships are critical to the development of sociality. People must want to spend time with others even if the tasks they are assigned are mundane or onerous. Gemma Edwards speaks of this as a friendship network that shapes one's movement career.[75] In describing the Gray Panthers, Roger Sanjek emphasizes the salience friendships have for the elderly. He notes that "experiences with illness or deaths were grist for conversations that might broaden to emotional support during health or family crises."[76] Those who claim to "get along with everyone," countering stereotypes of cranky seniors, demonstrate their civility by continued engagement.

To support the idea of the movement as a community, Chicago Seniors Together encouraged members to arrive at meetings thirty minutes early. Food was important, but the informal conversations, impossible during the structured and time-compressed meetings, were even more appealing. The relational questions posed at the outset of each meeting, while sometimes edging into the political, often proved personally revealing, such as "What's the most enjoyable thing you did over the holiday?" "What's your favorite kind of music?" or "What's your favorite fruit?" These are things friends might enjoy knowing about each other, as opposed to the more overtly political questions ("What's the worst thing about the tax bill?"). Strangers would find such "silly" relational questions uninteresting.

On occasion the desire for community became a problem when participants did not recognize as relevant the basis community is to be built on. The staff once organized a potluck for "Women of Color"; other members were not informed of the gathering. One attendee was disturbed because she felt it was a gathering of people who had little in common other than skin color. For her this was not a crucial connection: "My understanding is that they wanted to give voice and strength to Black females. I personally don't think I need it, but maybe some people do. At our first meeting I was a little bit surprised, to the point that I felt, 'Is this a social gathering or is this a mental health gathering?'" (interview). She had invited several friends, who were similarly disappointed. This admired leader soon left the organization.

One can see the desire for comity when the board spent significant time planning the winter holiday party and the spring luncheon. These events were fund-raisers for the organization, but their financial side had to be balanced with their role as parties. This ingathering supported a friendship culture, a form of the radical hospitality described above. How can the group create moments of fun, of financial support, and of community development within the same event? I attended a meeting of the Finance Committee that was planning the annual luncheon. This was the year's most important fund-raiser and included a large silent auction. The organization invited local progressive political leaders and recruited new members through invitations from current members. Jane, as executive director, reviewed the goals to be met if the luncheon was to be a success: raise money; honor longtime activists; build relationships with legislators and other allies; have fun; and welcome guests and make new friends. The theme—Veterans of the Fight—was important because it validated members' commitment. One member remarked, "Just take time to honor all those who built the organization. It's always good to reflect back on the people who have built the movement when we are facing new challenges" (field notes). The instrumental and expressive goals of the luncheon were intertwined. Although the event lasted only three hours, planning it took six months. Jane pointed out that developing the party was the members' job: "The planning meeting is really important, because otherwise it's like the staff are planning and not leaders. . . . [You need to make] sure that leaders were a part of every aspect of the planning."

These events contributed to a sense that the movement is not only about resistance but also about togetherness, overcoming potential isolation. The goal was to build a friendship network that inspired movement careers.[77] I learned that some members who lived in the same senior housing complex gathered for Saturday breakfasts. As these participants bonded, their mutual concern deepened. One staff member suggests the importance of relational organizing as well as its limits:

> The relationship-based organizing part of the work that we do is what keeps it together. It keeps it about people thinking deeply about each other in relationships instead of just bodies. . . . This isn't a club. This is an organization that works on really important issues. That social aspect is amazing to accompany our power building, but I would hate for Chicago Seniors Together to just be like a mingling kind of thing. We mean business. And there's like a bad stereotype of seniors as they go to bingo. (Interview)

This staffer pointed to the same potluck for women of color that was criticized above as a means of integrating sociality with political engagement. Whether it did so is an open question. What is important is that the gathering was organized to provide a space where those invited could develop camaraderie.

The Power of Group Culture

A belief in community and spaces for sociality is crucial in developing ways that values promote engagement. However, one additional feature deserves attention: the content of those occasions. Occasions matter, but they matter because they embrace shared content.[78] This connects to the role of a local culture that links sociality to shared, ongoing, and self-reflexive practice.

Group cultures provide interaction with a content that develops from the dynamics of participants acting together. Group cultures—what I have termed idiocultures[79]—reveal that culture is more than an amorphous mist.[80] In contrast, it is a recognized set of attitudes, feelings, and practices held by people with ongoing relationships. While some cultural traditions are widely known and utilized, they are known and utilized within group contexts. Other cultural traditions are particular to small communities. Whatever their spread, culture provides the basis for action: tools within a tool kit.[81] As a framework, idioculture

> consists of a system of knowledge, beliefs, behaviors, and customs shared by members of an interacting group to which members can refer and that serve

as the basis of further interaction. Members recognize that they share experiences, and these experiences can be referred to with the expectation that they will be understood by other members, thus being used to construct a social reality for the participants.[82]

Knowing that others share eventful experience can be empowering in creating civic commitment and a willingness to accept political risks. When many groups in similar circumstances have parallel experiences, this recognition can provoke a wider civic commitment or promote a shared demand for change.

Social movements strive to create common cultures and a set of practices that are treated as characteristic of the organization. This point is made clearly by Kathleen Blee in *Democracy in the Making*. Following from a survey of small social movement groups in the Pittsburgh area, Blee finds that local cultures support successful groups but destroy those in which no collective meanings bind members. Culture is the linchpin connecting participants and bolstering their willingness to support a set of values. Movements are sites of discourse and debate, and as these themes are recognized, group cultures are established.[83] Groups of all kinds—political and social—develop styles of interaction: the interaction order. These styles are recognizable through communal boundaries, group bonding, and speech norms.[84]

With regard to progressive social movements, we often find an admirable desire to create a diverse organization, and this push for diversity is linked to group styles that speak to those from a variety of interactional backgrounds. These contrasting styles are seen in a recent study of two immigrants' rights organizations.[85] Depending on whether their religious, class-based, and linguistic practices connected to those of their target groups, the organizations were more or less successful in incorporating targeted participants. To create comfortable cultural structures, diversity needed to extend beyond a rhetorical trope. As I discuss in chapter 6, the CST faced a similar challenge in becoming a diverse group, despite its sincere desire, as organizers struggled to gain the support of African American and working-class Chicagoans for a group that was often seen as having a White and middle-class culture.

Still, the organization did succeed in creating a culture that many participants found agreeable. Much culture swirls around charismatic social actors. Some figures developed personae that came to characterize the group. One example was "Dr. Ben." Ben Golden was about to turn ninety when I came to know him. He was a longtime active member of the organization and had been involved in progressive causes since the 1940s. Alongside his passion for racial justice and progressive policies was his enjoyment of lively conversation. Ben's frequent insights often derailed committee meetings, yet his generosity made him beloved even when his opinions could be seen as disruptive, as I discuss in chapter 5. Ben was known as "a character," and his involvement was integral the group's culture.[86] The accounts of Dr. Ben's bloviating and eccentricity were central to group lore. As Davey Gibbs, another longtime member, pointed out to much knowing laughter, "He's Ben" (field notes).

Davey himself had a reputation that shaped group culture. Hard of hearing and with vision problems, Davey, nearing eighty, demanded that events run on a tight schedule or he would respond dramatically, seeing corruption ("crap") everywhere he looked. Both men were central to the organization, but the group had to adjust to their peculiarities and grievances. As an organization of elderly men and women set in their ways, accepting eccentricity was part of establishing a harmonious culture and a soft community.

Beyond charismatic personalities, other elements of group culture characterized the organization. The leaders of the CST spoke of a "culture of questioning," a response to scandals at the defunct Chicago organization Metro Seniors in Action that resulted in all events' being carefully evaluated. On one occasion an active leader suggested it would be helpful if the new-member orientation included a glossary of all of the common local terms, noting that "we have all this jargon." While some of these phrases were widely used within progressive activism ("power analysis," "relational exercises," "feeling words"), others were specific to the CST, such as its being an "organization led by seniors for seniors" (field notes). Full integration depended on an awareness of groupspeak.

Chicago Seniors Together was not just any organization but an organization whose meanings and emotional appeal grew from a set of referents that allowed participants to feel they belonged to something other than a generic activist group. In contrast, they were a group of friends, and like all friends they treasured their relationships. As I discuss in chapter 2, part of this image resulted from the reality that they were elderly and defined themselves in light of this age category, their generation, and the collective identity that resulted. But another part resulted from their group history and idiosyncratic culture.

Commitments and Ideologies

The content of social movement beliefs matters, even if these beliefs are filtered through the demands of social relations and group culture. Committed groups connect minds and hearts, attitudes and communities, bodies and public spaces. Each of these elements must be present for a group to achieve its desired ends. This connects a social psychology with a meso-level local sociology. While a world exists outside the group, a topic of chapter 7, I begin with the recognition that activism is about something, and that something is motivating and contributes to the possibility of recruitment. Even though senior involvement is age-related, it is also idea-related. This links belief to culture.

It's not that a group culture must always be about ideology or the instrumental purposes of a group—it isn't—but its appeal to sociability must be consistent with the larger purposes that drive participants to join and to remain. Recruitment is more than simply friends asking friends: the asking occurs in a context where the asker and the joiner have something in common, a similarity that is deepened within the group. Tiny publics provide friendly spaces where values can be enacted. The instrumental and expressive faces of group life are joined.

We err if we ignore the issues groups fight for and the way these affect participants' desire to belong. Values were once central to sociology, and they must remain so, but in the context of social connections, local communities, and friendship strands. Chicago Seniors Together is not just any group of seniors, even though its membership was built through social networks. Ongoing participation is possible only if the community is important and if resisting *together* makes victories possible. Agitation is a team sport.

Building a sense of shared being is a challenge for any social movement group. The groups that can do this effectively survive, the others flicker out. In successful groups, voices of dissent must be moderated and controlled, exits kept to a minimum, and expressions of loyalty made a primary virtue. This matters even if not every member of the group privately supports each policy. While ideas and ideology matter, disagreement must be bracketed because of an overriding desire to remain with friends and to support colleagues. Belief, culture, and sociality join to support effective and lasting movements for change.

Coming of Age

Old age is an excellent time for outrage. My goal is to say or do at least one outrageous
thing every week.

MAGGIE KUHN, founder of Gray Panthers

Perhaps age is a state of mind, but it is also a state of body. As we age we become more vulnerable physically. Although this occurs at different rates and
with variable effects, the elderly face difficulties distinct from those facing
the young. Further, life stages have cultures, in part as a result of the structural positions age leads to, sometimes exacerbating inequalities.[1] Given this,
Deborah Carr questions the cheerful label of the "golden years" as she depicts
the disadvantages many seniors face as a result of race, poverty, or gender.[2]
Images of aging can be powerful: ennobling or sad, romantic or frighten-
ing.[3] Some have described being elderly as "the third age": the period after
retirement and before serious declines in health,[4] allowing for volunteering
and civic engagement. This can last ten to twenty years, a significant period
that has increased over the past decades, permitting self-expression, sociability, and political activism. Given their public presence, seniors need not be a
social burden, and they have not removed themselves from the community,
contrary to earlier disengagement theories of aging. Although gerontologists
once spoke of the prevalence of age-differentiated lives—social separation
based on generation—many seniors are integrated with younger people, and
they share similar values.[5] More roles are open to seniors, including being political provocateurs, like the Gray Panthers and the group I studied, Chicago
Seniors Together. Considering values, differences within age cohorts may
equal those between cohorts.[6] Much depends on the capacities of individual
seniors and the groups they belong to.

This chapter explores some distinctive features that make senior activism
potent, provocative, and problematic. Although this is not a study of aging
per se, to understand senior activism, understanding the lifeworld of seniors
is essential. Most seniors I met were in reasonably good health—sufficient to

participate in movement activities—and were financially stable. But despite their condition, they fervently believed that society has an obligation to moderate inequalities in the name of justice.

As I noted, much earlier writing on aging has suggested that it is a time of social retreat. There may have been some justice in this account when the retirement age was fixed and life expectancy was not as long as it has become. Current research recognizes that many seniors have active and long-term social and political lives. Some scholars even speak of the existence of a "gray political bloc with common consciousness, interests, and behaviors."[7] Current gerontology emphasizes the importance of civic engagement in creating well-being throughout the aging process[8] and recognizes empowerment in activism.[9] As Arlie Hochschild discovered in her examination of a senior citizen apartment complex, seniors who engaged in political activism, such as fighting for Social Security or better medical benefits, were more highly esteemed by neighbors than those who engaged in passive recreation.[10]

We may divide seniors into the "young old" and the "old old," as members of Chicago Seniors Together sometimes did, even while recognizing that some in their late eighties and early nineties were active in political protest, even civil disobedience. The period of old age incorporates considerable diversity in experience. Among my informants, some were young adults during World War II, others during the Korean War, and still others during the War in Vietnam. The age range in Chicago Seniors Together spans a quarter-century.

Age and even its bodily effects do not inevitably cause disengagement. Some seniors feel it is insufficient to sit in their rockers as the image suggests; they want to promote an altruistic future that stretches beyond their own horizons. A desire to leave a better politics and a more just society for future generations may be a powerful incentive for seniors beyond their personal interests.[11]

Age and Justice

Why should seniors care about a world they will not inhabit much longer?[12] Of course it's true that a sixty-five-year-old might be only two-thirds through her life span. Surely part of senior activism is tied to self-interest, reflected in the preservation and expansion of welfare-state programs for seniors.[13] Seniors are fierce in defending Social Security and Medicare, a concern that made the American Association of Retired Persons—now AARP—an influential lobby. Over the past several decades, seniors have voted and made campaign contributions at a higher rate than any other age group, even if their political preferences are diverse.[14] As Andrea Campbell writes, "Seniors are the super-participators of American politics."[15] To the extent that seniors vote alike—and this is not entirely the case—we can speak of the "gray vote,"[16] leading to what some see as a "gray peril" because of what are called their excessive demands.[17]

An organization like Chicago Seniors Together can be conceived in any of three ways—or in all three. Perhaps it is an organization composed of seniors, or perhaps it is an organization that fights for seniors' interests, or perhaps it is an organization that is run by seniors. As Richie Douglas, co-chair of the CST, remarked to a mass meeting the organization sponsored, speaking to other seniors he hoped would join the movement, "This is an organization of seniors, for seniors, run by seniors" (field notes). Richie wanted to claim all three, and he was not alone in this. In important ways he was correct: CST *is* all three, even if these multiple framings led to some tension within the organization, particularly with regard to the role of the staff in directing members, discussed in chapter 5. Debates over what it meant to be a "senior organization" had caused considerable strain among the Gray Panthers. The Panthers began as an organization of and for seniors, but over time it became intergenerational and broadly progressive, losing some of its core support among those who wanted it to be a focused senior group. These critics were upset because the group expanded the membership criteria and engaged with a larger range of social problems.[18] Similar decisions bedeviled Canada's Raging Grannies.[19] Perhaps because Chicago Seniors Together had an influential staff and was explicitly part of a progressive network, it was seen as an organization of seniors, but with a mandate that emphasized senior interest group politics, although it was not limited to these issues when the larger network was activated. Still, some members worried whether Medicare for All, legalization of marijuana, police reform, and the fight for a fifteen-dollar minimum wage were appropriate projects, even if most personally endorsed these proposals.

Members who had previously been involved in progressive activism were willing to extend their engagement beyond proposals that narrowly benefited seniors. These men and women saw themselves as part of a broader social justice movement. The tension between being a movement *of* and a movement *for* was crucial. In time, given the pressures toward conformity and the power of group culture, even those who joined because they wanted to protect senior entitlements supported projects that the organization defined as central to a progressive identity.

These decisions were made in the context of a community of seniors, a reality that gave Chicago Seniors Together power through its committed base. A longtime leader, Jeanne Hyde, explained the communal effect of seniors' banding together:

> You can find faith-based organizations to work on issues of racial justice and things of that sort. But for the really local issues I think the CST is really important there. I know that some of the people in the group go to the AARP meetings and I have been to some of those. But for me, Chicago Seniors Together has provided a community of like-minded people in working on issues, and I think that has been important in my life. (Interview)

As with most homogeneous communities, there exist shared understandings of the implicit rules of the group as well as a desire for mutual support by like-minded people. This was the basis of their tiny public.

In my interviews, many informants spoke of an intensely felt responsibility that comes with age. This ideal is not limited to progressive activists but derives from the belief that embodied experience can benefit future generations whether or not one can point to immediate material benefits. Lauren Dornbush pointed out,

> We're not only doing this for ourselves, and a lot of this we're never going to see. It's like Martin Luther King going to the hilltop. But we have children; we have grandchildren. My children do not believe that Social Security, even though they've paid into it, that it's going to be there for them. I said, "Yes, it is. We're going to fight for that." (Interview)

Those real or imagined grandchildren inspire the responsibility to act. Richie Douglas elaborated:

> We've been through a lot, and we can share with people younger than us, be they family members or whatever. We've experienced it. We know, and we can look out for dangers upcoming. So we bring that level of wisdom and understanding and a way of being able to deal with it and survive through it. (Interview)

These men and women "do the work of a citizen in a democracy" (interview). Not only do they speak for their own interests, they speak for others who lack the time, the health, or the voice to do so. In this they are role models in the words of housing activist Carrie Stanton:

> We need to show that we're not afraid to be activists. We need to stand up for our rights and the rights of our children and grandchildren. When I stand up for my rights, those rights are going to be my children's rights eventually. . . . When I stand up for HUD [US Department of Housing and Urban Development], [I mean a] fully funded HUD. HUD is housing; it's housing

for the disabled, it's housing for the single working mother, for children. I'm not just talking for me. So I have that responsibility. And I'm showing that single mother that I care. I'm showing that disabled person I'm with them. (Interview)

These sentiments edge toward a romanticism of seniors. If you can claim the "authenticity of wisdom" and can work through the vulnerability of embodiment, you can lead even when you fall.

Age and Activism

To see seniors marching on a picket line or engaging in civil disobedience is to be impressed. These men and women accept their weaknesses or even exploit them. To sympathizers they seem heroic because of their endurance of the burdens of age. This is what committed activists should be, and seniors are particularly noble in this regard. When the staff of Chicago Seniors Together planned an action, they took into account the limits and the possibilities of senior bodies. Actions suitable for those who are younger cannot always be managed by those in their eighth—or ninth—decade. Yet images of seniors engaging in politics can provoke a dramatic response from younger publics. These men and women care, despite the risks. Actions require flexible bodies, but also flexible minds. As Richie Douglas explained, "Although we have less muscular power, we still have a fair amount of brain power, and we need to use it and use it in quantity" (interview). In chapter 3 I discuss the varied actions led by the CST, but here I focus on how protests were structured in light of the reality of age.

Disadvantages are salient and compelling. While not all seniors are frail or dependent, these constraints loom as the changes of age advance. As I described in the prologue, those organizing a group of older men and women with canes, walkers, and motorized chairs must deal with limited mobility (especially in a snowstorm, as at the Racine protest). Falls, fainting, or other mishaps might occur at any time, changing the arc of the protest.

Organizers must prepare for crises that are less likely with those who are younger. This reality was an issue when the CST collaborated with allied organizations, a topic of chapter 7. Staff in those groups often ignored or did not recognize the needs of those seniors, whom they hoped to attract. On occasion this lack of foresight created tension. In planning a rally with senior participants, actions must be bounded in time: participants cannot be asked to stand for long or walk long distances, wheelchairs must be available, documents must be printed in large type, the sound system must be loud enough for those with hearing impairments, and water and food must be provided because of medical requirements.[20] Jane Tate, the CST's executive director, explained that both staff and senior leaders must be involved in planning:

> If we're doing actions, then the leaders will tell us when something's off the wall. Right? If we're talking about marching four miles, they're going to say, "We can't do that." So that's why you want to have leaders in those planning sessions [as well as staff], so that they can be really clear that this isn't going to happen. . . . Whatever the facility is, it has to be accessible. (Interview)

That protests happened without trauma is impressive, reflecting the commitments of seniors as political players. For a rally in downtown Chicago, the rented bus had to stop on the way for a "potty break," and then it parked only a block from the demonstration site to minimize walking. Still, as one participant noted, "It takes a busload of seniors a long time to get off the bus." Another explained that the rally would be short, "Because we are senior citizens and we can't stand very long. As senior citizens, we do not go on long marches. That's one of the things about being a senior. Your mind tells you that you want to do active things, but your body tells you that you can't" (field notes). When we were scheduled to return, not all the seniors could be found, eliciting complaints from those waiting on the bus. On another occasion a young organizer, planning a small demonstration outside a congressman's local office, explained,

> We're trying to find a space where we can meet up before the action because we don't want to travel very far, especially since it's going to be in February. It could be icy. It could be snowy. If I was organizing something just with my peers, we could walk twenty minutes and it would be OK. So [we're] sort of thinking about people's physical limitations and making sure this action is accessible to them. (Interview)

Events were planned in advance, often for places that lacked facilities for large numbers of seniors. This required diligence by the staff. Although important decisions were ultimately endorsed by the board, the staff did much of the day-to-day organizing that allowed actions to happen so that seniors could participate. The beloved mantra that Chicago Seniors Together is run by seniors must be understood in light of the behind-the-scenes work that makes this possible.

Old Lives Matter

Chicago Police Department officers do not always show a kindly face, despite a departmental desire to transcend memories of disturbing controversies from past years. Racial minorities may be treated with contempt, and on occasion—as in the case of the unarmed seventeen-year-old Laquan McDonald—even shot and killed. To be fair, the organizational culture of the CPD has altered from that of its infamous actions in battering demonstrators in the 1960s. Like any large organization, its employees have varying interpersonal skills and a range of biases. Over the years the CPD, along with other urban police departments, has developed tactics to control demonstrations without inflecting severe injuries, even if some horror stories remain. Despite occasional malign actions by police, officers do not begin their shifts with the desire to harm, maim, or kill. However, given prejudicial predispositions or extraoccupational frustrations, they can become emotionally heated or so frustrated that harm is more likely, especially when their authority is challenged.

Given the infirmities of seniors and the willingness of progressive elders to engage in confrontational and provocative forms of civil disobedience, described in chapter 3, how is the waltz between police and older protesters choreographed? For many, protesting seniors are picturesque. This phrase might be patronizing, but it reflects that images of the elderly demonstrating make for powerful visuals, as is true for ministers, rabbis, priests, nuns—and children. However, as opposed to occupational groups, it is the combination of moral authority—deriving from cultural images of wise elders—and bodily infirmity that leads to seniors' being seen as "profound" actors. As one staff member noted, "There's such a cultural narrative around seniors' being docile and nonactive that when a group of seniors marches or occupies or gets arrested it makes news in a way that when students or young people do, it's just like, 'Oh, young people. They'll find any reason to get outraged'" (interview).

The reality that seniors were willing to demonstrate, at their age and with their vulnerabilities, revealed a powerful commitment.[21] In this way the activism of seniors had strong reputational value. Esther Harvey, a woman with severe health problems, explained, "If it shows on TV, these people are really committed to the problem. This isn't just a bunch of people that like doing demonstrations. Here are these people out there and it takes quite an effort for them to be there and do it. So, I think it speaks loudly" (interview).

Recognizing the symbolic worth of participating in vivid actions, especially engaging in civil disobedience, some seniors considered being arrested a mark of honor, although the organization carefully warned members about actions where arrests were likely so they could keep a distance from the drama. In addition, they offered extensive training for those who planned to engage in civil disobedience, such as making sure to carry sufficient medications in case they spent several days in jail. During my research some members were arrested, but no one was confined for more than a few hours. In accord with Chicago's policy for dealing with nonviolent protesters, participants were released on their own reconnaissance, often without bail. If they weren't rearrested in six months, charges would be dropped. As a result, most protesters engaged in civil disobedience infrequently, following the advice of supportive lawyers.

Given the willingness to risk harm in the service of a cause, direct action was admired. As one enthusiastic senior remarked, "I'm looking forward to being arrested." While not everyone felt that way and few stood on the front lines, those who did received credit. One activist, now limited for health reasons, commented, "It's a reality that we age, and my knees aren't getting any better. It certainly affects whether I want to go to jail. If I had two [healthy] knees, I probably wouldn't think about that and [if I] didn't need my medications" (interview).

Referring to the thrill of street protest, Dr. Ben remarked,

> It's always exciting to go to Moral Mondays [monthly demonstrations in Chicago, inspired by similar actions of Rev. William Barber in North Carolina] to see people of our age making an impact. . . . I think our street drama is most effective, [such as] when we laid down dead in the governor's office. We might have old bodies, but we have young aspirations. (Field notes)

In this, senior activists have a cultural advantage in interacting with the police, who may treat them as harmless and nonthreatening.[22] In these fragile bodies, officers might find images of their parents or grandparents. At a committee meeting, a member suggested to laughter and applause, "We decided to do a flash dance in the middle of the street. . . . We are seniors. They couldn't take our fingerprints. They have all been worn down. We can do what we want" (field notes).

At another meeting I sat next to Davey Gibbs and Susan Locker when they were released after being arrested at the Chicago Board of Trade, where they'd chained themselves to the entrance doors (described in chapter 3). They reported that the police were nicer to them than when they were younger, and were more friendly than they expected. Despite their being agitators, the police were not the target of the agitation. The activists believed that the officers considered this a routine part of their job, that they might have been sympathetic to the goals of the protest, and that they did not feel affronted by the demonstrators. Susan admitted she'd put a copy of the *New York Times* in her pants so she'd have something to read in jail, but she said the police took the newspaper away, a uniquely mild punishment. Davey told me that when a policeman pushed him he asked, "Am I being arrested?" and the officer answered, apparently with good humor, "No, you're just being pushed" (field notes). Davey explained with amused and ironic detachment,

> I'm in that part of the population where they don't beat the hell out of you. I'm a privileged person. I'm a male. I'm White and I'm old. I'm not in their face calling them pig or something like that. I'm respectful. Oh, yes, I want to get arrested. "Do you want your hands in front or back?" . . . The police, they've got tremendous respect for old White men and old White women. I don't think they've got that respect for GLTB [LGBT] or people of color. . . . They see their grandma; they see their grandpa. . . . What you're doing is, you're seducing the police because they get paid by the elite to do certain things. . . . So, what you want to do is show the police that you're really not bad people. You're really on their side. I never see the police as pigs. (Interview)

Another senior leader explained, "[The police] have a gentler approach. I think they have more respect for us, when listening to us. We haven't run into any physical pushback at demonstrations from the police" (interview). African American senior activists did feel more vulnerable, in contrast to the White members, but even they were more protected by their age than younger people.

The Vulnerabilities of Unyouth

Attitudes toward senior citizens are complex. Seniors may be admired for wisdom and experience (the late Rush Limbaugh spoke of "seasoned citizens"), they may be patronized, they may be tarred with the stigma of dementia, or they may be ignored.[23] Of course, as I noted, many retain considerable economic, social, and cultural clout.

Perspectives on seniors—as with other social categories—constitute a tool kit that can be drawn on as needed. The images of seniors speak to the possibility of power, however effective or ineffective that power might be in practice. As Henry Dowdall, an organization leader, suggested at one of the Resist Trump assemblies organized by the CST, "I was so glad to find my brothers and sisters who are fighting together. . . . We refuse to be infantilized. We value each other not because we are different, but because we are alike." As Jane Tate added, "We're not slowing down because we're seniors. We're more energized" (field notes). Another leader, Carrie Stanton, remarked with pride after a demonstration with younger allies, "I told the young people I can stand up with them. At the end, they said I was a tough old broad" and that "I'd be glad to call you my grandmother" (field notes). For the relational exercise at one meeting, attendees were asked to imagine the title of a memoir that would describe their life. The titles reflected their commitments as aging activists and included "Keep It Up," "A Life of Challenges," "A Worker Bee for Justice," "Never Give Up," "I'm a Survivor," and, referring to his aging body, "Thanks for the Gift, but I Wish the Wrapping Were Better" (field notes).

As is true for other "model minorities," belittling may appear friendly, but it places seniors in a category where their voices are unheard. Jane slammed a bystander who described a member demonstrating for social justice by saying "He's so cute." She added, "it's so patronizing." He should have been seen as fierce, not adorable. Equally condescending was the claim that senior activists are "feisty." One older activist warned about politicians, "Don't let them pat you on the head," ignoring their demands as legitimate and believing, in the words of one member, that "seniors don't really know what's going on" and "we're just seniors, what can we do?" (field notes). Another, responding to the rules at her senior housing project that prevented residents from using the community room for meetings without staff supervision, asserted that "they're treating us like kids" (field notes). Davey Gibbs, nearing eighty, notes that "on a good day I can do fifty pushups. I walked seven and a half miles. I have to watch out when I go on the El [Chicago's subway]; everybody wants to give me a seat [*laughs*]" (interview). While this critique was often aimed at authorities or a generalized public, on occasion it could be aimed at staff members as well, particularly the newer ones: "We've had some very young organizers that didn't really understand that seniors know a lot, and so they have a tendency in the beginning to treat seniors like grandparents" (interview).

While I could detail negative views further, citing Robert Butler's "myth of unproductivity,"[24] I note the pungent belief of one of my informants, Barb Greene, that "our society as a whole does not appreciate seniors. We live in a throwaway society, and it's, 'Why are you living so long? You're using up our things' [*laughs*]" (interview). A second senior, Ralph Phelps, reflected on his younger self:

> When I was in my twenties, I used to look at senior citizens. . . . I had the attitude, "Well, these people are always complaining about being sick and how lousy life is. What's the point?" I used to look down at them. Then I became a senior citizen, and I realized I was a little naive and a little ignorant. (Interview)

A third snorted that many younger adults would like to "send us out on an ice floe" (field notes).

Whatever those attitudes, age does carry with it physical limitations. These people are activists, of whom Jane pointed out, "Our members are aging and getting sicker." They have—and discuss—magnifying glasses, hearing aids, walkers, and wheelchairs. As I noted, for seniors to be an effective public, participation must be tailored to their needs and abilities.[25] I begin with the serious discussion of vulnerabilities, then discuss how these weaknesses are transformed and tamed by joking, essential to the culture.

Not having previously spent time in an organization of seniors, I was startled at first by how unpredictable attendance at various committee meetings and political actions could be. While for all grassroots organizations achieving a target number requires overshooting commitments, a message widely taught by organizers, attendance was a particular difficulty in galvanizing seniors, for whom attrition was expected. Staffers who had not previously dealt with such a group had to be patient when promises were broken. I do not suggest that the reasons given were inappropriate, but often illnesses, doctor's appointments, or simply "feeling poorly" prevented attendance. As Richie Douglas, one of the most committed leaders, confessed,

> I've been guilty of this. I might wake up and I just ain't feeling good. It might've been something that had been scheduled two to three weeks down the road, but once that time gets here, I might wake up and I just don't feel it. I don't feel right, I might have a serious headache, my blood pressure might be up and whatnot, so therefore I might have to call in, and the staff would say "OK, we understand," but I know they're a little disappointed at the same time. (Interview)

This situation even included those who were scheduled to lead a meeting or to speak at a rally.

One seriously ill leader, returning from the hospital, described it as his second home. Another leader, an eventual co-chair of the organization, could not attend meetings when it was raining heavily because of his motorized wheelchair. Several meetings were canceled for lack of attendance. At one meeting only two people showed up. I was one. As Jane said, sighing at a meeting of two, "It doesn't make sense to hold the meeting. We have a committee of ten, but it's seniors" (field notes). Some rivalry was involved. One senior confided privately that she "competed" with those who were older and in better health, feeling that "I better get myself in [to meetings], get myself in order, so I've been working on it" (interview). These super seniors were treated as role models even if their bodily aches often won out. Hope bows to reality, as Barb Greene attested: "I may think I'm eighteen or twenty-eight or fifty-eight, but I know I'm not, and if I forget that my body tells me. So, basically, even though you may want to do those things, you don't have the stamina" (interview).

Medical discussions were common, and for many members they were not considered embarrassing: cancer, encroaching blindness, heart surgery, even incontinence were all legitimate topics during social hours. For younger people such conversations might reveal humiliating bodily failings, but for the members of CST they raised topics everyone could contribute to. They were survivors.

In previous ethnographies I have been fortunate not to have to confront the death of any informant, but that was not true here. Several friends and confidants died during the research or immediately afterward. Beyond being both an emotional strain and methodological problem, this attrition was also an organizational matter and a cultural topic. As with illness, the death of members—individuals and in general—was an acceptable topic. This became clear when the organization considered honoring longtime members at their annual fund-raising luncheon. Jane Tate remarked in a board meeting, "We're having a midlife crisis. We have a lot of victories and a lot of people who have passed away. We want to celebrate them." Eventually they decided that what was most important was to celebrate longtime members. At first they considered honoring those who had been members for fifteen years but, considering the small numbers, ten years was chosen to include enough honorees. As the board member in charge of the luncheon admitted, "We realized that sometimes people have died before we could honor them." Another board member suggested, humorously but significantly, that perhaps we should require only three to five years of participation.

This was also taxing for the staff, as the young staffer Dan struggled:

> We lose members because people die, and seniors are thinking about "people my age are dying." . . . I don't think about that a lot. I'm twenty-five years old. . . . I think seniors are seen as people often who don't have any vision for the future because they're going to die. . . . I think the CST challenges that, because I think the coalition says that seniors care about the present and they care about the future, and they have a vision for the world. . . . And, you know, they're not just holding out until they die. (Interview)

The COVID-19 virus transformed much of society, but for seniors the threat was even more immediate. Although the pandemic occurred after I completed the main body of research, I remained in touch with the organization, occasionally attending meetings and watching its effects as the organization held supportive online "Healing Circles" to cope with fear and isolation. As a result of the pandemic, the organization shut down all face-to-face meetings and relied on Zoom calls, a problem for seniors who lacked secure computer access. The virus trimmed some of the organization's activist power even as the politics of Chicago city government became steadily more progressive, allowing some of its key goals to be achieved. That the virus hit seniors—and especially those living in congregate housing or in nursing homes—with special ferocity emphasizes the dangers to aging activists.

Joshing Around

One way a community is built is through establishing a jocular culture.[26] Cohesive organizations are characterized by laughter and teasing. When targeted at elites and forces of control, these are weapons of the weak,[27] but humor also creates cohesion, even when directed internally. Laughter—difficult to fake—indicates that individuals see the world in similar ways. Life at Chicago Seniors Together was filled with banter and with a comic recognition of a shared worldview. Although some humor was directed against the powerful, other forms of humor—which I discuss here—were specifically about seniors' infirmities. Participants would often make fun of their own limitations in ways that were understood not as being self-critical but as embracing their collective identity. These remarks occurred at virtually every meeting and addressed most senior weakness, with the notable exception of sexual dysfunction and physical attractiveness, topics that were never mentioned during my observation, although they are a source of amusement in other domains. Members might attribute errors to a senior moment or to brain freeze, phrases that were common and congenially understood. Within this group, bodily decline was noted without awkwardness.

While examples can readily be offered, I heard one leader comment, "We act in a knee-jerk fashion, but I can't do knee jerks anymore." Another said, while leading a meeting, "I'll give you a minute or two, but I can't see my watch." A third joked, "We may need training to remember each other's names" (field notes). This same joking occurred between the members and the staff. Jane Tate, then fifty-nine, was teased by a member who claimed, "Jane could be having a baby." She punched him playfully and responded, "Most of our staff is young except for me" (field notes). This group teasing was a means of taming aging by viewing it as so natural that it could be a source of fellowship. Its presence suggested that aging is central to accepting group culture and belonging to the organization. Even though the topic might seem distant from the goals of the CST, it was essential to defining the distinctive nature of the group.

Activist Careers

Theories of work help explain moral careers, skeins of behavior that extend through the life course, tied to communal practices.[28] Even mental patients

have moral careers, shared behaviors that evolve over time.[29] Applying the
concept to the social movement literature, we can speak of an activist career.[30]
This term acknowledges choices in the forms and extent of activism one engages in as well as the continuity or gaps in one's involvement. Biography
is important in creating an activist career, as in the accounts of influential
promoters of social change such as Frederick Douglass, Margaret Sanger, or
Betty Friedan.[31] As Caroline Gatt emphasizes in her ethnography of Friends
of the Earth International, agentic individuality provides the basis through
which activists present their own life stories to themselves and to others.[32]
The ability to achieve a coherent selfhood permits stories to be treated not as
idiosyncratic, but as tied to one's local publics.[33] Ultimately, while personal biographies are narrated, many times with considerable panache, they often are
presented in a context where others are sharing as well. Cohort biographies
matter as much as individual ones.

The politicizing of life experiences provides the grounding for ongoing
activism.[34] In this regard, Natalia Ruiz-Junco points to the significance of
biographical identity integration. Activists apply frames for constructing a
meaningful identity, a personal narrative that sustains activism and links to
larger cultural themes. But collective identity does not simply happen, it is
generated through group-based dialogues.[35] When identities are politicized,
they motivate participation in contentious actions, even costly ones.[36] A
movement group fosters self-anchoring within a tiny public.[37] The age-related
identity of seniors draws on a collective sense of being "old."[38] One's age category is embedded in an imagined social world. These constructions link aging with ways of understanding social problems, options for volunteering,
and the desire for political engagement.[39]

Studies of activists focus on those who have chosen a politically engaged
life. Those who make other choices or who rapidly leave the scene also have
a meaningful biography[40] and a comfortable identity.[41] In examining activist
selves, we must consider the connections between collective and individual
identities. To be engaged in activism, one must see oneself as part of a group
and embrace a shared injustice frame. While this is true for all activists, seniors can look back over the course of a life and find their choices especially
salient at particular moments, providing templates for current engagements.
The past, present, and future are knit together, as they are for those many
members of the CST whose early civil rights activism provided a model for
current activism. Beyond this, the self-anchoring frame chosen—"responsible
grandpa" or "caring granny," for example—was not only a means of seeing
oneself, but also a claim to the way others should treat one's actions.[42] Internal
selves and external identities became linked.

Engagement depends on two fundamental features. First, the individual must believe that participation in an activist group is desired and desirable. This is not a belief everyone shares. Second, they can imagine acting on their values. When and how this occurs varies widely, but it can produce a long-term commitment to activism and a sense of moral responsibility that justifies that choice.[43]

Seniors help us understand the dynamics of volunteering because of the unstructured time tied to retirement. With the alteration or erasure of other roles, volunteering is a space where seniors are welcomed.[44] By contemporary standards, seniors are expected to stay busy. Activity is equivalent to living well. Seniors volunteer in large numbers, devoting more time to these efforts than younger people, although a smaller percentage overall choose to volunteer.[45] They become the "nation's civic legs," with estimates that approximately 25 percent of seniors volunteer with community groups.[46] Those who consider themselves activists were more likely to be educated, female, and wealthier.[47] Of course, even with the best intentions and enthusiastic beginnings, seniors, like others, may not continue. One study finds that about 30 percent of seniors stop volunteering after a year.[48] Still, this leaves many available volunteers. Nancy Morrow-Howell's research shows that volunteering has benefits for seniors, such as higher reported levels of well-being[49] and general health.[50] These advantages include reduced mortality, better physical functioning, decreased depressive symptoms, and increased life satisfaction.[51] Other studies find that volunteering boosts self-rated health and mitigates dependency.[52] While one might be skeptical of volunteering as a cure-all, engagement with a community, developing diverse social ties, and participating in a vibrant group culture surely are desirable. Cause and effect are linked. Healthier seniors are more likely to volunteer and, in turn, they gain the most.[53] Even though seniors with more human and social capital are especially likely to volunteer,[54] some evidence suggests that positive effects may be most powerful for seniors who are less advantaged in social, economic, and health resources.[55]

Not surprisingly, the activist careers of seniors vary both in pattern and in intensity. I address three broad types of activist careers as forms of engagement and provide examples of each through the biographies of members of Chicago Seniors Together. Some seniors have lifetime commitments. They have remained politically engaged, and this is crucial to their identity. Political engagement is a primary, salient basis for a sense of self. Research suggests that activists from the 1960s maintain their ideological commitments for decades, whether or not they remain involved in political organizations.[56] Their engagement is an ongoing and defining aspect of the self and reflects a belief in moral responsibility. According to Roger Sanjek's account of the Gray Panthers, its radicalism forced the organization to depend on longtime activists. Deciding between a more extreme politics and a more centrist one poses a fundamental dilemma in determining how expansive the group's appeal should be: a large organization or a devoted one.[57] Sanjek writes,

> It was not involvement with senior citizen issues that brought most people to the Gray Panthers. It was rather lifetimes of engagement with labor struggles, civil and human rights, economic justice, health care, and peace—from the 1930s onward for the older Panthers and during the 1960s and early 1970s for younger members. Participants in a long American activist tradition, they were persons for whom the political was personal—a part of daily thought and conversation—over years of organized action with others.[58]

While this is true for some conservatives as well,[59] it seems to be more common among progressives, who rely on a more extensive movement infrastructure.

A second group shared these beliefs but prioritized other life domains. They were activists when young: in college, before marriage and children or the rigors of a career. This constitutes *punctuated activism*. The third group chose to be active only after retirement, sometimes as a result of a moral shock that compelled involvement. They found a late calling. With the "free" time that retirement affords, lacking institutional demands, they chose progressive politics that perhaps had already been appealing, but with lower priority. These three paths converged at the CST, with members bringing along their identities, experiences, and memories. For each one, as seniors activism now had priority. In line with the argument in chapter 1, whichever category individuals belonged to and however they came to be recruited, their political perspectives were stable over their lifetimes, at least in their telling. What they required was a vehicle where these personal beliefs could be activated in the company of generational peers.[60] While those who once participated in a movement—such as the 1964 Mississippi Freedom Summer project—are more likely to continue with activist engagement,[61] some join along the way. Still, although the form of involvement may change, general political orientations typically remained stable. I found no reformed conservatives who'd had an epiphany that produced progressive activism. These careers paths were reflected in an interview with Jane Tate, CST's executive director:

> A lot of leaders who wish they were active in the sixties [1960s] and weren't, it's the moment for them to become active. I don't think you ever met Justine Adams [a member who died in the course of my research], but I remember the first time Justine did civil disobedience; she said to me, "I stood in the background during the Vietnam War, and I'm no longer willing to sit in the

background. The way for me to do my activism is to be in the forefront and to do civil disobedience, because now is the moment for me to do it and now I feel brave enough to do it. I'm ready to do it now." So, I feel like for some of our leaders, in particular different leaders with different experiences, it's this moment that they get to do [protests] because they didn't feel like they either had the support or the capacity or whatever. They didn't do it when they were younger. Then I think you have people like Ben and Jeanne who have this long history of doing it who, it's like, "I did it and I like this." I feel like there's a lot of people who did it in the sixties and then there's been this lull, so it's like this moment to come back to that work. . . . Justine said, "I'm ready to roll up my sleeves for the first time in my life and risk arrest." . . . Then for someone like Ben [it's] to say "I did this. I'm ready to do it again." (Interview)

As Jane pointed out, different dynamics brought seniors to political participation, tied to the priority of an activist identity. To understand the articulation of a political career, I discuss several cases in each category, referencing general principles from these life histories.

LIFETIME ACTIVISTS

I begin with "Dr. Ben" Golden, whom I came to know when he was about to turn ninety and who became a key informant, appearing throughout this book. Ben, lean and athletic, was known for riding his electric scooter around town. He was a charismatic member of the organization, given to making windy pronouncements and pushing his always progressive agenda. Dr. Ben was born in Chicago to Hungarian Jewish parents in the late 1920s, served in the army in Europe as an infantry rifleman, then attended medical school. He explained that he had long had a progressive worldview and activist agenda:

> I've been doing some kind of protesting ever since the 1950s. I started out with a protest when the Rosenbergs [Julius and Ethel, accused atomic spies for the Soviet Union] were on the line to be executed in 1953. . . . I was an intern at County Hospital at that time. I was trembling because I had never done any real political work, even though I had my opinions [developed from watching comrades die in World War II]. The whole idea of war made me realize how I had a mission to stop it. . . . Subsequently I was appalled by what was happening in the South. (Interview)

His early activism became more sustained with a commitment to civil rights and racial justice:

> I was incensed, of course, with the lynching of Emmett Till. It was terrible. I said, "Oh, God. The South will never change." But then, shortly after the marches, the civil disobedience in the South started taking place. Finally, in

1966 I was already in the middle of practice and already had a house. We already had four children. I finally said, "I'm going to march with them." I went down for two weeks. I marched in Mississippi in June of '66 with [Rev.] King. We got tear gassed. . . . I just felt I had to do it. I actually performed medical services down there as we marched and as the police attacked us. (Interview)

Dr. Ben reviewed his life as an activist, telling about desegregating some Chicago hospitals, and recounted how he maintained his activism for sixty years. Of all those I met, Dr. Ben was the one with the most intense activist career.

He was not alone. Richie Douglas was a widely respected leader, serving as co-chair of the CST and of its political action arm, United Chicago Seniors in Action. An African American, Richie grew up in the Englewood neighborhood on the South Side of Chicago but eventually moved to the North Side, where he worked for local government. Unlike Dr. Ben, Richie began with a concern for his neighborhood rather than with an expansive political perspective:

I came to the organization with the previous experience of being what I considered at that time a community activist. All of my community involvement has been here in the Edgewater neighborhood, as well as in Uptown. I was involved with a block club in the area. . . . I was told to be involved with that group because I was having some problems with the apartment that I lived in. Because of that activity, I was asked to be on the board of the Uptown Chicago Commission, which was a community organization that was about quality-of-life issues within the Uptown area. So I got started there. (Interview)

In his work in Uptown, he met the activist mother of the current alderman. When Richie moved to Edgewater, just north of Uptown, she asked if he would join the Edgewater Community Council. He agreed: "Hence started my real community activism. Since my involvement at the council, we did get other African American people to be on the board and active in the organization, but when I came on board, that wasn't the case."

Richie later served as the first African American president of that largely middle-class organization. Being a community leader and promoting social justice became central to his sense of self.

Jeanne Hyde grew up in a southern home imbued with Christian activism. She laughs in recalling that her activism began as a child during the Second World War:

I'm a member of the United Methodist Church, and the United Methodist Church, even in the South, had a fairly strong social justice arm to it. During the Second World War my brother, who's younger than I [am], and I would go out collecting scrap iron and scrap paper and selling war bonds. Then, through church committees, social justice committees, I have maintained an involvement. I think it's not unusual to see a number of people like me who grew up in faith-based social justice movements of one type or another. . . . Then a lot too is where we find ourselves in history, and I actually was living in Alabama when the Montgomery bus boycott began. I moved to Chicago when the civil rights movement itself was in pretty full swing and churches here were quite active. . . . Civil rights have always been extremely important for me. (Interview)

While the commitments of these three developed along different paths, each was motivated by the wish for racial justice. Indeed, racial justice has been the motivating force prompting generations of American activists to commit to progressive politics. This became a core value that determined their sense of self.

PUNCTUATED ACTIVISTS

It is impressive that over the course of a life, given changes in work, marital, and parental roles, some people never leave political action. Others, with similar values and politics, drift in and out of activism in response to external demands. As Doug McAdam argues, activism often emerges at specific points in the life cycle as involvement depends on biographical availability.[62]

Consider the case of Jerry Hackworth, a retired professor at one of the city's community colleges, now living near the University of Chicago. Early in his adulthood, Jerry was an activist. Like others, he was active in the civil rights movement. As he put it, "I was an activist in the sixties, and now I'm back." He continues,

I'm somewhat less of an ideologue than I was in my younger years. Even teaching in the city colleges and seeing what a lot of my students have gone through over the years, and their families, sensitized me to a lot of that stuff. . . . In the period of the 1960s I was very active. In fact, so active that I actually ended up getting fired at Tender High School. . . . I became active within the university system . . . for the most part as they call them a "chairperson liberal," and most of my activism then was focused over the years in unions [the American Federation of Teachers]. So that was pretty much the limit of my activism. Then with the buildup to the Iraq War in 2003–4, I was active again at demonstrations. (Interview)

Recognizing his progressive obligations, Jerry returned to activism after his retirement.

Women had different problems in their punctuated activism, since their personal and family responsibilities were often deeper and more demanding than men's. Consider Stephanie Moore, office manager of the CST:

At the beginning of '65 Dr. King had sent his advance team up to Chicago. . . .
I met some of them, and I started doing volunteer work for them. We really
started organizing when Dr. King came in '65. So we did some organizing
work there about open housing. . . . I was in my twenties. . . . [I'd] just met
somebody that was an organizer from Dr. King's organization, and I started
volunteering there and I got on staff. [GAF: "And have you been an activist all
your life?"] No, not at all. [GAF: "So there was a gap there?"] A big gap, because once Dr. King was assassinated . . . people were really depressed, including myself and my husband. Then we did the Poor People's Campaign in DC,
which was a total disaster. It was just traumatic. It was just a horrible, horrible
time. So at that point I had gotten pregnant. I could have stayed with SCLC
[Southern Christian Leadership Conference] and gone to Atlanta. I just decided not to. Then my husband and I ended up getting divorced, and I had two
young kids to raise, so I went and got a job. [GAF: "How did you get back into
activism?"] I didn't get involved until I came back to Chicago. I moved back
in 2009 and became a member of Chicago Seniors Together. One of my best
friends kept saying, "Come to these meetings." For a year I was just like "No,
I don't want to be bothered. I don't want to be involved." So finally it took her
a year and I did come to the meeting. Then I [*chuckles*] remember walking in
and saying, "These people are really old" [*laughs*]. I said that to her. She said,
"Well, what do you think you are?" [*chuckles*]. I really had not been in a group
of older, active seniors. So then I got involved in the Housing Committee and
went to my first action, and the rest is history. (Interview)

She found a group, and "the rest is history." These were typical examples,
again emphasizing racial politics in generating a moral demand, true for
many members. However, life demands increase identity salience. These activists never lost their core values, but they decided when and how political
engagement was possible, given external pressures. With family and work involvement less central, the freedom of retirement permits values to become
practices.

LATE CALLINGS

Relatively few Americans engage in any form of sustained political engagement, even at those moments when society seems to be in turmoil. Yet identities can be rearranged, especially if one finds a tiny public to belong to. As one
member explained,

Most of them are so ensconced in raising a family and making a living for
themselves that they really don't have time to think about what's going on
around them. That's a full-time job raising a family and making a living. They
never have time to get politically involved, even though they're decent people

and they're righteous and they know right from wrong. It's just a matter of energy and time. (Interview)

However, turning points may shift the direction of a life,[63] representing a late calling and a group context that demands activism. Some event or relationship sharpens or ignites what might have been inchoate beliefs. Perhaps it was President Trump's election and concerns about MAGA nativism that contributed to activism, or perhaps it was something more local or personal. Concerns about housing or retirement often provided a jolt to activism, and in time new recruits discover unexpected benefits. As Jeanne Hyde remarked, "The people who become activists after they retire, they get involved with Chicago Seniors. They develop their own voices and begin to really feel a sense of enhanced dignity, more self-worth, self-esteem" (interview).

Perhaps the most dramatic of these epiphanies is the experience of Ralph Phelps, radicalized by the experience of his brother:

> I was apolitical, really. I thought [activism] was only for somebody that had fire in their belly; I didn't have any fire in my belly at that time. But my brother started getting sick. He had trouble swallowing. He had an incident where the police found him sitting on a sidewalk and he had a six-month growth of beard, which meant he had a mental problem. I couldn't get him to seek any help about it, so I moved out after a month and he stayed there himself for a while. He was in the army earlier, so he went to the army facility in Waukegan for a while, and he stayed there. Then he went to a facility in Chicago for a while, and they placed him in this place where people go to [if they] can't take care of themselves. . . . He started having incidents of falling down. Finally the place where he was staying realized that they couldn't take care of him. [He eventually went to a hospice.] Finally he told my sister he was ready to die. A few days after that we came to visit him, and he was gone. [GAF: "Obviously that changed you."] I already started attending some senior meetings because when Trump came into office I could see that seniors were at risk in a lot of areas. The mental [health] clinics in Illinois have been shut down. There are threats to Social Security and Medicaid. And I lived in a senior building, and I was on Social Security. That's my only source of income, and that was threatened. I realized I had a stake in the outcome of this. I realized I just can't sit idly by anymore and take it on the chin. I'm going to at least put up some resistance on this and participate. Probably [my brother's] passing away is what made me more active, probably a little more angry. That really motivated me. . . . After that I started doing senior actions. (Interview)

It was not the death of his brother by itself that caused Ralph to become actively engaged. He had already started to attend meetings of the CST before his brother died. The death was coupled with Ralph's concerns about the

Trump administration. In his case a dramatic event merged with an underlying perspective to create a willingness to engage directly and intensely in an activist community.

Less dramatic was the case of Esther Harvey, a medical professional who moved with her husband from a small midwestern city to be near their daughter. She had not been active in politics before living in Chicago, but eventually she became an officer of Chicago Seniors Together. Esther reports:

> For me, during the civil rights movement, I remember seeing it on TV at the time. But it wasn't something that was very relevant to my personal life at that point. In terms of the Vietnam War, I'm not sure I really understood it. I knew I was against it, but I don't know that I could tell you why. I did one demonstration in high school about the Vietnam War.... When we moved to Chicago, I needed to get involved in something to have something to do. Our daughter had worked for Chicago Seniors before, so she suggested maybe I could come volunteer, like stuff envelopes. (Interview)

Esther embraced progressive politics in a vague way without seeing politics as her calling. Activism was left to others. With the network connection through her daughter's activism, she started to participate in the CST and then found a home—a meaningful civic public—but without a strong desire to engage in public actions.

These cases reflect how diverse activist careers shape and are shaped by identities and opportunities. They reveal the inflection points of lives, coupled with the power of an organization to incorporate seniors into what we might metaphorically describe as an engaged family. For some, like Dr. Ben, activism was a central part of their identity; for others, like Stephanie, activism fitted into a life as time was available; and for still others, like Esther, activism was motivated given her availability, establishing a new identity. Those who were supportive, yet passive, must decide to become active promoters of change. But in each case an activist career was constructed that allowed identity to be linked to willing participation in a tiny public of commitment. These differences were not just personal but provided well-trodden recruitment paths to senior organizations that allowed each person to feel—to know—that they belonged in light of the group culture as reflected through their life experiences.

Coming of Age

In this chapter I provide a template for how to think about the aging body and the aging mind as central to civil society and, in particular, to those tiny publics that direct seniors to activism. I start with how the elderly are seen in the wider culture. To their colleagues they may be heroes; to their opponents they are nuisances, but without the threats of younger people.

Like every sizable demographic group—women, southerners, African Americans—there are many frameworks one can draw on, depending on the perspective of the person selecting and the audience being appealed to. Seniors are powerful and they are weak; they are friendly and they are depressed; they are rich and they are needy; and they can be political or they can be apathetic. These contesting images provide alternatives for how seniors fit into civic life.

But seniors face a chronological reality: they never get younger. Of course that's true for us all, but decline becomes more apparent as one is defined as elderly. This reality was brought to screaming attention when it became clear that seniors were primary victims of the novel coronavirus that decimated residents of congregate living sites. Any group that organizes seniors must consider this embodied reality.

For Chicago Seniors Together, this affected determining how senior members could best participate in progressive actions. What is assumed to be possible for younger activists—although some have limiting disabilities as well—must be carefully considered when one is organizing a gathering of seniors. As a result of issues of mobility, energy, stamina, and capacity, the sociology of aging is linked to the sociology of disability, conceptualizing what individuals and their tiny publics are capable of and how their vulnerabilities might be addressed to avoid their being swept from the public square.

Responding to the images and abilities of seniors are the forces of control. In this seniors have an advantage in being perceived as "mostly harmless." Even when engaging in actions that might otherwise elicit a vigorous response from authorities, the reality that seniors are chaining themselves to doors or lying down on public thoroughfares may seem charming, not dangerous. While African American seniors are aware that they might provoke an aggressive police response, both Black and White elderly people appear to be better protected from the malign attentions of police than younger ones.

Finally, aging seniors have varied activist careers. For some seniors, being unruly and troublesome is central to their identities. They have been committed to activism throughout their lives. These men and women serve as the heart and soul of the organization: they are the most devout members, and they prod others to become engaged. These activists often have the sharpest and most extreme political beliefs, demanding immediate social change, whereas others who are not so committed would be satisfied with gradual improvement. Lifetime activists stand in contrast to those who have arrived through an epiphany, either some traumatic event in their life or because of a newly emergent need to get involved in a social world after retirement or a change of residence. If they join, they will be encouraged to accept the group's political and social culture. A middle group, punctuated activists, have their youthful passions reignited as retirement permits this. These seniors must determine whether their newfound activism fits their lifestyle and their embraced identity.

My purpose is to address the political engagement of seniors: to determine how this group contributes to civil society. Older citizens can be politically active even when their activity varies from that of younger people. Although this is not a comparative ethnography of older and younger groups, by drawing a detailed picture of how elders are politically engaged despite being physically vulnerable I describe how seniors as activists constitute a realm of tiny publics, not to be ignored. If they are confronting an end game, it nonetheless is a game, one with strategies, tactics, and the possibility of victory. In chapter 3 I turn to the way actions of Chicago Seniors Together are organized and the beliefs that stand behind these choices. Whether or not the rallies have profound effects on policymakers, they are a point of pride for those who participate and, as I discuss in chapter 4, a basis for collective memories.

Where the Actions Are

Without the organization of abolitionists into societies, the cause will be lost.
WILLIAM LLOYD GARRISON

Any depiction of a social movement must be attuned to the range of actions the movement supports and the organizational culture through which members believe means and ends are linked. This is what Charles Tilly speaks of as repertoires of contention.[1] Movements enshrine certain forms of action that have been successfully used, and these constitute templates for future engagements. Sharon Nepstad speaks of a "theology of resistance,"[2] by which she suggests that resistance, however disruptive, must be judged ethically acceptable. Even if this is not grounded in religion, as it was in the Plowshares movement, focused on resisting war, moral boundaries stretch beyond the individual, grounded in standards of sociality. This resistance can include civil disobedience or, in some cases, collective violence. In describing the propriety of resistance, we speak of activist movements—and not merely participants—as having a "rebellious career," achieving influence through a shared injustice frame.[3]

Tilly's influential phrase recognizes that few social movements are limited to a single form of action; most have a tool kit that leaders draw on as appropriate. While these standards are group based, groups do not create actions from whole cloth; they consider what they have done in the past and what others are doing in the current moment. There is an isomorphic quality to movement activity as one group borrows from another. Social movements are laboratories of contention. However, the borrowing is never simple copying. Movement participants must learn about the choices others make and transform them to fit their own cultural style and interpersonal preferences. In this way repertoires of contention become routines, part of the circuit of action any activist group relies on.

In this chapter I examine the repertoire of Chicago Seniors Together with particular attention to those forms that seniors adopt and define as appropriate. In the case of senior activism, any planned disruption or large gathering, as I noted in chapter 2, must be consistent with the participants' capacities and limitations. Still, following an established repertoire of action too closely might prevent novel, innovative strategies that fit the moment.[4] Ultimately the form of action is a situated choice that affects not only the movement's audience but the community of activists. The personal and the sociohistorical are linked through the forms of interaction endorsed by group culture.[5]

For a movement to be effective, it must encourage *movement*: collective actions are rituals of involvement. Eventful experiences should clarify and magnify shared engagement.[6] Further, they need to be planned in light of their spatial components. A social movement must find places to gather, and these spaces must be suitable for disruption, publicity, education, or recruitment, whether in a public square, a meeting hall, or a church sanctuary. As William Westermeyer demonstrates for local Tea Party groups, social movements become vibrant motivators of commitment when individuals interact in settings where the group culture is built and the presence of others promotes a belief in political efficacy.[7] Movements produce "local spaces of practice."[8] Often these places are chosen because they prove their local relevance as the very spaces their protests will improve.[9]

The concept of action lies at the heart of sociology. Social movements, particularly those that develop from community organizing, are fine-tuned to building on local traditions. The Alinsky model and those that derive from his approach focus on the meso level, conceiving the activist group as standing between the person and the state. The goal is to energize local communities as tiny publics. One need not focus on minds and structures: if one can establish groups, minds and structures will follow. Organizers like Saul Alinsky's associate Ed Chambers argue that activism arises from local institutions: churches, union locals, clubs, and hospitals. The Alinsky approach treats the movement group as the hinge between macro and micro. Once groups develop, they can be networked.[10] The goal of the organizer—the agitator—is not to create spontaneous grievances and unpredictable action, but rather to have a group join together in common cause. While establishing group culture is not always explicitly mandated in advice to organizers, the core of leadership is to gain followers who share goals and will work toward them.[11]

Organizing theory did not end with Saul Alinsky's death, and criticism of his style is common, particularly noting that he ignored the voices of underrepresented groups, listening instead to those who aspired to speak for them, as well as his willingness to collaborate with groups that discount the experience of minority populations. Still, the goal of creating group solidarity, shared values, and a grievance frame remains powerful. The mantra "think globally, act locally" heeds the importance of group action as the engine of change. Communities can achieve what individuals cannot. This was evident at a session I attended, aimed at building the allegiance of members, that was titled Organizing 101, metaphorically akin to a freshman seminar on confrontational politics. At this class Davey Gibbs, an organization leader, asked us to write down a problem we wanted solved. Davey, portraying the conservative Republican governor Bruce Rauner, approached several attendees and, as they announced their problems, ripped up their papers. After a few insults, he collected the sheets from each of us. He demonstrated that he couldn't rip up several dozen papers at once, illustrating that if we worked together our demands couldn't be ignored.

Three sessions of five hours each were planned, hoping to train the CST leaders to think like organizers. Training was treated as vital, even if it was not the way most members preferred to spend their days. Perhaps the most charming evocation of the use of movement power—the inchoate process through which groups gain influence—came from Jane Tate, the CST's executive director, who explained, "Organizing is messy. It's sort of like playing in mud. I was one of those kids who liked playing in mud" (field notes). With mud one can build elaborate structures, but of course one can also throw it at others.

Organizing is a process by which people are encouraged to accumulate power—to act together in their shared self-interest and that of their community, developing an oppositional consciousness opposed to the status quo.[12] The activities of the CST were designed as collective strategies to produce change, overcoming the blockage of resistant authorities. While mass demonstrations are personally thrilling, energizing, and visually impressive, such as the 2017 Women's March, they rarely produce the lasting commitment and empowerment that smaller actions can deliver.

The staff at Chicago Seniors Together were not scholars of community activism, nor did they talk much about the theory of organizing. Several of the more senior staff were familiar with the core ideas and debates in the area, but this was less true for the younger and newer staff members, for whom activism was more intuitive. The turnover among staff led to diverse perspectives on whom and how to organize. Over the years, meetings that addressed these topics, such as one called Popular Education in Organizing, attempted to interest members but met with modest success. The staff organized popular education training sessions, originally in concert with Tennessee's esteemed Highlander Center, for over a decade with varying effects. Most members simply wanted the experience of action rather than its theory, despite Saul

Alinsky's emphasis on education and training.[13] At one point Dan lectured on popular education. Topics included Listen to Individual Experiences, Share Experiences and Look for Patterns, Gather More Information, Make a Strategic Plan for Action, Take Action, and Reflect and Evaluate. Dan asked six volunteers to read a sheet about each process with regard to a housing campaign. Attendees seemed confused. Dan admitted, "I know this seems really theoretical, and you don't see how this operates in the real world" (field notes). At times Jane suggested that "training is really critical," but at other times she admitted that "we can't have too much training." Finding a balance proved difficult.

Movements must be about more than talk. To have effect, talk must be based in community: the belief that others share these ideas and that those who participate accept risk in the attempt to alter societal arrangements. The status quo has considerable weight, making change onerous. But even lacking success, seniors can be proud: *to act is to be*. If it doesn't make them feel young, at least it makes them feel vital.

The transition from the pleasure of talk to a commitment to action is what defines an activist, but as I noted in chapter 2, it can be an arduous transition, since action may lead to injury or arrest. Such experiences may be new to seniors with secure lives. Petra Daggert reported how impressed she was with her own bravery: "I never in a million years thought I would do some of the things I was at. I never thought I'd make a speech. I did four last year. I did one in the rain" (interview). Petra had a powerful story to share with others, depicting her personal challenges, and she proved a lively speaker with happy results.

Despite the satisfaction some found in resistance, other leaders were unwilling to protest, although they made significant contributions behind the scenes. There were always tasks to be done in the office. It was commonly noted that progressives love to complain, but the organization required public bodies if it was to matter. As one member remarked, "Talk won't boil the rice" (field notes), but cooking can be messy. Davey emphasized this point in describing his three-hour bus ride to protest at the Illinois State Capitol in Springfield despite his multiple frailties: "I don't like going. I'm always looking around for a bathroom. I'm always afraid of getting lost. But they're not going to get away with it. I don't like to do this, but we want to look them [the legislators] in the face, so they know we're there" (field notes).

The goal was to take part so that "we can be active and proactive in our role as seniors" (field notes). One activist described her first major action as a baptism. Once one bridges the unknown, further participation is likely and often pleasurable.

Talk is insufficient for a sense of accomplishment. Barb Greene, one of the most committed members, declared, "We are a group of people who are here to take action. We are an activist group. We are not here to talk. I encourage people to take risks. I encourage people to get outside their comfort zone." Or, as Davey affirmed, "The main fun thing we do is going on actions" (field notes). Recognizing this desire for excitement, community organizers speak of their demonstrations as "high-spirited and fun."[14] Politics must be embodied and emotive to deliver the pleasures of disruption.

A contrast between talk and action is often strongly drawn. Doug Lucas, a former union organizer, exhorted us, "It's time to put our boots back on." Luisa, a key staff member, echoed his sentiment: "No one in this room can only think about things. We have to have boots on the ground" (field notes). Slippers aren't enough.

While movements that are the most militant have advantages in creating new forms of justice,[15] these groups demand commitments from members to generate that militancy. At first—and later—participants must bear the costs of disruption. For seniors, perhaps protecting Social Security and Medicare was sufficient motivation when the programs were enacted in the 1930s and 1960s. Yet achieving each program took boots on the ground. However, the nation has changed—or has it? For the CST, boots are still essential.

What strategies are appropriate for elderly activists? Answering this question involves recognizing that every social movement is situated historically, technologically, and demographically. Given the increased online activity of many movement groups, Chicago Seniors Together was an "old-fashioned" organization.[16] Perhaps this is part of its charm, and perhaps traditional tactics are still effective. Many of their strategies would have been familiar to Saul Alinsky and his midcentury comrades. To be sure, ideologically the organization has no interest in a Communist Popular Front; members do not call for state ownership of the means of production. However, as was true for Alinsky's Industrial Areas Foundation, Chicago Seniors Together believes that the government—federal, state, and local—has a moral obligation to provide for needy seniors, to redistribute resources, and to ensure that all pay their fair share. These ends are to be achieved by mass meetings, demonstrations, civil disobedience, and political campaigns: techniques that have long been part of the activist's tool kit, borrowed from labor protests and the civil rights movement.

In this chapter I describe four activities that Chicago Seniors Together engaged in: the meeting, the endorsement, the rally, and the action. In chapter 4 I return to the demonstration in Racine, Wisconsin, and consider one at the State Capitol in Springfield, Illinois, when I discuss the politics of memory.

These cases are just a few of the actions the organization sponsored, believing that a strong movement is continually active. Before the COVID-19 virus struck, barely a week passed without a protest. Sitting back and watching—and talking—was insufficient. Smaller actions included bird-dogging politicians (the mayor and the secretary of HUD) by disrupting public meetings; a ("silly, fun") event in which members stood outside the mayor's home singing political carols; and a "die-in" at the convention of the American Medical Association to demand health care for all. Effective demonstrations had a hook that leavened the protest with humor.[17]

As community organizer Michael Gecan argues, activists—particularly senior activists—must "demand the respect you've earned and deserved."[18] Given the presence of group cultures, the question is how demands can be linked to the pragmatics of protests in ways that reveal emotion, develop empowerment, leverage policy change, and increase the power of the challenging group while being appropriate for those who choose to perform in public.

The Mass Meeting: The Senior Power Assembly

Aside from the memorable demonstration in the "Wisconsin blizzard" and the protest at the Illinois State Capitol, the most memorable event that Chicago Seniors Together held was their Senior Power Assembly in September 2017. This was a quiet political period, a year from the midterm elections, eighteen months ahead of the mayoralty election, and more than three years before the 2020 presidential election. The CST hoped to gather supporters and recruit new ones through a large community meeting. But several elements of timing had to be considered: the gathering could last no more than two hours, and it could start no earlier than 10:30 a.m. to encourage turnout.

At the time, the organization was emphasizing the need for affordable and safe senior housing.[19] The Chicago Housing Authority and the US Department of Housing and Urban Development were top targets. The CST had been developing what it labeled the Senior Housing Bill of Rights. This consisted of demands for housing justice for the vulnerable elderly who required government subsidies. While the proposal covered homelessness, it also addressed rent control, affordability, safety in public housing, and nursing home policies. While the Bill of Rights evolved, it included (1) The Right to Be Treated with Dignity and Respect; (2) The Right to Truly Affordable Housing; (3) The Right to Secure and Safe Housing; (4) The Right to Organize; (5) The Right to Live Free of Discrimination; (6) The Right to Needed Services; (7) The Right to Physical Accessibility; and (8) The Right to Transparency, Accountability, and Democratic Control. These were aspirational goals, but ambiguous enough that they could be used to address many perceived threats to senior welfare. Achieving a proper level of ambiguity that appeals to many constitutes a dilemma of articulating policy. "Affordable Housing" and "Dignity and Respect" have some of the rhetorical qualities of demanding a Fair Share. Movements have no endpoints and no fixed goalposts. As constructionists emphasize, there is no end to social problems.[20] When a problem is seen as rectified, others appear. Activists are never satisfied.

Housing was central to the organization's agenda. A committee met each month to discuss challenges, share victories, plan actions, and encourage participation in demanding change. Demonstrations against policies of the Chicago Housing Authority (CHA) and the US Department of Housing and Urban Development (HUD) occurred throughout the research. At demonstrations the members, wearing bright blue CST T-shirts, held up signs, banners, placards, and posters reading "Housing Is a Human Right," "Lift the Ban on Rent Control," "Full Funding for HUD," and "CHA Stop Killing Us."

The original purpose of the meeting was to present the Housing Committee's Bill of Rights, but the idea of a mass meeting proved so appealing that other topics were included. Trina Davis, a senior leader, noted, "Dan wanted to roll out the Senior Bill of Rights, and over time it morphed. It expanded from there" (field notes). This gathering became the most significant meeting of the year. Through their extensive planning, the original modest idea developed into a plan for a citywide assembly to which politicians were invited, with the hope that they would be forced to embrace the organization's agenda. The event was intended to be a rite of solidarity.[21] Extending from the Senior Housing Bill of Rights, the Housing Committee called for fully funding HUD and renovating CHA housing.

The Health Care and Economic Justice Committee, the organization's other major policy committee, demanded scrapping the cap on social security taxes, supporting a caretaker credit, and pushing the fair tax (allowing for a progressive state income tax). A range of progressive proposals, focusing on those related to seniors, would be on display at this town hall setting.

During summer 2017 the CST developed plans for what became their largest event during my research. The goal was to fill the expansive and elegant sanctuary at the Chicago Temple, a historic building in the heart of the Loop, home to the United Methodist Church. By mid-July commitment to this rally had the explicit support of the Housing Committee, which originated the plan, and the Health Care and Economic Justice Committee, which supported the event unanimously.

Although CST's partisan sister organization United Chicago Seniors in Action, a 501(c)(4) non-tax-exempt organization, eventually chose not to endorse a candidate for governor in the Democratic primary, the original plan was for it to announce its endorsement at the mass meeting. If CST could fill the sanctuary and have politicians attend, its power would be evident. As Jane Tate explained to the Board of Directors, "We want to get three hundred people into a space. The goal of this is to have these elected officials walk in and see our power." A colleague supported her, remarking, "This will be an occasion to brand ourselves. To show stamina. To show our power. This is about our organization, the Chicago Seniors, coming together and building power as an organization, and to put senior issues on the [City Council] agenda" (field notes). Bea Barrett, a leader, remarked, "We have the power. If we have three hundred people showing up, we have the power. I'm going to say 'Senior,' you're going to [respond] 'Power.'" While power is hard to measure,[22] its display was essential, as indicated by the title of the event, Senior Power 2017. Still, arranging such a meeting was an organizational risk, and each member of the board was exhorted to contribute.

The event required extensive planning over two months. First the site had to be rented at a cost the organization could afford. But this was only the start. As I described in chapter 2, a gathering of seniors has special requirements. Since this was a church building the structure was suitable, but the organization had to consider how many spaces were needed for wheelchairs, snacks and juice had to be provided, an area had to be set aside for children or grandchildren, and materials had to be printed in Spanish, Russian, and Hindi. Translators and sign-language interpreters had to be hired, and the church hall had to be adorned with signs and posters without defacing the space. Each of these was a task for the organization that if ignored could be used to criticize the event.

This was not all. The event organizers met to develop a program addressing the themes the policy committees wanted to emphasize. Since the claim was that the CST was a senior organization run by seniors, the speakers had to demonstrate this as well as reflect its multiracial membership. Relying on the advice of the staff, the Planning Committee selected two African American leaders to chair the event. The CST hoped to have politicians attend, not to give frothy speeches but to respond to a set of frosty demands. Despite the invitations, I wasn't surprised, given these conditions, that neither Senator Dick Durbin nor Senator Tammy Duckworth attended (or even sent representatives from their offices). Only one member of Congress was present: Congresswoman Jan Schakowsky, an organization favorite. (A second, Congressman Danny Davis, sent a letter supporting CST's goals.) The date was chosen to coincide with a congressional recess so elected officials could attend. Their absence was treated as an affront, an indication that they didn't think the organization mattered, although one might equally believe these politicians didn't want to be confronted or embarrassed.

Creating successful gatherings is essential for movements, possibly leading to new perspectives.[23] As Jonathan Wynn points out,[24] occasions are critical for defining a community and establishing a shared identity. In this regard the members and staff of Chicago Seniors Together thought the success of the program was so vital that presenters held a rehearsal to practice their speeches and discuss the order of the program, allowing them all to feel comfortable in their roles. Leaders saw the assembly as a performance that defined them. It was not simply a set of individual presentations, but a team drama.

As with many effective performances, conflict was thought to increase the audience's attention. While the talks—sad tales and atrocity stories[25]— included villains and victims, a visible opponent was needed to create interest and generate emotion. The dramatic crux was to be the contentious questioning of those politicians who had been invited. The Planning Committee intended to place an empty chair on stage if either senator was absent (neither showed up, and the plan was shelved). A more moderate congressman, Michael Quigley, who had said he might attend, would be challenged with hard questions, allowing him only brief responses. The idea was to raise the level of tension, hoping to get the congressman to commit himself to the organization's agenda, notably support for Medicare for All. Perhaps foreseeing this plan, he didn't appear.

The next challenge was to fill the sanctuary. Can a meeting in an empty hall be counted as successful? Surely not. Gaining an audience was critical. At this time the CST had about six hundred dues-paying members, but only about fifty were actively engaged. The organizers had to motivate enough supportive seniors to travel downtown on a Saturday morning for a political meeting. While some proposed placing newspaper advertisements and distributing fliers in senior housing, Jane insisted that direct communication was essential. Networking would recruit attendees to an event that in itself might not have sufficient appeal. Members were to commit to inviting friends, neighbors, and fellow parishioners to ensure that the event would be judged successful. Jane emphasized, "I want to make sure we have actual conversations with people." This desire for personal appeals also led to phone banking to potential supporters and former members, held each week but of uncertain effect.

The weather on the morning of the Senior Power Assembly was perfect, a deliciously mild Chicago autumn day. The leaders of the organization, wearing bright blue CST T-shirts, began to arrive at 9:30 a.m., an hour before the meeting was to start. We anxiously shared our hopes for a successful event, discussed the possibility of media attention (there was little), and set up tables with flyers and snacks. Speakers were full of nervous energy, especially since they couldn't read their speeches but needed to "speak from the heart," having memorized written remarks. As Dan informed us, "It's hard to get energy if you're reading. Practice, practice, practice." Before the event I found Ralph Phelps sitting alone in an alcove, anxiously rehearsing his three-minute speech.

By 10:00 a.m. the sanctuary began to fill. All but one of the seven hired school buses arrived on time. The room was decorated with a large banner reading "Senior Power! For Dignity and Justice." By the invocation, the pews had filled with seniors, caretakers, and other supporters. Attendees were asked to sign in, both to get a count for publicity purposes and to gather contact information on potential supporters.

The care that went into constructing the program was evident, emphasizing the theme of "housing justice." This was the primary message and the way the CST hoped to define itself. Organizers deliberately avoided the mundane routine of speech after speech, believing that mere talking heads would depress the crowd. We were welcomed by the pastor of the Chicago Temple, who praised the Senior Housing Bill of Rights and intoned, in line with the CST perspective, "We encourage our members to vote their values." The assumption was that personal values ("equality," "justice," "fairness") would be transformed into policies the CST supported. As I noted earlier, "freedom" and "faith" were not cited as values, as they would have been at a conservative gathering.[26]

The rest of the assembly was a carefully curated mix of speeches, music, sing-alongs of civil rights-era songs ("We Shall Overcome," "We Shall Not Be Moved"), chants, and a short speech by CST's beloved ally Congresswoman Jan Schakowsky, followed by gentle questioning. She was the only politician who chose to attend. The diversity of activities kept the audience attentive for nearly two hours. The meeting was formally divided into two parts: the ostensibly apolitical Chicago Seniors Together meeting and the partisan United Chicago Seniors in Action event for the final thirty minutes.

Talks given by members, standing behind a lectern in front of the congregation, dripped with emotion and emphasized the advocacy frames of the organization. Most were no longer than three minutes, and many were shaped by the advice of staff and sometimes by their backstage speech writing. To demonstrate the CST's commitment to diversity, more disabled people and more African Americans were given the stage than were reflected in the organization's membership. Rather than being treated as individuals, the speakers were a team with shared vision and a communal culture that demanded social justice. These elderly men and women, few with extensive public speaking experience, were passionate and inspired. Erik Stanton, not known for his eloquence, gazed at the audience and intoned, "I am the face of hunger," demanding that food stamps (now named SNAP: Supplemental Nutrition Assistance Program) be supported despite funding threats. Ralph Phelps recounted the lack of institutional support for his mentally ill brother, and Francine Doe shared an atrocity story about problems at her decrepit Chicago Housing Authority building: "My manager continually harassed me and tried to get me evicted. I want all seniors to be treated with respect, and that's why I support the Senior Housing Bill of Rights" (field notes). Perhaps there was an institutional justification that might have refuted these stories of uncaring bureaucrats, but given the impassioned narratives, there was no space to ask.

Chants ("Seniors Matter," "That Ain't Right," "Time to Take on Corporate Greed") bracketed the talks, augmented by slides and the voices of leaders. Despite the desire to challenge politicians, Congresswoman Schakowsky, a veteran of progressive activism, commanded her moment, giving a rousing—and brief—address, inspiring her audience with their own influence:

> What do you feel today? Say "powerful." This is bigger than the civil rights movement. This is bigger than the antiwar movement. It is much larger than the Tea Party. Our people are so mad, and that's a good thing. We can see the dawning of a new progressive era. . . . Elections really matter. We are fortunate to have two great senators. (Field notes)

In answering questions, she grabbed the microphone from Richie Douglas, who was on stage to control her presentation. He admitted that this was his most challenging responsibility, and he felt he'd failed. Chagrined, he confessed, "We just had to let her do her thing." Despite Congresswoman Schakowsky's praise for other officials, the leaders of CST expressed frustration that no other politician had joined her. Hazel Windblatt, soon a co-chair of the CST, called for the audience to target the more moderate congressman, Michael Quigley, who chose not to attend. Davey Gibbs, aggrieved as usual, remarked that their senators didn't "have the decency to show up. . . . It's time to cook or get out of the kitchen, because we are raising the heat. . . . We're just not that important to them" (field notes). Although realistic, he was not uplifting.

The meeting closed with Richie imploring the audience, "We urge you to join us on the front lines of change. This represents a strong show of senior power." Angela Knight demanded, "Who's ready to take back government?" The crowd, though thinning, responded lustily. Given that seniors' energy had begun to flag, it was perhaps for the best that there was no endorsement for governor and no need for a march.

Did the organization reach its attendance goal, the mythology of numbers as a mark of triumph? They nearly succeeded, and the sanctuary was impressively filled. An organizer admitted at a debriefing, "We had about 265 at the church. . . . It won't be three hundred, but it will be close." This was based on a head count taken at 11:00 a.m. "Our goal was to have about one hundred new members or people who'd had little contact with Chicago Seniors. . . . This was completely on us. No one else could take credit for it." Later, through some creative accounting, perhaps reasonably assuming that some people did not sign in or could not be counted, the newsletter announced that they had three hundred attendees, close enough for movement work, as one might joke. Crowd estimates are a form of fiction, a triumph of desire over reality. The audience included more African Americans than the organization itself did, perhaps because some Black churches publicized the gathering.

As was true for many events at Chicago Seniors Together, much time was devoted to debriefing. The Organizing Committee did not simply move on: it discussed what went well and what did not, even if the event wasn't to be repeated. For the CST this served as a test of what the organization could achieve, despite the absence of politicians and media. Most responses were enthusiastic. Although the late bus was noted and some overhead projections didn't work as planned, Richie said we deserved to celebrate. The speakers, nervous novices, praised themselves for staying calm, and there was widespread agreement that the brief but emotionally jarring narratives were effective. When asked for "feeling words" about the event at the debriefing, leaders were aflame: happy, amazed, empowered, moved, powerful, and beyond words. Aside from the emotional benefits and increased commitment, they raised $600 from donation baskets. This was not enough to pay for the event, but it indicated widespread support. They congratulated themselves on how smoothly the staff and leaders collaborated, which, as I note in chapter 5, was sometimes a source of tension. The Senior Power 2017 gathering was a significant achievement, even if its impact could not be measured. Whether or not they were due to the assembly, the organization could point to progressive successes in the subsequent municipal election that installed a progressive mayor and city council, so perhaps it did energize seniors to buck the traditional Chicago Way.

The Endorsement: A Marker of Weakness?

An early reason for holding the Senior Power Assembly was to let the organization introduce itself as a player in Chicago politics: seniors with big shoulders. An election for governor was coming a year later, and eight serious Democratic candidates had announced they were competing for the position. By then the CST had formed a political arm, United Chicago Seniors in Action, a 501(c)(4) that would permit them to endorse candidates and engage in electoral politics. These two organizations, although linked, were legally and financially separate. However, there was much concern that if partisan political action was linked to the ostensibly nonpolitical Chicago Seniors Together, the group's tax-exempt status might be threatened. The reputation of one could seep into the other, but the finances had to be kept separate. As a result, defining the UCSIA was vital if the group desired to influence local elections. The CST could protest the policies of elected officials, but only the UCSIA could support or oppose candidates. The line was thin but consequential, since it involved tax-exempt status. It was also complicated in that the two organizations had the same staff and had to create practices of cost-sharing when only contributions to the CST were tax deductible. The divide was hard to enforce, since casual and caustic comments about politicians were common. It took time to become sensitive to the division, and members were warned about "entrapment." Perhaps CST was too small to be entrapped, but the issue was frequently on the table.[27] The rules were complex. As a strategic planner emphasized, "We can bash Trump all day. We can't say we are working to defeat him. . . . Be aware of entrapment. [Don't share your] dirty laundry" (field notes). Their worry was so profound that when members attended a candidate forum they were told not to wear their CST T-shirts for fear they might be seen as partisan. The two organizations distributed different buttons and T-shirts (one yellow and one blue), and members were informed which to wear to events. This concern was linked to fears over President Trump's reelection, where they were afraid they might be "witch hunted" by his reelection committee and lose CST's tax-exempt status. As someone said, referring to one of Donald Trump's noxious supporters, "You only need one Steve Bannon [to lose your tax-exempt status]" (field notes). Although this seemed unlikely in Chicago, some fretted about undercover videos.

Unlike the Senior Power Assembly with which it was linked, the endorsement process did not proceed as planned. Many members considered it a failure and, worse, thought it showed the organization's lack of power, at least in statewide elections. Perhaps it was useful as a learning experience, since the CST decided to focus on local races where the group had more influence.

Defeating the Republican governor Bruce Rauner, economically conservative although socially moderate, was a high priority for progressives, even if the group believed—following the Alinsky mantra—that they had no permanent friends and no permanent enemies. (President Trump tested this belief.)

Governor Rauner was not invited to fill out a questionnaire for possible endorsement. While the eight candidates were liberal, two of them, potential
allies, were notably progressive.

The Movement Politics Committee of the newly formed UCSIA worked
diligently to develop a questionnaire asking candidates about senior issues
and progressive policies. Despite the claim that this was an organization run
by seniors, staff exerted considerable control in the process of endorsement.
Luisa, the staff member in charge of movement politics, pushed the key decisions. When Luisa said that in making their decision "we have [been] sworn
to secrecy," Carrie joked, "She's threatened to kill us." Later Carrie noted, "We
need someone talking to the press," and despite organizational claims Luisa responded, "That's my role." Later Luisa disinvited me to the committee
meeting where they were to decide whom—or whether—to endorse. After
the meeting one friendly committee member pulled me aside and whispered
the decision, not wishing to be overheard. Not every staff member would
have been so directive, but a balance was always necessary between staff and
leaders on who made decisions, a topic I return to in chapter 5.

Under Luisa's direction the group spent considerable time phrasing the
questions so as to challenge the candidates and to require specific responses
about topics such as changing the state constitution to allow for a progressive
tax increase. This questionnaire was sent to all eight major Democratic candidates. Only four responded, and one of the progressives ignored it. (This was
a fairly low-budget campaign by a Chicago alderman who might have lacked
sufficient staff to respond.) The four candidates who submitted responses
were invited to be interviewed. The seven-member Endorsement Committee
was selected with recognition of gender (three men) and race (two African
Americans). Each person was given prepared questions and rehearsed with
another member role-playing the candidate, prompting laughter with irre-
sponsible answers (the worth of immigrants was "food and fiestas"). Other
members of the CST could attend the interviews but were seated in rows of
chairs behind the committee.

The plan did not go well. All four candidates who submitted answers
agreed to be interviewed, including two of the three leaders. Interviews were
scheduled on two days. The first day was particularly disappointing. One candidate canceled that morning, citing a meeting with a group of veterans in
southern Illinois. Although not a first-tier candidate, this man had suitable
credentials. The committee members arrived to find that only one candidate
was scheduled to address them; fortunately this was the candidate they were
most inclined to support. We spent an hour building our community and
discussing politics, waiting for 1:30 when the candidate, State Senator Daniel

Biss,[28] was scheduled to arrive. At the scheduled time, Biss didn't appear. He never called. As someone who once worked on political campaigns, I was somewhat nonplussed: schedules could be approximate in the heat of the political moment. However, this was not how it was interpreted. As we awaited Biss, frustration turned to anger. After fifteen minutes, Luisa asked the group how long we should wait. When someone suggested another half-hour, noting, "We're new at this; we don't want to be so rigid," she chided the group, and they decided to give him another fifteen minutes. When Biss didn't appear they rescinded the invitation. ("If he's not here, he's out.") In fact Biss arrived at 2:05, thirty-five minutes late, while the committee was still present. I assumed they would have him apologize and then question him. I was wrong. His tardiness had been transformed into an issue of organizational respect. A staffer and a group leader went into the hallway to inform him that he was not welcome and would not receive the CST endorsement. Despite their hopes for the endorsement as a sign of the group's political maturity, his not calling overrode their desires. Their anger was palpable. As one participant remarked, "The value is respect. It's not what the candidate says that counts; it's what they do that counts." When Richie returned after giving Biss the bad (and surely unexpected) news, he swiped his finger across his throat to show that any possible endorsement had been killed, adding, "Many of us feel we're not being listened to. . . . We're really beholden to nobody." One member noted, "At this point it's done." Biss's apology notwithstanding, he was not permitted to meet the committee, even if he might have brought desired progressive policies to the state. Jane insisted that Biss had disrespected the organization: "What you're doing is showing candidates that how a candidate treats an organization [matters]. We don't have to endorse anyone. You can do what you want to do. There's the sense that you have to treat politicians with kid gloves" (field notes). One might doubt that the incident conveyed this message as opposed to revealing the organization's immaturity, but Biss wisely made no comment. The desire for respect had become more significant than supporting a candidate they agreed with, who was fighting for progressive policies. The episode was best summed up by Luisa, who remarked, "I was seething in my chair."

On the second day, two candidates did attend: a minor candidate—a school administrator from southern Illinois—and the leading candidate, J. B. Pritzker, a wealthy moderate liberal who was eventually elected governor. Each was on time, but the energy level and enthusiasm were distinctly lower, since neither was seen as a progressive champion. Both men made articulate presentations and supported senior issues, though not as firmly as the staff and some leaders wished. Like many politicians, they chose to speak as they wanted and answered questions other than those asked. Pritzker in particular was chided for not addressing senior issues sufficiently in his opening remarks. While he was respectful toward the organization, his values were not seen as matching its own closely enough. In this light Carrie proclaimed, "They didn't speak to senior issues, so we decided not to endorse" (field notes).

After the decision, Ralph Phelps noted about the failure of the endorsement process, "We're small potatoes" (field notes). Some suggested that the failure mirrored the lack of respect that seniors often receive in political campaigns. Perhaps this is true, but it also reflected a degree of inflexibility and perhaps even naïveté. Jane suggested that not endorsing a candidate who did not share their values was "a huge accomplishment," and Luisa insisted, "Everything starts at zero. We're not at zero, but we need to ramp up." However, these excuses rang hollow to some members, particularly those who admired and supported Daniel Biss. As one senior member noted with some asperity, "We're satisfied because we've rejected all of them. That concerns me." In the end it might not have mattered, but the plan was a failure. In this case the perfect was the enemy of the good. As I noted, the lesson learned was that they should focus on the local level, where their impact might be felt. The organization later endorsed a progressive aldermanic candidate who successfully toppled a more conservative incumbent, while choosing not to endorse in the presidential election of 2020, despite virtually unanimous agreement on the preferred candidate.

The Rally: Resist Trump Tuesday

As I discuss in chapter 7, the 2016 presidential election was cataclysmic: joyous for some but dismaying for my informants. Afterward, energy bubbled up on the left, even during a cold winter. In Chicago as elsewhere, protests were scheduled each Tuesday, organized by various groups that composed the People's Action coalition, of which Chicago Seniors Together was a member. The demonstrators met at a scheduled time and marched to a chosen corporate location in the Loop that was said to support the Trump presidency. By April participation had dwindled, and even some staffers admitted they were burned out from attending the repetitive demonstrations.

However, in the early weeks of the Trump administration the rallies bred community, even if they were soon ignored by most media, although occasionally reporters from the local CBS channel, Fox News, and Univision were present. Whenever the media were present, attendees were satisfied that "we got our point across."

I will discuss a larger, more disruptive example of civil disobedience later.

At this rally, held near the end of March on a cold early spring afternoon, there were arrests as some members of the CST and their allies briefly blocked four revolving doors at the front of the downtown Bank of America building. After forty-five minutes the icy crowd began to melt away.

Because this week's event was sponsored by Chicago Seniors Together, the organization took it seriously and held a planning meeting the week before to strategize and to make signs at an informal "Art Party." We sang songs and cheerily made posters for the rally using colorful markers, perhaps channeling our middle school selves. We also constructed a large articulated effigy, an amusing caricature of the target, which several seniors carried through the streets. Participants were proud of their construction, and one delighted friend reported that she had helped carry the "puppet." Supporters were called on to encourage a robust turnout, and the members of the CST gathered early to strategize at a meeting room of the Grace House Ecumenical Center, an Episcopal-affiliated prison ministry. Although the demonstration was supposed to look spontaneous, it was carefully staged, as is common in Alinsky-inspired protests. About one hundred activists showed up; most were older White women.

These weekly demonstrations assembled at the downtown Federal Plaza. This spot was chosen both because of its central location and because the final destination could be hidden so police could not prepare, increasing the likelihood of disrupting traffic. Signs mentioning the target were not distributed until after we arrived at the site. We gathered in front of a large banner reading "Housing for All" (figure 2).

The rally began with an invocation, and as we listened participants held up signs (Trump as "Agent Orange"; "Support HUD, Not Homelessness"). This was followed by short speeches from group members and allies about housing justice, since the theme of the march was "Housing is a Human Right." One speaker cried out that "Trump wants to take housing away from the poor." CST speakers were being groomed for leadership positions by their public participation, even though one inexperienced speaker admitted, "This scares me to death." Despite her fears this senior, Petra Daggert, gave a moving address describing living alone on Social Security: "I couldn't afford my rent. I have also some health care issues that had to be put on hold because I couldn't afford it. . . . People elected the worst president in American history, and he appoints people without qualifications—as a case in point, Ben Carson [the HUD secretary]." Other speakers included ministers with experience in giving militant sermons.

We then marched to the nearby office of the US Department of Housing and Urban Development, where the marchers placed yellow sticky notes

FIGURE 2. Resisting Donald Trump on Tuesday

on the windows ("We Love HUD"; "Fully Fund HUD"). These notes were to be taken as tokens of love, supporting the department's mission as understood by progressives. Soon the windows were covered. As Carrie Stanton explained, "We're going to be good at HUD and bad at the [Bank of America]."

As we seniors marched several blocks through a heavily trafficked area, the CST had trained marshals wearing bright orange- and lime-colored vests to stop traffic while demonstrators crossed streets. They also had the charge, perhaps no easier, of ensuring that marchers remained on the sidewalk. This was critical given the limited mobility of many seniors. Marshals are crucial in contemporary protest, since they understand the trip lines that will provoke a police response and since as group members they receive respect from protesters. Movements have their gentle forms of social control, and some are trained for this role.

From the HUD office we headed to the nearby Bank of America building where the main rally was held. In contrast to rallies of the 1960s, I sensed no animosity toward the police, and comfortable communal camaraderie was established. The police, a more politically diverse group than often imagined, would at times hint at sympathy or support for the goals of the demonstration when their tasks were not obstructed by civil disobedience.[29] Davey Gibbs saw the police and protesters as being in league, a negotiation that is now common in planning organized rallies and demonstrations: "You're making an allegiance with the police. We even get arrested. The police, they know we got to do work, but you're really making a bargain with the police. . . . We're going to arrest these seventy-five people and we're all going to get tickets or whatever you're going to do" (interview).

Even blocking the sidewalk had a festive air, done without hostility. I was told that as working-class men and women, the police were potential allies (figure 3).

The likelihood of producing immediate change was slight, but the feeling of affiliation was real. The rally became the subject of conversations and stories over the next weeks. This may have been its larger purpose: to create a beloved community of resistance.

At the plaza in front of the Bank of America there were speeches and chants, ignored by the passersby. I was puzzled at the choice of location, since the issue was not mortgage policy. Instead, the site was selected because a man whom I choose not to name rented office space in the building. He was not a major figure in Chicago politics or business, not a central member of the power elite, just someone few of the protesters had heard of before the rally was planned. The reality that he chose to contribute to conservative causes and that he served on the board of the Heritage Foundation, which shaped

FIGURE 3. The police presence on Resist Trump Tuesday

the Trump administration's housing policy, was sufficient. We chanted, "President Trump is a puppet of the Heritage Foundation. We are here today to reject the Heritage Foundation" and held signs that proclaimed, "Heritage is Heartless." Other signs called for this man to meet with us. As Dan, a CST staffer, remarked, "I want to make life uncomfortable for him, if only for a little while." Perhaps this otherwise anonymous businessman was honored by the attention, perhaps not. The group hoped he could hear the chants and see his effigy and the placards with his picture. We never did learn if he was even in his office during the demonstration or if his staff was bothered. I was troubled by the realization that the (admittedly minor) grief we caused was related to his right to associate with whomever he pleased. I suspected that few Chicagoans had a clear sense of what the Heritage Foundation stood for, why it might be worth a protest, and whether the disruption might have led to resentment. I also considered why, in a democracy, a private citizen's politics should be a source of attack, not debate; but the Alinsky model is to create enemies and to build tension. As Saul Alinsky argued, when one deals with middle-class power brokers, their aversion to rudeness, vulgarity, and conflict might make them more willing to negotiate.[30] Attacks on decorum are a tool. However, one's own supporters must be willing to use these tactics, distasteful for senior social movements.

After that action in 2017, the target's name was not mentioned by the CST; he merely personified Trump's housing policies. Three years later he remains on the Heritage Foundation Board of Trustees. However, the targets of these rallies were not the point; a crucial goal was to create a group culture of shared engagement. As rallies became routine, their effect in building an activist community diminished. Resist Trump Tuesdays soon became just another weekday.

The Action: Moral Monday Civil Disobedience

Although civil disobedience and a few arrests occurred at the Resist Trump rally, here I describe a larger action that was designed to be more contentious: mass civil disobedience at Chicago's Board of Trade on LaSalle Street in the heart of the Loop. As Craig Jenkins and Michael Wallace point out, there is now a greater tolerance for civil disobedience in the repertoire of contention by educated professionals (and possibly by those who have retired) because of their work autonomy.[31]

Such events are designed to produce civic disruptions. Movements need to plan action,[32] and the action is where angry protesters congregate. These occasions stem from what a group considers legitimate in its interaction order. At the least, the disruption means that bystanders will attend to the demonstration—a key feature of movement influence[33]—whether persuaded or offended.

While this was part of a movement repertoire that leaders felt was strategic, not all members of Chicago Seniors Together supported civil disobedience and disrupting the lives of fellow citizens, even if they admired the passion of those who engaged. As a result, the CST, like other organizations,[34] recognized that these events might cause contention within the group. Civil disobedience was used infrequently, and it rarely was highly disruptive of city life or economic activities. These moments were intended to constitute short bursts of public trouble.

Demonstrations were held once a month on a Monday during spring, summer, and fall of 2015 (typically the first Monday of the month; eight times that year) and were part of the activist movement of "Moral Mondays," originally organized by North Carolina's Reverend William Barber, a leader of the NAACP in that state. The demonstrations gained moral authority because they used religious discourse in the service of progressive economic policies.

This was the first civil disobedience action I observed, early in my research, and I was excited to attend even though I was not participating in the attempt to shut down the Board of Trade. The action occurred on a mild day in early November 2015, a year before the 2016 election. It had little to do with national politics, but rather supported a progressive plan ("the LaSalle Street Tax") to raise money to solve Illinois's desperate fiscal crisis by taxing each financial transaction. This was proposed to force the rich—at least those who bought stocks and bonds—to pay their "fair share" of state revenues. Activists considered taxing the rich to be a low-pain means of achieving social justice. Given that few people define themselves as "rich," this approach should provoke little opposition while exposing the power the wealthy wield.

The demonstration, along with the civil disobedience, was organized by the progressive coalition the CST belonged to. Desiring a strong turnout, the CST arranged for buses to drive from senior housing projects on the North Side of the city. Jane estimated that over a thousand activists were present. Most were White, although the crowd was diverse in age, including protesters from numerous activist organizations.

Those who planned to engage in civil disobedience[35] had been carefully trained on what to do if they spent time in jail. They were promised support at all stages of the process. This is particularly important for seniors, who might be injured, and for civil disobedience "virgins" facing their first arrest. Protesters were warned about possible consequences, and those who were participating practiced role-playing.[36] While a few activists spent a night in jail, most were released on their own recognizance. However, those who chose this course prepared for the worst. For many the trial date was slated six months or a year away, and if they were not arrested again in that time, charges were dropped. If given community service, they could even serve the time with Chicago Seniors Together. In Chicago, resisting arrest is a misdemeanor in most instances, although it remains on one's record. Although the threat was small, each participant signed a form absolving the organizers of responsibility should injuries occur. Lawyers from the National Lawyers Guild, a progressive group of attorneys, were prepared to help those who were arrested, and observers were present to monitor the police response. A member of the staff was selected as a liaison with police. Those engaging in civil disobedience needed to decide whether to leave when the police ordered them to, whether to respond politely or hostilely, and whether to go limp, the last bringing a strong likelihood of arrest. In discussions of civil disobedience, going limp was described as "hard-core" protest, a true commitment to disruption. Carrie Stanton remarked, "If we go limp we'll get more press, and that would serve the action. It will draw a crowd, and people will be talking." A staff member added, "If we don't go limp it will all be over in fifteen minutes," hardly worthwhile. The worst that could happen would be for the police to ignore their protest: "It should not be that the police are ignoring us. That seems very powerless" (field notes). The response by agents of control, and its depiction in the media, has more impact than the action itself, and these responses contributed to stories that were subsequently told and retold.

Protesters were informed that "it's important that you don't say anything aggressive to the police. You could say, 'You're hurting me,'" but they were told not to engage otherwise. Jane Tate told those protesting, "Keep saying, 'I'm not resisting arrest, I'm just protesting.'" I learned from observing training, rehearsals, and the actions themselves that civil disobedience, once impulsive and spontaneous, has become a well-scripted performance for all parties. As one police officer noted, "If I have to drag you, you go to jail." This sentiment allowed for some predictability. Although instances exist of violent protest, most protests organized by movements are contained, even if disruptive. This has been a substantial change over the past half-century, especially recalling the drama of the 1968 Democratic Convention in Chicago. While now there was some aggressive crowd control by the police—pushing or picking up demonstrators (in one case I was told that a police officer ran a bicycle into a demonstration marshal)—there was little violence by either group. It was not Grant Park 1968.

The goal of the action was to block the entrances to the Board of Trade, making it inaccessible, at least for a while. Dr. Ben Golden exaggerated warmly when he announced, "We practically stopped the whole world" (field notes).

Trading at the Board was shut down for an hour, a short-term achievement that inspired pride. The estimate was that as many as seventy people were arrested. Some of those who chained themselves to the doors were members of the CST, including Davey Gibbs, Dr. Ben, and Susan Locker, longtime protesters. In the words of a staffer, "Some of us put our bodies on the line" (field notes). I was not one of them.

Susan, in her late eighties and frail, relying on a motorized chair, is known as the "Action Queen." For the police, handling such disabled demonstrators is particularly tricky. She reported that she challenged the police: "I was saying, 'Am I under arrest?' They said no. 'So, I need my chair.'" The police carried her, wheelchair and all. Demonstrators were told that the police "will try to make it scary for you." Even Jane Tate shared that "I'm ready and I'm nervous" (field notes).

Although there were speeches, I was impressed by the joyful atmosphere, as is true at many protests, and by the way the crowd milled about, lending the event an air of congenial disorganization. While the civil disobedience team was well organized, the rest of us stood around chatting with friends and moving to the site of activity, chanting when encouraged to do so by movement marshals: "Shut It Down," "Tax the Rich," "Greece Got Bailed Out, We Got Sold Out," and the inevitable "Pay Their Fair Share."

Those engaged in civil disobedience chained themselves to doors. Eventually they were removed and the protesters, having expressed their opinions, dispersed to buses, cars, or public transport. Within a few hours, business was back to normal at the Board of Trade. The proposed tax still hasn't been passed.

For these vulnerable seniors, civil disobedience was status enhancing. At a committee meeting, seniors were asked what they had done during the past month. Davey announced, "On Moral Monday I was arrested." He was vigorously applauded. He reported that he was in a cell for several hours before being released. Praise for those who placed their bodies at risk was common. Jeanne Hyde, like Davey a longtime activist, declared that "civil disobedience [is] a civil responsibility at times." She disclosed that she had engaged in it with the CST a half dozen times (interview). This is another case of old bodies and young aspirations. Luisa made a powerful case from the standpoint of the staff for the importance of seniors' engaging in civil disobedience:

> Civil disobedience is about putting your body on the line, and there's something about saying that my body matters; that my body has a value. So, when I put it on the line it's valuable and not just young bodies and not just able bodies, and that I can take just as many risks. I think there's something way more powerful about a senior in a wheelchair blocking a door than there is about

young people who [can] move out of the way. . . . Why not use the body? If you're going use the body of a senior, use it in creative ways, in the same way that people with disabilities in wheelchairs climbed up the stairs of the Capitol building in DC. They knew exactly what their body was worth, and they used it as a visual symbol. (Interview)

Not all seniors—not even most members—were willing to risk arrest, but those who did were honored. After Gina Pirro—a previously law-abiding senior—was arrested she announced, "I did something I never did in my whole life. I engaged in civil disobedience." She received a loud ovation. In contrast, Davey could joke sardonically about another action, "I blundered—I didn't get arrested." (We laughed.) Those who were active in the organization but had not been arrested were teased in a friendly way about when they'd take the plunge. When Richie Douglas talked about expanding a demonstration, Jane joked, "I think Richie is saying that someday he'll be arrested." Willingness to engage in civil disobedience seemed more common among White activists; African Americans knew (or at least believed) that they might be treated with less deference by Chicago police officers, a conclusion that much research supports. Tara Lamont, an African American leader, said of Dr. Ben, White and age ninety, "I remembered that he was the first person I ever saw get arrested [for civil disobedience] [*big laugh*], and that's something that scared me to death" (field notes). Richie agreed, as he pointed out the greater danger that Black protesters face. He said he had talked to White activists:

Of course, their experience would be a lot different than what mine would be. [I] might be kept longer in jail than others, knowing what's happened over the years. That is really a deep concern of mine. I look back to when Dr. King was doing civil disobedience and a man of his caliber and stature, a man of the cloth, and he wasn't always treated in the right manner while in jail. (Interview)

The choice of tactics is linked to perceived—and real—dangers in a society in which race affects the way police are likely to respond. Even though civil disobedience raises one's standing, it is shaped by White privilege and structural racism.

Action Worlds

In this chapter I examine how social movements—and in particular Chicago Seniors Together—rely on a tool kit of events to achieve their ends: their repertoire of contention as appropriate for senior bodies. Whether any of these events had much effect is difficult to determine, but they kept members involved in a symphony of occasions. However, social movements thrive or fail depending on whether their actions engage their members, supporting a group culture.

I have emphasized that collaborative events are never set apart from social relations or group cultures but are integral to them: a culture of action that constitutes a tiny but meaningful public. Members believe they are the kind of people who do these things, changing the world for the better. Without this belief that involvement might leverage a new society, few would bear the costs. When there is explicit or tacit recognition of failure or when the action is ignored by the broader public, frustration results. The exit is open.

Few social movement groups find immediate success, and many disband without achieving their goals. The field of politics is littered with the bleached bones of advocacy groups. Persuading people that they need to be "where the action is" is essential. And so, as Saul Alinsky understood, achieving one's goals, however local, is a movement high. Those forms of contentious repertoires that do this are prized.

The Senior Power Assembly I described began with a large gathering, people packed into pews. It was a glorious and happy morning. Whether or not a sociologist could demonstrate its effects, those in the sanctuary devoutly believed. Nearly three hundred progressive seniors met to demand the rights they felt entitled to. These elderly activists organized a production—an entertainment—that captivated a large group.

This was a rare occurrence. It hasn't happened since. More common were the rallies that brought seniors together in joint action to support (or oppose) national, state, and local issues. The speeches, rituals, and intimacy were important whatever their political consequences, as on that early Resist Trump Tuesday. The failed endorsement process suggested that in the world of elite actors an organization with a modest membership might hold little sway. This reality was made salient because of their demand for respect that perhaps they had not earned: yipping puppies of protest.

Perhaps it is better to work with coalition partners, as at the Board of Trade disruption. Was this a disruption for change or merely a disruption of city life? A disruption *of* or *for*?[37] Many examples of civil disobedience turn out to be disruptions *of,* whatever their original intent. However, with a coalition civic agitation can have greater impact, generating attention for public betterment, whether or not change results.

The range of actions considered legitimate and effective contributes to the legitimacy of a tiny public. An array of possibilities exists, a repertoire from which contentious moments are selected. Ultimately those chosen must connect to a belief that they just might change the world. Actions matter, but they matter because they are part of a meaningful and recognized skein of civic involvements.

4

Movement Memories and Eventful Experience

> Strictly speaking, there is no such thing as collective memory—part of the same family
> of spurious notions as collective guilt. But there is collective instruction. . . . What is
> called collective memory is not a remembering but a stipulating: that this is important,
> and this is the story about how it happened, with the pictures that lock the story in
> our minds.
>
> S U S A N   S O N T A G

Social movements depend on transforming experience into motivated action.
The action in snowy Racine, described in the prologue and later in this chapter, is such an example of persuading seniors of their power. The march in the
"blizzard" is recounted often, as movements ride on participants' awareness
of their shared histories. These collective pasts create distinct self-reflexive
group cultures and selected action repertoires, means through which movements frame their pasts and futures.[1] As a result, participants and their audiences consider this network node a tiny public that attempts to shape civil
society. Emplotment, revealed through narrative, is central in defining legitimate collective action;[2] movements could not exist unless members embraced
an organizational plotline, a sense that together they are heading toward desired progress and that they can describe and promote this hoped-for future.
Movements thrive when they transform events into experience, experience
into narrative, narrative into action, and action into imagination. This last
transformation permits a temporal horizon of inspiration.[3]

Collective memory is essential in allowing participants to treat themselves
as an influential public situated in time and space. The eventful experiences
of members and their presentation of those experiences are critical in building affiliation and promoting a desire for joint actions. As Lauren Dornbush,
an organization leader, remarked at one gathering, emphasizing that values
must become personal, "The stories mean much more to those holding them
than the values. It puts a face to it" (field notes). This chapter is a story about
stories.

Despite the claim that Chicago Seniors Together depends on shared
values, Lauren correctly intuits that public narratives reveal values.[4] This is
particularly evident in movements where members draw on their lengthy

pasts. They have "decades of experience," meaning decades of stories. Luisa, a staffer and committed activist, admitted, "We are standing on the shoulders of people who were in this fight before. I was too young, but there are a lot of people who have been in these fights before. There is a lot of experience in this room" (field notes). These seniors can draw on deep layers of embodied knowledge. As a long-standing activist explained to applause, "Our first strength is age and experience." Jerry Hackworth, retired professor and organization co-chair, adds to laughter, "Experience. I don't know about age." These contradictions reflect both the physical limitations of being a senior and the advantages of recall that come with having coped with life's vicissitudes and dramatic political upheavals.

Eventful experience as a resource for engagement is pivotal in how activist cultures are solidified, particularly those that treat these events as central to political activity. Although movement participation is frequently described in light of present motives, interests, strategies, and resources, activism inevitably has a storied component that is revealed through sharing memories. How, where, and when stories are told matters in generating commitment. Poorly told or with the wrong message, stories can limit the amount of activism perceived, making participation seem less heroic and challenging the potential identity of activists.[5]

Recognizing the historicity of movements in their local context creates opportunities for political engagement through the culture of the movement group.[6] By means of sociality, groups transform inchoate political perspectives into muscular movements. The reverberation of events establishes meaning.[7] Through the richness of their implications, events are markers for societies, institutions, and groups,[8] making engagements real, memorable, and shareable. These markers address the implications of chronological change. But they do more than this; they provide reference points that historicize events for a community, sharing a timescape in which accounts of joint action—and the veneration of these accounts—demonstrate the potential for progress.[9] Jointly experiencing and recalling events reveals how temporality as a feature of group cultures builds cohesion and a commitment to a better future.

Through eventfulness and its potential for narrative, individuals perceive themselves as a collaborative circle. They become a group with a linked trajectory and a shared future.[10] As a result, commitment and discourse are central to identity work: belonging reflects one's core self.[11] In movements this is essential, since the pressure not to be a free rider depends on close allegiance despite costs.

While memory work is a feature of all movements, it is particularly evident among those at Chicago Seniors Together. Senior activism is an exemplary site for examining memory in movement work, since many participants, as I described in chapter 2, have had lengthy activist careers in which their past engagements serve as identity markers and resources for the group they participate in. Confronting issues relating to inequality in the second decade of the twenty-first century, many politically engaged seniors had participated in the civil rights and antiwar movements of the 1960s, feminist activism in the 1970s, antinuclear movements of the 1980s, and the LGBT movement of the 1990s. Their perspectives were forged by movement memories, and this past defined their responsibilities in the current moment.

Movements and Their Temporal Horizons

A focus on temporality as a social phenomenon has a recent history.[12] However, it is now well established that references to the past and temporal expectations are determined in an interactive context.[13] Chronology is communally shaped, not merely "one damn thing after another." Although once ignored in the analysis of movements,[14] time—experienced pasts, lived presents, and imagined futures[15]—is an organizing principle.

The study of social movements, building on the rich literature on narrative and identity, suggests that focusing on temporality as outside the social is inadequate.[16] Collective memory not only reveals an imagined past but directs future action,[17] providing moral authority.[18] Barry Schwartz concludes that collective memory involves not only a mirror exposing a community's history, but a lamp lighting the way forward.[19] Whether the original action is seen as heroic or as a failure, shared accounts support the movement's legitimacy. This is the heart of the claim that the eventfulness of the past generates mobilization.[20] Past strategies justify current protest traditions. As Randall Collins argues,[21] strands of memory, building on emotional moments, lead to collective action.

These cultures are often stronger in social movements than in other organizational types, given that participants choose to be linked through their common goals and their desire for community.[22] Members recognize that they share experiences and that these experiences can be pointed to with the expectation that others will understand the reference, creating a self-reflexive reality and a local culture.[23] In Ann Swidler's influential metaphor,[24] this shared awareness belongs to the tool kit from which participants select strategies for collective action. This is especially true during unsettled times, when contending groups have distinct agendas and images of a better future.

Collaboration arises from a community of discourse. Iddo Tavory and Nina Eliasoph argue forcefully that goal selection depends on temporal landscapes that are collectively understood as opening and closing potential paths.[25] Shared recall establishes frames that justify actions within a moral order and an organizational repertoire, in a process of prefiguration.[26] Further, local cultures result from awareness of which metaphors of justice are persuasive,[27] linking the challenges previously experienced, current constraints, and a vision of an ideal future. Movements require the sharing of provocative memories and awareness of injustice, making the past insistent in the present.

Sharing Experience

Eventful experience cemented in memory and narration characterizes all communities, but it is especially salient when facing obstacles. As an organization recruits members, it also recruits their experiences. This is the process that Natalia Junco-Ruiz terms "biographical identity integration." As she notes, "If activists elaborated personal experiences that predated activism into their biographical stories to sustain their activist identities, they also integrated past experiences with activism predating their current activism for the same identity purposes."[28] From this perspective, past activism and present activism are joined, but so are distinct domains of experience: those that are tied to the movement and those that stand apart.

Experience, history, and narrative intersect to shape senior activism by making the memory of events and references to them relevant to collective action in three distinct ways. First, biographical memory situates activism within the context of societally significant events,[29] emphasizing historical awareness. Second, biographical memory connects events to the stories activists tell, inserting presence into biography. What might be antiseptic, distant information becomes lived experience. History is powerful when it becomes embedded in moments of the life course. This is especially true for seniors, where sharing narratives is a means of making their biography coherent, both to others and to themselves.[30] Finally, the past is a communal resource in that participants share experiences through collective narratives. We can speak of a *community* of narratives as each supports (or challenges) the next, suggesting directions for justice. As Patricia Ewick and Marc Steinberg point out,[31] narrative provides communities with mobility and traction, developing "paths of redress" to correct injustice. In Jeffrey Olick's terms,[32] this is the realm of *collected* memories, which when institutionalized are transformed into *collective* memory. When experience is shareable, drawing on common emotions and trust in the speaker, personal relationships aid movement goals and strategies.

These three elements—history, experience, and narrative—underlie movement participation. Although this applies to all social movements, it seems especially prominent among senior citizens, with their long arc of experience. Political awareness, both personal and acquired through the media, contributes to a movement culture that organizers use strategically. Self-referential narratives, capable of being accessed and repeated, have power in building culture. These stories are prominent when colleagues ritually share their demotic commitment, although they are in danger of being defanged—depoliticized—to permit all to embrace what might otherwise be a conflictual tale.

History as Predicate

In examining how history as a form of collective memory shapes movements, I describe organizational discourse in light of the way these elderly Chicagoans recall major historical events. In doing this I am not analyzing activities participants themselves have engaged in; rather, I consider knowledge of historical events that have a broad impact and inspire remembrance. Today's challenges have a lineage of events of past decades. As Todd Fuist points out, this involves imaginaries that become shared representations. Jointly held images allow "actors to conceive of times they didn't experience, people they haven't interacted with, or events that haven't happened yet, serving as a lynchpin for the coordinating of social action."[33] Imagining those communities that surround us can be powerful. This form of collective envisioning is essential for intersubjectivity, the basis of a common culture. By being a part of a community, one gains access to a wide variety of moments of consequence, including those outside one's own experience.[34]

Inevitably, the choice of which values to embrace is historically contingent. As people learn of momentous events, their politics are shaped. Those in the same community are likely to develop similar views of how the future will unfold. This is what Iddo Tavory and Nina Eliasoph refer to as trajectories of action.[35] We speak of this process of integrating images of the past, present, and future as futurework[36] or foretalk.[37]

Because of their longevity, senior citizens have greater awareness of events and their consequences than younger people do. Even if societal change appears at times to move gradually, recognized only in retrospect, core values do shift. Glacial alterations may become recognized as constituting dramatic transformations. Further, nodes and junctures are found in which change is rapid as some event constitutes a decisive turning point that forces rethinking.

For Chicago Seniors Together, references to the temporal landscape were common, ranging from allusions to the antiwar and civil rights movements of the 1960s to feminist activism in the 1970s to recent LGBTQ crusades. These events as they came to be defined—minor and crucial, local and national—shaped collective consciousness. Even if not personally experienced, they provided templates for understanding.[38]

Iconic events are memory markers,[39] but for this to happen members of the community must recognize the references. A dramatic example in local memory was the infamous 1977 march that the National Socialist Party of America threatened to hold in Skokie, Illinois, a Chicago suburb that at the time was predominantly Jewish. Although this Nazi group won the well-publicized legal right to hold the demonstration, they canceled the event and gathered on the less hostile Southwest Side of Chicago. Forty years later, during the summer of 2017 when board members of the CST met to discuss how they should respond to the alt-right and neo-Nazi march in Charlottesville, Virginia, Jerry Hackworth, the White co-chair, referred to the earlier march as a similar moment of fascist provocation. This permitted him to assert that race relations have worsened over the past four decades. His co-chair, Richie Douglas, an African American senior, added, "All this hatred on the streets, I've lived that." Both used their awareness as a form of *experiential authority*. The claim is that President Trump had said "there were very fine people on both sides" linked 2017 to the 1930s, implying a long-term connection between the Trump administration and those who planned to march in Skokie. The organization composed a statement that captured this moral outrage. The same was true in their memories of attacks on civil rights protesters. The CST statement read in part, "Many of us remember when Dr. King came to Chicago in 1967 and someone threw a rock at him. We as seniors must fight together to make this a better place." No one in the group was present at the attack on Dr. King, but their collective recall ("many of us") permitted them to use history to suggest disturbing—and relevant—parallels with the present. The march by White nationalists in Charlottesville reminded some of Nazi demonstrations, recalled from anxious childhoods, suggesting that, as happened with Holocaust survivors, trauma could reverberate across generations. Activists use memorable events to reflect on the present in order to increase their collective commitment to justice.

The White nationalist march in Charlottesville was a particularly dramatic moment for galvanizing progressive movements during my research, but it was not the only memorable occurrence.[40] The election of Donald Trump inspired memories as these activists attempted to place the outcome in the sweep of history. That election, with its unexpected—and, for many, dismaying—outcome, allowed salient comparisons to other elections. At a committee meeting discussing how this progressive group should respond to the election's aftermath, members struggled to find an appropriate context for understanding the new Trump administration. One activist suggested, "This is not completely unprecedented, the Trump administration. There have been other cruel administrations. I think we need to have a historical perspective about this." A staff member endorsed this reading, reminding seniors of the connection between memory and commitment: "We are standing on the shoulders of people who were in this fight before. . . . There is a lot of experience in this room" (field notes). A speaker commented at a large public rally that resistance is always grounded in history:

> We made it this far, but we have to keep focused. We don't have to accept it. We can move forward. . . . When I went to sleep it was 2016. When I woke up it was 1957. We are in a reactionary moment. . . . All we have to do is mobilize the power of the people. We are the generation to do it, because, you know, we vote. We have to lobby for people learning their history and learning their civics. . . . He [Trump] has been president for eight weeks, and it feels like he has been president for thirty-four years. I'm that tired. . . . If I die, I die. . . . We have to make it local. We have to make it personal. (Field notes)

One senior added sharply, "Wake up, my generation." Through these remarks, the speaker asserts a shared commitment to history as a basis for activism. The parallels between 1957, during the stirrings of the civil rights movement, and 2017, as the Black Lives Matter movement was expanding and resistance to the Trump agenda was building, appealed to the applauding audience. For older members the 1955 murder in Mississippi of Emmett Till, an African American boy from Chicago, was a powerful memory and brought several of them into civil rights activism. Several recalled the visit of Dr. King and battles over integrating Marquette Park on Chicago's Southwest Side. Social movements inevitably draw on temporal imaginaries, connecting them to contemporary issues.

Embedded Experience

While many salient historical moments are learned indirectly through media accounts or secondhand reports, activists participate in memorable events that justify future actions. This makes broad social trends personal and builds the culture of the movement by one's embodied presence.[41] As one staffer explained, "We're all a composite of our collective experiences. That's what I bring to the table. That's what you bring to the table. . . . It would be a lost opportunity if I ignored that" (interview).

Even if these moments do not generate organizational action, they are personal in a way that mere exposure to history is not. Experience is a resource through which one can claim expertise by virtue of having been there. Most explicit was Dr. Ben, when asked about his pathways to activism:

> It was my experience in World War II. I almost got killed. Two of my buddies were killed. I was playing poker with them an hour before, and it made me think about war. It was awful. My great change was that in the 1950s, I thought the South would never change with Emmett Till and then the Freedom Riders. I walked with Reverend King in Mississippi in 1966. (Field notes)

Other attendees chimed in with snapshots from their own mental photo albums. Some accounts presented at a meeting of the organization's Racial Justice Leadership Team involved exposing systems of White supremacy, making clear the historical basis of structural systems of racial bias. One White leader of the organization described with passion how as a young man working at bank he interviewed clients applying for loans. His supervisors instructed him to mark the loan applications of Black clients, which would then receive extra scrutiny by loan officers. (He admitted candidly that he would sometimes neglect to note their race—if he felt the client was worthy—but on other occasions would make the mark.) In another case an African American activist explained how he learned community organizing by participating in the uphill, but eventually triumphant, progressive campaign of Harold Washington, the first African American elected mayor of Chicago. Many activists had "racial narratives"—vivid and personal stories that were upsetting, poignant, heroic, or hurtful—about how they adjusted to the complex and trying racial politics of the city. These lived moments had dramatic effects—wise epiphanies and moral shocks—that inserted individuals into the sweep of history.[42] Whom one meets and how one responds alters one's lifeworld, establishing identities and commitments.[43]

Eventful experience provides for a more powerful sense of commitment than simply eventful awareness. Being where the action is matters more than information that everyone can access. Experience creates an insistent reality that becomes part of a personal lifeworld and justifies claims of expertise. Having participated in a meaningful event justifies a self-image, but it also lets one share that image with others. This is crucial for social movements in which one's personal equation looms large: the political is personal. Having lived through the 1960s civil rights movement as a protester justifies supporting the contemporary Black Lives Matter movement, as was true for Stephanie Moore, who had worked with Dr. King and the Student Nonviolent Coordinating Committee in Chicago and in the South in the 1960s. She was treated as an oracle of racial justice.

Likewise, those who had protested (or experienced) poverty or hunger have authority to judge contemporary protests against inequality. Movement participation depends on these moral assessments. Having spent a lifetime demanding a better world and promoting dramatic change provided status within this group culture. In Chicago Seniors Together, where many members have participated in collective action throughout their adult lives, these experiences justify continued activity.

For Chicago Seniors Together, the 1960s—a half-century before my observations—constitute a repeated point of reference and a moment of personal pride, a time when many of those active in the CST were demonstrating in the streets and in which they recall their youthful selves, often with a warm glow of nostalgia. The 1960s have a profound meaning in the history of American activism. Dramatic events from that decade continue to resonate. Whether these seniors were longtime activists or newly returning to the streets, their youthful engagements legitimated their current ones. After a successful demonstration, one activist announced proudly, "Baby boomers, you're back. I'm glad to have you back." Another claimed, "I needed some activism. It takes us back to the sixties." Both referenced their activism from that iconic decade. Thinking of the hundreds present at an action, still another reminisced, "I turned in a thousand draft cards in Washington. . . . Doesn't this remind you of the 1960s?" A recent recruit explained that she joined for "two words: Women's March. I was a marcher back in the sixties. [*Looking around she notes:*] Many of you were active too in the 1960s. I was guilty of complacency. We have to keep fighting battles." As one movement leader pointed out, "The 1960s. . . . You have all lived this" (field notes). Perhaps these claims were a means of establishing coherence given a wide range of experiences and a set of diverse memories, but a shared understanding of activism in the 1960s made this possible as a way to create a stable organization. No one referred in the same way to the less iconic 1950s or 1970s. This public talk served as a control mechanism, permitting Blacks and Whites, women and men to articulate a vision of the future in light of the past. The sixties, a complex and diffuse time with competing strands of change and stasis, was transformed into a meaningful decade with a set of solidified and energizing meanings.[44]

In part this reflects an anodyne nostalgia for a period when political resistance was valued in a progressive subculture and in which these seniors could recall their young, limber, hopeful selves. However, these references to a half-century before also link to a belief in the relevance of current events and the importance of shared perspectives. This was clear in the comment one activist made in an informal gathering: "I've been a lifelong activist since college.

The impetus in high school was the Vietnam War. I hated Nixon so much. Anything that could limit Nixon's policies, I did. I've never been so frightened for the future of my country [as] I am now" (field notes). She recalls her visceral distaste for President Nixon, but through this emotional memory she judges the present moment, suggesting that 2017 is even more dangerous than 1969, although both times are linked in their moral threat. Perhaps more to the point, given aging bodies and their effect on future engagements, is the longtime activist who notes, "We may have one foot in the grave and one on a banana peel, so we shouldn't be relied on to be there forever" (interview). The future is recognized, but so is the vulnerability of the present.

Shared Memories

To this point I have focused on the recall of experiences that are separate from the current activities of the community. But memory is most powerful when it is shared: when it truly contributes to *collective* memory. Put simply, memory matters when it enters a group culture.

As I spent time with these activists, I learned that memory of demonstrations burned bright as a means of demonstrating their moral virtue. Esther Harvey, a recently minted activist, explains her admiration for Dr. Ben, who had devoted much of his life to protest:

> I think you'll find those people have probably been activists over their lives like Ben; [they] are probably much more gung-ho than some of the newer ones, because this is kind of more part of them to be an activist. It's kind of their makeup [more] than maybe some of the people that are just starting when they're becoming seniors. If you talk to some of the people that are really gung-ho, you'll find that they were doing things earlier in their life. But I think having lived their lives and experienced what they have experienced gives them more insight into things than somebody who may be young; they have more wisdom about kind of things and how things can be. (Interview)

Personal commitment becomes the basis for judging subsequent protests. One member, recalling a recent demonstration when he and seven other members of the CST were arrested, referred to himself at a committee meeting as "one of the infamous Chicago Eight," referencing the trial of antiwar demonstrators at the 1968 Democratic National Convention in Chicago. He wondered how many listeners recalled the Chicago Eight, but it was clear from approving nods that fellow seniors understood.

Another way experience matters is through organizational development. Local movements, including Chicago Seniors Together, rely on the experiences of members to justify participation. This was evident when the organization chose the themes for the spring luncheon, their annual fund-raiser. One year, on the fortieth anniversary of the organization, speakers at the event lionized the movement's founder ("Mother Joan") and recounted the group's successes over the decades. Judging by applause and enthusiastic comments, this proved inspiring for current members, especially since few knew the founders. After the fortieth year, what does one do in the less iconic forty-first year? The decision was to connect to organizational history once again. The fund-raiser honored longtime members, defined as those who had participated for at least a decade. The luncheon speakers, including those honored, invoked the successes of the organization, giving credit to those who contributed and sharing their stories, including achieving nursing home reform and preserving affordable senior housing. Recalling history built organizational capacity. As one leader remarked, "Just take time to honor all of those who built the group. It's always good to reflect back on the people who have built the movement when we are facing new challenges." These longtime members were labeled "Veterans of the Fight," and each was asked to recall a CST victory: shutting down Jackson Street, organizing the Die-in at the AMA convention, demonstrating in the rain, infiltrating one of Mayor Rahm Emanuel's supporters' breakfasts, shutting down the Board of Trade, and the snowy rally in Racine. Given that few demonstrations produce immediate results, and given that, at least in the near term, activists often tend to "lose," these expressions allow the experience of one to become the experience of all.

Narrative Facility

The experience of shared events solidifies beliefs and identities. To involve others, however, history must become a basis for collective action. Narration generates emotion, constructs shared meaning, and builds group cohesion.[45] This is particularly evident in social movements where narratives strengthen the members' commitment to potentially costly organizational goals and status-based identities that can be contested.[46] As the staffer Luisa explained in generating commitment to oppose federal budget cuts, "We have to talk about how it affects us. If we talk about corporate loopholes, people's eyes will glaze over. They'll go do the dishes." In contrast, she notes, "'This is a true story.' All of a sudden we're bonded." Longtime leader Barb Greene uses the same metaphor:

> You have to touch the emotional feeling; it's not just the intellect of people when you're trying to get them to understand, you know, why they want to be

involved in this. . . . When we talk just facts, people's eyes kind of glaze over, but when you talk a personal story or you ask them to give their own personal story and how they feel about it, I think that's much stronger than any facts you can give people. (Interview)

As executive director, Jane Tate comments that members of the public have similar stories and that they identify with the stories activists share: "One thing we know is that door knocking sessions work. We need to connect the stories [we tell] to what they know" (field notes). As an example, one activist reports, "I lost my house that I inherited from my parents. They wanted to leave me a place to always live in. I couldn't keep up with the property taxes." On another occasion a member says that three residents in her senior housing building have died in their apartments because a manager refused to install a buzzer at the front desk so that they could call for help. "He said it was too expensive." Those listening groaned in sympathy (field notes). Because they believed in the power of stories, on several occasions members collected narratives that they hoped might move others to commit to active citizenship.[47] The CST held sessions to train members to tell effective stories with heightened emotional resonance and personal impact. While some tragedies are too heartbreaking to use, sharing accounts of death, disease, and impoverishment can advance movement goals. The caution was that the stories should never elevate sympathy for a particular victim over the structures the group wished to change. As a staff member phrased the task, "Are we sharing our stories as if our lives depend on it? We all have our stories that brought us here" (field notes). But the troubles of individual lives must translate into something more than sympathy.

A group with a robust narrative tradition can better mobilize because the memories inspire applicable behaviors, effective strategies, and desired identification.[48] On one occasion a staffer asked us to close our eyes and imagine the most compelling action we'd participated in with the organization. We claimed to feel closer and more hopeful as a result of the exercise.

People narrate in order to process experience within a sociable context, a space of shared reminiscence that participants believe will interest others. Stories are part of identity work, including war stories, triumphal accounts, or even atrocity tales.[49] One source of movement allegiance is anecdotes. These need not be strictly personal; they are fundamentally collective although, as I noted, members relate their own experiences.[50] As sociologist Sujatha Fernandes points out, these personal stories must become more than idiosyncratic; they must recognize structural constraints. Pointing to villains is not sufficient if the injury is only personal. Fernandes argues that to generate activism, stories must incorporate conflict. The danger, she suggests, is that "curated personal stories shift the focus away from structurally defined axes of oppression and help to defuse the confrontational polities of social move- ments."[51] Effective stories are a means of understanding the world in ways that might be missed if the conversation is only about good and bad actors. Jane points to their multiple strategic consequences:

> You can understand what are the experiences that led them to work on these campaigns. And sometimes people by sharing their stories actually under- stand their own story in a different way. I feel like there's been leaders who've been sharing stories with me that their father died when they were younger and their mother had to raise them herself. And then for them to unpack a story in a different way. I think stories, for me, it's about understanding peo- ple's values, trying to understand what's important to them in their lives. Is it church? Is it their children? Is it their grandchildren? I think that stories and sharing stories are really important when you're going to meet with elected officials: advocates like to share numbers; I think stories are more compelling to elected officials. I think stories of seeing somebody in their district who is being hurt by a policy and understanding that this person ended up home- less because of this policy has a different impact than hearing the number of people in the city of Chicago who are homeless. (Interview)

Members own a stock of relevant narratives claiming that a desire for change is an ethical imperative. Narrative facility is a skill that channels the life of the group. In this they draw out appropriate emotions, a process sociologist Orrin Klapp terms emotional hitchhiking.[52]

The relations among participants permit narratives to cement personal bonds. A social movement organization such as Chicago Seniors Together is a site of sociability and fellowship. As Nina Eliasoph argues,[53] the enjoy- ment of others constitutes a "close to home" forum in which politics can be embraced or avoided. The group provides a setting where many forms of talk are judged legitimate and, through courtesy relations, are treated as an ac- curate and relevant representation of others' lives. Social ties overcome po- tential skepticism of collective action. This deference creates strong bonds of community on the local level.[54] The effect is magnified if external obstacles are perceived,[55] whether real or imagined. Thriving movements—indeed, all forms of communal engagement—require established cultural traditions to mobilize members by appropriating, situating, and personalizing memory.

Relying on an interaction order based on shared experiences, every ongo- ing social movement has to develop collective identity.[56] Engagement in social movements demands the ability, as C. Wright Mills argued,[57] to demonstrate that what might otherwise be minimized as personal troubles (victimhood) are actually instances of a widespread social problem (failed structures). For example, Patricia Ewick and Marc Steinberg point out that sexual abuse by priests is not simply a set of troubled churchmen and victimized believers, but a structural condition that shapes the consciousness of many people.[58] What matters more than this linkage of troubles and problems is that it is salient in a group that communicates together. Protest groups do not merely sponsor events; if these gatherings are to have effects, they must be recounted:[59] a library of recall. Telling stories incorporates larger forces within a communal lifeworld, linking the external and the local in a way that is immediate, intimate, and identifiable. Talk transforms beliefs into a demand for action, and as actions become memories, additional talk is possible.

In every cohesive organization, members are encouraged to be a sympathetic audience, welcoming narratives that support recognized priorities. These stories have an emotional punch, a memory hook, and a cultural authenticity that mere recitation of facts lacks.[60] This speaker-audience relationship establishes a tightly knit group, a central goal of much community organizing and relational activism.[61] Telling a story and making it stick is a skill that adds to the speaker's authority. Emphasizing skills privileges the ability to bond by creating empathy. Effective narratives both rely on and deepen relationships, providing a context in which audiences willingly incur costs.[62]

As I noted in chapter 3, many events sponsored by Chicago Seniors Together included members' sharing sad tales about the tragic contours of their lives, gaining sympathy and support, and bolstering the belief that collective action and institutional pressure can make the world more just. Lacking trauma caused by systems of oppression, are social movements truly needed? These narratives reveal the value of struggle and the possibility of heroism, but they require a set of demands. Shared references, extending movement idiocultures, become the basis of a history that expands from the lifeworlds of participants to become the basis of collective organizing. Movements encourage a *performative world* in which the willingness to present one's struggles indicates the authenticity of one's emotions. In this, narratives work by illuminating the speaker's willingness to link a private self with a public identity.

For Chicago Seniors Together, many believe that narrative helps gain support for progressive, senior-friendly policies. Members are exhorted to tell their stories to "document their lives." This assumes that talk is relational and not merely transactional. As Luisa explains it,

> I think one thing that it shows is the long history of the fight. Like seniors'
> Social Security. There are seniors who can talk about when it was passed and
> that long march toward what people are doing now. There are seniors who can

talk about housing. Barb grew up in Lathrop Homes. She could tell the story
of subsidized housing through the history of her life. You don't need to read
the history books; it's all there in front of you. . . . I think it inspires people.
(Interview)

The emphasis on narratives is framed by treating others as "people, not numbers" and "making it personal." While dramatic statistics may attract momen-
tary attention,[63] accounts of those under strain and in pain magnify personal
troubles so they can be imagined as applying to others. A story about me
becomes a story of us. This involves, as literary critic Hayden White suggests,
history as a form of imaginative narrative.[64]

At a training session for movement organizers, sharing values through
life experience proved central, drawing on events in one's life to demonstrate
the consequences of social ills. One leader shared how the burden of having
ADHD that was not properly diagnosed had affected her life, making her
question her ability and limiting options until others helped her overcome
the psychic challenge and public stigma. Another related a history of family
abuse and her mother's struggle with addiction.

Although these stories were moving, there is a concern that the emotions
can be too raw. Francesca Polletta emphasizes the danger of privileging a
victim self.[65] She suggests that accounts of suffering must be modulated to
be effective. Too much distress, and audiences turn away; too great a claim
of victimhood, and sympathy dissipates. At one training session we were
warned that community organizing should not constitute the "Oppression
Olympics." The demands should produce a desire for justice and structural
reform, not pity for the needy. Sympathy must lead to struggle. "Victim storytelling" is widely believed to be ineffective by social movement professionals,
in contrast to accounts of resilience and determination.[66] The most moving
stories are those that touch on victim status, even if deeply depressing stories
are often the most personal and most memoirlike narratives. Effective stories
should recount inequalities that need to be altered, not merely point to hor-
rific but unalterable happenings.

Attendees at this training session learned that emotional talk was a valuable means of having listeners validate each other's lifeworlds: "Reflect on
your own experience and know what you want to share. Meet their emotions genuinely and share your own." As one trainer explained to eager activists, "We are embarrassed and ashamed to share our stories. That's why
we have Trump. At the end we are in a war of values." In a relational context
it was hard to deny another's hurt. Pointing to the transition from talk to

action, an organizer emphasized, "Storytelling is how we take on the political situation" (field notes). Part of socialization is to account for the world as lived by justifying experience as the basis of collective action. It was hard not to sympathize with those who have had to choose between housing and medical care, or between possible forms of care available to them. A senior who has COPD told how, given his straitened financial circumstances, he had to choose which medicine to take, since he lacked the $300 a month copay for the one his doctor preferred. An organizer wept openly as she shared her fears for her undocumented immigrant husband: "I fell in love with a person who has no status in this country. He was treated as expendable. It made me so angry. Things are not OK. His life is disposable. I don't know if, when I come home, he'll be there." Statistics do not carry the embodied history of a tragic experience that is shared. Averting one's eyes and closing one's heart against a crying sufferer is harder when surrounded by supporters.

Narrated experience is not inevitably persuasive, but narratives that come from those who passionately describe their suffering create relational barriers to rejection. Sympathy requested is often sympathy granted—at least to a point.[67] Survivors' ability to share their pain in ways that cannot be denied constitutes a potent force. These stories suggest the harms in existing structures, but they also show the reality that some reflected on them[68] and were strong enough to share their troubles in public. Denying their story denies the teller, an affront in any supportive community. As a result, most movement stories go unquestioned, honoring the teller while increasing commitment.

Telling Actions

I return to the demonstration in Racine and describe the one in Springfield as examples of how memory work and narrative facility mattered for achieving cohesion and inspiring protest. The joyous references to these events recognize that both were central to group culture. For their tiny public justice burned brightly, at least in communal memory.

To examine this celebratory process, I address the experiences, memories, and stories of these seniors, examining how these two major events became integral to group cohesion. Chicago Seniors believed in social change and stood for it Together. The march in Racine during the "blizzard" of March 2017 and the demonstration the CST and its allies held at the State Capitol in Springfield two months later were the two actions that best reflected how the organization represented itself to itself.

RACINE, WISCONSIN

The demonstration in Racine, described in detail in the prologue, began with the claim that "We're taking the message that we want medical care for all." Even though Medicare provides for seniors, seeing health care as a right is a core belief. The demonstration, held outside the district office of Paul Ryan, then Speaker of the House, with the goal of "taking the streets" brought back memories of the sixties. It barely mattered that few others were on those streets. In planning the event, sharing personal stories was central. As Luisa pointed out that day, "We want to continue to tell these stories. . . . People who spoke keep your stories because that keeps our movement going." One activist told about his kidney and pancreas transplant, resulting from childhood diabetes and renal failure. He moved us, saying, "I can't afford life without health insurance. I'm healthy now, and I feel very well. My insurance literally saved my life. Millions of people will lose their insurance in Paul Ryan's plan." Another speaker described her daughter's epilepsy, proclaiming that government health care is a right. After the rally a friend declared, "The weather, cold as it was, wasn't as cold as Paul Ryan's heart" (field notes).

The intersection of frigid weather and heated rhetoric proved powerful, but its broader appeal to a moral order that transcended the local was uncertain. Huddling in the blowing snow, I wasn't sure whether workers in Ryan's office were even aware of the protest outside their windows or, given the absence of reporters, whether the public in Milwaukee or Chicago would learn of it.

As I noted, this demonstration occurred in mid-March 2017, soon after the election of Donald Trump, while Republicans controlled both the House of Representatives and the Senate. Most demonstrations during this period occurred in downtown Chicago and had become routine. A field trip to southern Wisconsin promised a change of scene. The organization rented buses to travel together. As I described it in the prologue, the lake effect snow was routinely referred to as a "blizzard," exaggerating the chill for dramatic effect. As Carrie Stanton reminded us, "Remember how cold it was. We should applaud ourselves." We did. As we watched the events unfold on video in a heated meeting room, there was loud applause and cries of "I love it. I love it." Some called the demonstrators "Nanook of the North." On another occasion an activist remarked with admiration, "We can put up with anything to make our point" (field notes).

Residents of the small city of Racine ignored the outsiders; only a few police officers were present to watch the events unfolding in "whiteout" conditions. Publicity depended on the media, and the mainstream media didn't consider the event newsworthy. However, one progressive journalist did film us and circulated the images. As with many demonstrations, the broader public was not the primary target. More important was how the visuals could be used for the group's ends and how our participation might motivate supporters. From our photographs, the CST developed a slide show. Jane Tate reported to the CST board of directors, "It was a very powerful moment seeing all these seniors trudging through the snow with their canes and walkers. The energy of the chaos of the day was so beautiful. It's the moment that gives us hope that we will win. . . . People should know how much fun we had." Doug Lucas admitted to me,

> I was standing there with those folks in the blizzard, and there was nothing in my mind that said, "Well, why are you here when it's this bad? Why would you be involved?" That's the time that I really felt part of it and really proud of myself for being there and being unwilling to give up (interview).

In a similar way, Kate Bibb remembered,

> The people that are in those situations, they seem to just go with the flow. . . . It doesn't seem to handicap them to be there, and I admire them for it. Especially when we went to Wisconsin and it was a snowstorm and all that. I couldn't even imagine when we were pulling off the highway that we would even get off the bus, never mind actually walk the streets to protest. (Interview)

As one senior later remarked,

> What I carry with me is how empowering it was to see our people out there with their best canes, walkers, and prosthetic legs in fourteen-inch lake effect snow. It wasn't a weak demonstration, but a powerful one. People spontaneously gave us what we needed. The more I did it, the more empowering it was. (Field notes)

Dr. Ben Golden, ninety years old and with a lifetime of protest, proudly emphasized his age: "We're not twenty years old anymore." Seventy years had passed. Another recalled, "In a strange kind of way, the snow worked in our favor," making the protest more dramatic, providing "images that the [progressive] media used in two states." What made it count was "the scene of seniors slogging through the snow" (field notes). Richie Douglas remembered, "You couldn't have asked for a better photo op than that, walkers in the snow." As Ralph Phelps told me, "I can remember the people in town looking at us like we were from Mars." Thanks to the progressive videographer, we even received brief attention on Rachel Maddow's MSNBC broadcast as well as in the *Chicago Sun-Times* and Milwaukee newspapers. Compelling visuals of the elderly are catnip for the media. If we couldn't claim that "the whole world was watching," at least media representation meant someone was, and in a minor way the group made history.[69] As William Gamson and David Meyer declare, "fire in the belly is fine, but fire on the ground photographs better."[70] Or in this case canes in the snow.

These seniors felt heroic—deserving of reportage—for braving the elements despite their frailties to demand secure health care and a firm commitment to Social Security in the face of potential cutbacks. Stephanie Moore, the CST office manager, recalled,

> That was a great action, but I swear to God when I came in that morning, I had seventeen messages, and I said, "Oh, this person's dropping out. That person's dropping out." But I think it was galvanized by this whole Trump thing, and what was going on was people saying, "Are you guys still going?" We had a full bus. We had people who showed up. People were in their gym shoes and walking in the snow [with] walkers, and one guy didn't have a leg. It was so powerful to me. I thought that was really, really good. In a blizzard, you know. (Interview)

Jane Tate provides a similar account:

> I remember when Luisa called me that morning and said, "Should we cancel it?" and I'm like, "I don't think so. Let's just take whoever shows up. Let's see what happens." We had a lot of people; I think we had almost seventy people [on the buses]. It was huge. So, here's this moment that I remember: I was watching this whole experience happen, and there was a guy who'd had an amputation, and I thought to myself, "Tomorrow morning you are going to be inundated with calls from our leaders who are so angry that we did this action." And I got not one phone call. As a matter of fact, there are people when you say, "What's your favorite action?" they'll say Paul Ryan. So I think it's the moments when I sort of realize that sometimes you plan things and sometimes things go a little different than you expect them to. What I do remember about that is I watched people help each other, I watched people that probably today would be like, "I could never do that action again" were there and were really excited about it. Nobody complained to me about it. Even that day I remember being in that church thinking, "I'm going to have people coming up to me yelling at me, screaming at me." Because that's typically what happens when people get angry; the next week I got phone call after phone call after phone call. People were thrilled. So it's this moment that you just have to realize that sometimes you plan something and it doesn't go the way you want or you sort of envisioned it. We had envisioned it would be like a block and a half and we were going to bring some buses down there for the people who couldn't walk. (Interview)

Over a year later, stories of the demonstration were still being shared. Members recalled one senior who wore a sneaker in the heavy snow because her foot was swollen, and another demonstrator who walked the two blocks with an artificial leg. While some imagined the demonstration might be canceled, they recalled Luisa yelling, "No way!" These images were seared into group memory, a resource for the camaraderie that movements depend on.

SPRINGFIELD, ILLINOIS

I was present for the frigid protest in Racine but was away during the springtime march to Springfield, although I attended the planning meetings and subsequent evaluation meetings and heard about the overnight action at the Capitol from many informants: informally, in in-depth interviews, and in group discussions.

I briefly describe the Springfield action, held in May 2017. The state of Illinois has for many years had financial problems, connected to generous retirement packages for state employees and a constitutionally mandated income tax that does not allow for progressive taxation. All citizens pay the same percentage of their adjusted income. In addition, the state had not had a budget for two years because of a continuing conflict between the fiscally conservative Republican governor and the Democratic legislature, adding to its financial woes.

To illuminate the problem, Fair Economy Illinois, with the support of member organizations in the People's Action coalition, including the People's Lobby and Chicago Seniors Together, decided to hold a two-week march from Chicago to Springfield, a distance of over two hundred miles. The march was planned to start with a rally in downtown Chicago on May 15, and listening sessions were held in small towns along the way. The plan was to reach Springfield on May 30, where there would be a concluding rally and an attempt to "take over" the Capitol building through nonviolent protest and civil disobedience. While some younger protesters marched the entire distance, seniors were encouraged to walk as far as they wanted or, in the case of ninety-year-old Dr. Ben, to ride a motorized scooter. Ben reported that his goal was "to tell that our government is making people suffer." The marchers and those traveling by bus or car were to assemble at the State Capitol, where they would meet supportive legislators and then demonstrate in the halls of the Capitol, as had happened in Madison, Wisconsin, challenging the policies of Governor Scott Walker. Since Springfield is a smaller and less political town than Madison, far from the state university, the demonstration would be smaller. Still, some seven hundred people were estimated to have descended on the town to demand what was described as a "People and

Planet First Budget." The protesters were met by police who were assigned to protect the Capitol, excluding demonstrators from the legislative galleries and preventing them from blocking the hallways. The actions of the police led to some accounts of mistreatment.

As Jane declared, "We need progressive revenue and a budget that is fully funded. We need to show our power. On May 30, we're going to take over the Capitol. . . . It's not Governor Rauner's Capitol, it's our Capitol" (field notes). Several times during my thirty months of observation, the CST made the trek to Springfield. (They have not done so since the election of Democratic governor J. B. Pritzker.) This trip was not a favorite activity, since it required a long early-morning bus ride. Jane sympathized, "I know nobody wants to go to Springfield. [*She adds sarcastically,*] I know many of you are very excited. I can see the joy on your faces" (field notes). However, this march was to be different. They wanted an action of a thousand people, with perhaps one hundred from the CST. This turned out to be an optimistic goal (the numbers were somewhat over half of those forecast), but organizers thought the numbers could motivate members to see this as a shared and consequential event. As Dan explained, "This march is about our survival. Are people in this room willing to fight back? We are in a crisis, and we need to do something about it." The marchers applauded loudly.

Similar to the Senior Power Assembly described in chapter 3, this protest required intense planning for over a month. Those members of the CST who chose not to march (only Dr. Ben traveled the entire distance, riding his scooter) were bused to the Capitol in the early morning, leaving Chicago at 6:00 a.m. Many stayed overnight in a makeshift dormitory in a local office building with only sleeping bags or blankets for cover. Were members to be jailed, a quick return would be impossible. As I noted, some members claimed they were roughed up, shoved, or pushed down by the police. Eventually twenty-seven protesters were arrested for blocking access to the governor's office, including four members of Chicago Seniors Together, but no one spent time in jail.

In the end the activists could not point to any policy change, but the march and demonstration received considerable media attention, underlining the state's financial troubles. Perhaps the march had some effect on the 2018 election, in which Democrat J. B. Pritzker was elected governor and the Democrats gained seats in the legislature. However, what was most significant was that those involved believed the event had been successful and returned with stories. Dan summarized his satisfaction as a staffer: "So many people in this room took great risks. We were the images of the budget crisis" (field notes).

In contrast to the stories about the demonstration on the deserted streets

of Racine, much of the discussion about Springfield dealt with how the protesters were treated. Although the responses of the Capitol police were fairly
mild, given occasional police brutality law enforcement was treated as an
adversarial force. One eighty-year-old demonstrator, Hazel Windblatt, contrasted the response with the way they were treated in Chicago: "When we
got to Springfield, [the police] made it difficult for us" (field notes). These
were brave accounts of resistance. I heard many over the months after the
action. Perhaps the most expansive was from a conversation with Petra Daggert, a lively septuagenarian living quietly in senior housing on the North
Side of Chicago:

> Springfield was amazing. I ended up staying overnight. I was on the radio.
> I was on WGN. Long story short, we did the walk to Springfield, the march
> to Springfield. I took the bus, and I was going to be a marshal. That was dif-
> ficult, but I did it. We got off the buses, we got our stuff, we put on our [CST
> T-shirts]. . . . We got to the Capitol and we got everybody in and, long story
> short, we went to the governor's office, and we were there for all day; well,
> hours. [The governor] left early. I mean, there was more than one entrance
> to get out of the office. . . . Some of the people went up, went to the House [of
> Representatives], and they were kicked out. A couple of people were hurt, not
> badly, but they were hurt. And we demonstrated. There were people who were
> going to do civil disobedience. They were in front of the governor's office. We
> were there, we were chanting, and most of the people went home on a 2:30 to
> 3:30 bus. I decided to stay because I said I would [stay] overnight. I think Dan
> asked me if I wanted to go home because there was a later bus, and I said no.
> I stayed. (Interview)

However, this was not all of her account. Petra became a media star for the
moment and for the movement:

> There were reporters. Patti Vasquez has an 11:15 show [on WGN] during the
> week, 11:15 p.m., and she came in. And I listen to WGN and I listen to her, and
> she came and she was interviewing people there. . . . We were all in front of
> the governor's office, and she was by the railing. . . . She's talking to someone,
> and I'm sitting down because it's hard to stand. There were no chairs up there;
> there were downstairs. She's talking to somebody, and I'm exhausted. I'm sit-
> ting there and I said, "Oh, I know Patti Vasquez." And she comes over and she
> sits down and she starts to interview me. She starts to talk to me. She says,
> "You doing anything Friday night? Come on my show." . . . We were supposed
> to be there for an hour; we were there for almost two, until 1:00 in the morn-
> ing. They drove me home. (Interview)

It's easy to see how her travails would remain with her, suggesting that her
pains were worthwhile. Perhaps she felt young again:

I stayed [in Springfield], and the Capitol security made an announcement—we were there until 10:00 p.m.—made an announcement (they wouldn't let us bring food in, so these people hadn't eaten all day). We somehow got some sandwiches in. Anyway, they made an announcement that everybody was going be arrested unless we left. So this was 10:00. They did all this on purpose. We all left except the people that were sitting in front of his office. I think there were a total of sixty of us. It was raining, but we waited for the other people. We had our blankets and sleeping bags in a couple of vans. Then, little by little, they gave them citations because the jail in Springfield isn't very big, apparently. They gave them citations, and they sent them out. They sent people out like a few people at a time. Definitely on purpose. We didn't leave there until midnight. And luckily, we did have a contingency plan. Dan had a friend who had this office building not far [away], and some people walked and some people drove there, and we spent the night in this unfinished office space. There was a big room, and they had restrooms, so it wasn't outside. We were able to get pizza delivered. . . . Midnight in Springfield. Let the people who hadn't eaten yet, eat, but we had plenty. Then apparently Starbucks in the morning donated boxes of coffee, and we had bagels and we had breakfast. Then maybe about 9:00 or 9:30 buses came and took us back to Chicago. It was a great feeling. . . . Everybody was on the floor but in the halls. We were warm. We certainly weren't expecting a hotel. . . . It was a great feeling. And that interview [*laughs*], I was just dumbfounded. She asked me questions and I knew the answers. (Interview)

Petra was awed by her experience, feeling that she had finally become a real activist, flattered by the requests to retell her story to groups of friends and colleagues—and to the residents of Chicago. She and other demonstrators became heroes, fighting for justice against those who were counted as villains, such as the Republican governor. The emotional tenor of Petra's report was repeated in an account from Ralph Phelps when I asked him about his most memorable action:

We went to Springfield, and we had a sit-down outside the quarters of the legislature to protest Rauner's inability or resistance to [passing] legislation and establishing a budget. . . . They did a budget recently over his veto. They overrode his veto, but he just wouldn't give at all. I felt very proud and strong about that one. . . . We took a bus ride to Springfield where we had a sit-down. It was actually a lay-down. They let us stay there for about five minutes, and the police said we had to leave. [GF: So that was an act of civil disobedience?] Yeah, actually it was. They actually had designated people that they wanted to be arrested because we wanted to get recognition and publicity about the event. (Interview)

What Ralph referred to as a "lay-down" was also termed a die-in, designed to claim that the governor's budget cuts would kill seniors. Dr. Ben noted, "We wanted to show the governor that we were dying." Even more dramatic was the account from another committed activist, Carrie Stanton, one of those scheduled to be arrested:

> When we were in the State Capitol . . . those guards on the second floor in the House [of Representatives], they were rough. They were throwing those young men down on the marble floor. They could have broken their backs. . . . I'm sure they were bruised. The one guard took me, we were in front of the rail, and he grabbed my walker and just threw, pushed me. If there hadn't been a rail there, I'd have gone down onto the first floor. I mean, he got taken out [removed], but I'm just saying. . . . He grabbed someone else. . . . I would've been dead, you know. . . . they still were pushing me around rough. I'm always scared because you never know. Now, most guards or police in Chicago, they come up and say, "Do you want to be arrested?" and I look at them like, "You dumb fool. What do you think I'm doing sitting here?" And they're polite. But that's because they're used to it. (Interview)

What the governor learned from this demonstration is uncertain, but being there inspired the protesters. As Angela Knight, an African American in her seventies, said, "Going to Springfield was really good for me, because it let us know what we could do. I think that was the biggest thing for me. I had never been to Springfield before. . . . I think it made them think, if nothing else" (interview). Perhaps nothing else, but that belief was something in itself.

Admittedly, the same intensity of narrative does not apply to all events or to all social movements. The degree varies with the articulateness of the participants, the drama of the performance, the time members spend together, the strategic arenas they operate in, their shared or diverse backgrounds, and the responses of authorities. Of course the culture of the movement shapes the content, but in all cases there is a moral narrative that makes the story relevant to local politics,[71] providing a problem and the possibility of redress.[72] Chicago Seniors Together, with its rights orientation, with an explicit goal of utilizing emotion as a strategic method of commitment, and with many in its members having long activist careers, reflects the power of experience as a resource to motivate action.

Experience as Resource

Public history and personal experience constitute a means of forming the identity of movements and potentially affects their success. Experience is local and so, ultimately, is movement culture. That reality is the focus of this chapter, linking memory and narrative to group culture and forms of interaction. By weaving an eventful past into the present, both through histories that activists are aware of and those moments they have participated in,

movement groups develop a vision of eventful progress. The more experience, the more they have to draw on. This applies to much collective action,
as is evident in listening to the discourse of friends.

For older activists the linkage of past, present, and future is vital. Seniors'
experience and personal knowledge is more extensive than their juniors,'
even as their imagined future horizon edges closer. Because of the distinctive features of senior activism, the link of narratives and histories may be
stronger when considering social movements that depend on the arc of age.

Movement culture and the rules of interaction are powerful forces that
bolster internal cohesion and promote a commitment to action, transforming biography into history.[73] Incorporating the past into the present discourse
underlines the salience of personal relations, establishing a temporal arrow in
which past events and their consequences strike a target. The experience of
one can, in the right circumstances, extend the imagination of many. Local
narratives provide unarguable proof of the moral rightness of movements'
claims, presenting injustices so as to brook no dissent.

In addressing the temporality of movements we must treat memory—as
felt and as expressed—as a social accomplishment integral to political activity.
Memory can be individually or institutionally "owned," but it is crafted in local
spaces. The ability to narrate in a compelling way aids emotion work and mobilization. Treating narratives as invitations to identify allows for embracing contentious action. Shared experience and common awareness bolster dramatic accounts that promote collective identity and in their turn facilitate group activity.

To think of an effective movement that is unmoored from history, that
lacks a local culture, whose members do not share their experiences, and
in which this sharing does not channel later action is virtually impossible.
Such a view stands apart from an approach that recognizes the power of local
cultures. Movement groups are fraternal and sororal clubs. There are many
genres of talk in activist communities, which is part of the satisfaction they
provide. This includes both formal stories and more casual genres of conversation. But talk is not enough; it must bolster action.

Connecting pasts and futures applies to all domains of joint activity, even
if it has particular power in the politicized tiny publics of seniors. We act on
beliefs that are part of our histories and are linked to the conditions of the
present with a rough and hazy pathway that leads to the future. The memories
we regard as relevant and the narratives we treat as worth sharing connect
eventful experience to the present through our social relations. Constructing
a future depends on recognizing an eventful past and being willing to invite
others to embrace a common memory. Social movements, when successful,
achieve this with confidence and flair.

Staff Power and Senior Authority

A critical element in nearly all effective social movements is leadership. For it is through smart, persistent, and authoritative leaders that a movement generates the appropriate concepts and language that captures the frustration, anger, or fear of the group's members and places responsibility where it is warranted.

DAVID WILKINS

Social movement organizations are organizations: magical and mundane, nimble and normal. They must solve routine problems while inspiring members to do brave and consequential things. Their group culture must inspire a culture of action. When effective, movement organizations create events that reverberate. To this end, movements must demonstrate flexibility and reflexivity.[1]

Given the limitations of seniors as political actors, establishing organizations that are stable and lasting is a challenge. Of course one finds bureaucratic, staff-driven organizations like AARP that have had long and influential histories. Occasionally activist groups such as the Gray Panthers, the Raging Grannies, the Older Women's League, or Metro Seniors in Action emerge, but they are surprisingly few.

In this chapter I detail the operation of Chicago Seniors Together, dependent on the interests, abilities, and aspirations of seniors, incorporating staff and member-leaders in a structure that promotes an injustice frame. The organization, though modest in size, addresses multiple issues of significance to seniors and beyond. As I noted, this multi-issue focus adheres in large part to the Saul Alinsky model of community organizing.[2]

I emphasize the relationship between the younger staff and the older members. This recognizes that intergenerational communities exist and can be influential. This is not an organization in which the older and younger participants have the same roles, but the interconnections are central. However, the difference in their perspective, expertise, and capacity occasionally leads to delicate relations between younger staff and senior leaders concerning the authority to make decisions. Of course not every social movement group is able—or chooses—to hire staff. There must be a resource base and a commitment to organizational longevity that will survive the turnover of members and allow for a transition of staff.

In well-functioning organizations, staff and members operate in concert, but on occasion leaders may feel that staff members overstep their bounds, and staff may feel that leaders lack the background or expertise to make decisions. The task is to fit these role sets together in ways that build on the skills and commitments of each. In a sense, each group must contribute its fair share to make their tiny public effective. This can be particularly difficult when the differences are not only in expertise and responsibility but in age and generation as well. These distinct roles contribute to competing visions of what leadership should entail in a multigenerational organization. The divisions constitute a topic little explored in social movement research.[3]

Members of Chicago Seniors Together claimed repeatedly that the organization is senior led—owned by seniors, as it were—but this can be hard to achieve in practice, given the expertise of younger staff. How is authority to be distributed? One view is that of Richie Douglas, the African American co-chair of the CST who (frequently) remarked, "This is a senior-led organization. It emphasizes that you [the members] control the organization. Chicago Seniors is an organizing organization that relates to senior issues" (field notes).

What does senior led mean in practice? What is the relation between an organization that is run by seniors and one that focuses on senior issues in a world where injustices bleed into each other? Does this hold true when the organization hopes to be expansive in its politics, supporting progressive allies, and when staff play a prominent role? If seniors are in charge, can the staff rule? The influence of the staff was to be expected, given their skill and the reality that they, unlike the leaders, were employed full time. To what extent did seniors run the organization, how was control negotiated, and was it essential that every issue addressed be a senior issue?

Structuring Seniors

During my research, the number of dues-paying members of Chicago Seniors Together more than doubled, from approximately 280 in 2015 to 650 in 2017. As I noted, this sizable jump can largely be attributed to the progressive energy generated in reaction to the election of Donald Trump. Although membership has decreased and energy has flagged, especially in the midst of the COVID-19 pandemic, the CST remains a midsize social movement group with the ability to organize events that have political impact, though rarely as much as desired. During the pandemic, after my research had concluded, the office closed, and organizing was done through video events, Zoom invitations, and phone calls.

Most active leaders were women, and most were Whites from the North Side of Chicago or from Hyde Park, the South Side location of the University of Chicago. As I describe in chapter 6, despite their desire for an inclusive multiracial community, the CST had trouble recruiting African Americans from the West and South Sides of the city, and during my research few Latinx or Asian Americans participated.

In this period the annual budget of Chicago Seniors Together hovered around $500,000, made possible through dues, contributions from supporters, and a variety of grants from progressive foundations. Thus the organization, while not large, was stable. Once the CST established its political action sister organization United Chicago Seniors in Action, it could raise money from political units such as supportive labor unions, although these contributions were not tax deductible. I was surprised at the range of foundations in Chicago and nationally that contributed money to community organizing. The fierce politics of the CST did not frighten those in charge of dispensing grants from these charitable groups. A progressive infrastructure exists, sufficient to support medium-sized activist organizations. One of the primary tasks of the executive director was to submit grant applications to these foundations, and the CST had considerable success under Jane Tate's leadership. Grants came from religious agencies as well as from groups with particular policy goals such as promoting health care or retirement support. During my research the CST received funding from the Catholic Campaign for Human Development, Evangelical Lutheran Church of America, Service Employees International Union (SEIU) Health Care, Chicago Foundation for Women, Chicago Community Trust, Center for Community Change, LUSH Cosmetics, Polk Brothers Foundation, and Field Foundation, among others. Most of these grants were modest, typically about $20,000, but they totaled $250,000 a year. The organization also held an annual spring fund-raiser as well as fund-raising drives, including one on Giving Tuesday, the week after Thanksgiving. Staff and board members were assigned fund-raising goals; each recognized that they were obligated to raise money, what Jane termed taking "ownership of the organization." In a movement with many members on tight budgets, internal fund-raising was hard.

A "culture of fund-raising" never materialized, even when Jane exhorted leaders, "Which is harder, asking for money or not having Social Security?" Board members were selected based on their commitment, not their finances, and the organization was proud that it did not "chase money" by shifting its positions to appeal to potential donors. Even though many disliked fund-raising, with some preferring to donate money themselves rather than asking friends and neighbors, birthday parties proved a successful strategy. Davey Gibbs raised $1,500 from his party, and Dr. Ben Golden raised $3,000 from his bash. The goal was phrased by Jerry Hackworth, an English professor and the witty CST co-chair: "We need boots and bucks. Boots on the ground and bucks in the till" (field notes). While both needs were challenging, members at least had boots.

Staff salaries ranged from approximately $65,000 for the executive director to about $45,000 for others, near the median for similar organizations, and staff received valued benefits. In the early period of my research, the CST relied on a sizable bequest of $290,000 from two supporters. Surprisingly, these benefactors were barely known, and their names were never mentioned. They had once been members of the CST but not leaders. The money was referred to as the "bequest" or the "windfall." While the money was useful during the three years it was available, when it was spent the organization had to reconfigure its budget, limit projects, and delay hiring staff. As in many fiscally cautious organizations, there was a desire to keep more money in reserve than might be essential—an irony, since the CST pressured the Chicago Housing Authority to spend its reserves.

The Finance Committee was central to the organizational structure. Only responsible members were asked to serve, since the group culture emphasized preserving economic stability. Jane, as executive director, defined the committee as the "most intense" in any of the organizations she had been involved with. "We have to protect the organization," she told members: "If there are budget items that you see as out of line, you can ask questions" (field notes). They did so at length. While many members would have liked to see money taken out of politics, it had to be brought into the movement. Leaders recognized the inconsistency.

Raising and spending money is central to any social movement group, but it was particularly salient at the CST. This need resulted from what Dan Ryan speaks of as the "ghosts of organizations past," recognizing both the collective memory within organizations and the collective memory of the actions of allied organizations.[4] Several decades earlier, as I noted in the introduction, another senior progressive organization was active in Chicago: Metro Seniors in Action (MSA). Several of the longtime members of CST had once been members of MSA. That organization collapsed owing to a series of financial and leadership crises, including, I was told, embezzlement by a staff member and the failings of an executive director who was honest but "in over her head." This led to the organization's demise[5] and the movement of activists to the CST, along with the belief that financial probity is essential for "good" so-

cial movements. The scandal, fixed in shared memory, underlined the importance of trustworthy staff, but also the need for accountability. The collapse
of Metro Seniors in Action meant that as part of its organizational culture
the CST, never profligate with funds, became exquisitely sensitive to financial responsibility and auditing, holding lengthy, detailed budget meetings.
The Finance Committee met each month, setting the organization's budget
and reviewing it in detail. Each month the committee dutifully examined the
organization's expenses, asking about line items that seemed higher or lower
than expected, including office supplies and travel expenses. How much the
CST should provide for staff health care and holiday bonuses was discussed,
not from hostility to the staff, but to protect the budget. Their culture treated
this issue as fundamental and the most obvious area in which members had
authority, in contrast to planning political actions. Once a year the Finance
Committee met with the auditor, and the committee held several meetings
whose main agenda was budget and audit training. At times the close scrutiny seemed excessive for a midsize organization, but it ensured that finances
were scrupulously considered in light of the members' collective anxieties.

As I noted, during my research the CST had five to seven staff members.
With the exception of one White male staffer who was employed for part of
the research time and the executive director, who was sixty years old, the staff
members were younger women. Many staff were Jews or Latinas[6] who had
previous full-time or part-time experience in community organizing, activist groups, or social service agencies, such as those for the homeless or the
disabled. Hiring was done through a multistage process of interviews with organization leaders and with the executive director. The member-leaders had
ultimate authority, but in practice staff evaluations weighed heavily. Although
the pool of applicants was not wide, multiple candidates were interviewed
for each position. During my research, several interns worked there, paid by
other agencies or funded by university programs.

The headquarters of Chicago Seniors Together was a suite of offices in a
small office building on the gentrifying Near North Side of Chicago, close
to the wealthy Gold Coast and near bus and subway lines. The five-story
building was owned by a nearby church, a liberal Protestant faith community with which the CST negotiated for space. The building held the offices
of several community groups as well as a neighborhood day care center. The
CST rented four office spaces, one a conference room where small meetings
were held; the room was bright, with yellow laminated walls on which agenda
items were written with erasable markers. On one wall was the hopeful plea,
"Chicago Seniors Together envisions a world where all seniors can age with
dignity and safety, free of ageism, racism, and other forms of oppression." The

organization also had access to a break/lunch room and a larger shared meeting space that could seat over one hundred. There was a private office for the executive director and a comfortable, if somewhat disorganized, office for the other staff, with six desks and a bookshelf holding volumes on community organizing. The walls were festooned with posters, including those for Black Lives Matter, Fair Budget Now, Fight for Fifteen (minimum wage), and other progressive causes. This space was neither elegant nor expansive, but it was sufficient for the staff and their meetings.

A Culture of Meetings

As an ethnographer of organizations, I was struck by the existence of a *culture of meetings*. Structured gatherings promote interpersonal cohesion and permit consensus and adjustments. Put simply, meetings provide a structure for organizational interaction. This constituted the "pull" factor I described above, creating the CST as a desirable community to spend time in. Strong organizations promote inclusion, comfort, and ease, and this was a goal of the CST, supported by sharing reports of successes at meetings and by socializing (and sharing food) before them.

Gatherings are essential ways organizations formulate rules for interaction and promote a shared culture. Meetings were said to democratize the organization, allowing those in attendance to help set policy. But they also served as social control by encouraging attendees to share the vision that those in charge embraced and pressing them to agree to participate in movement work. Meetings generated collective meaning and commitment to organizational labor.[7] As Jane exhorted committee leaders about recruiting for their next phone bank, "Can we make sure that we have people sign up before we move on to the next issue?"

Meetings could be informal, dyadic engagements (one-on-ones, as I described above) or more formal events. Each week several meetings were scheduled to discuss programs or to plan upcoming actions. The most active members visited the office several times each week. As I sat in the main office watching the staff work, I realized that most of their tasks involved setting up meetings with leaders, grants administrators, residents' groups at senior buildings, donors, politicians, and allies of the organization. The staff were continually on the phone or visiting those with links to the CST. Over the course of a month, some staff members scheduled up to a hundred meetings by phone or in person. This became clear at a staff meeting when Luisa said she had met a senior who said, "I've been waiting for a political group. Do you have meetings?" Her colleague laughingly exclaimed, "Do we have meet-ings!" (field notes). Connecting in shared space contributed to the sociality that was vital to the local culture. The problem, as I noted in chapter 2, is that seniors did not always attend meetings when they weren't feeling well or lacked transportation.

As part of the culture of meetings, the organization held weekly staff meetings, a monthly meeting of the Board of Directors (ten members elected for two-year terms), a monthly Finance Committee, Leadership Committee that met several times a year to nominate members for major positions, a monthly Housing Committee, a monthly Health Care and Economic Justice Committee (these committees occasionally met jointly), a quarterly Move-ment Politics Committee meeting, a monthly Racial Justice Leadership Team (disbanded toward the end of my research), and meetings of various ad hoc committees established when actions were being planned. I attended meet-ings and actions most weeks, sometimes several times a week. These occa-sions allowed the organization to be tightly networked.

I came to recognize the importance of these meetings, often tied to an informal social gathering and luncheon. While the meetings were tightly scripted, allowing little discussion, the "potlucks" (some homemade dishes and other food from grocery deli counters) promoted informal socializing. Their importance meant more than plying seniors with food:[8] by establishing lines of sociability, it was harder to be a free rider who avoided responsibili-ties. The social hour encouraged members to attend what might otherwise be dry reports detailing ongoing projects.

These meetings also defined rules for legitimate interaction. Attendees were often required to endorse a set of "group agreements." These prac-tices, sometimes presented by staff and sometimes by leaders, were never debated and were always unanimously adopted by a voice vote. Although some changed over the course of my research, when I started there were ten rules: (1) Be prepared for the meeting; (2) Be on time; (3) Be nonpartisan (i.e., no comments about political candidates that might threaten the group's tax-exempt funding); (4) One person speaks at a time; (5) Step up, step back (don't dominate the floor); (6) Stick to the topic; (7) Disagree, but don't be disagreeable; (8) Use "I" statements for you; (9) Use "we" statements for the organization; and (10) No cell phones. These rules evolved, and "Celebrate confusion," "Ask questions," "One diva, one mic," and "Land the plane" (Don't talk too long) were added over the months, although I never learned who inserted them and why the changes were made. On occasion, "No cologne" was added. Leaders relied on the elementary school technique of "clap once," "clap twice," "clap three times" to capture the attention of those present. These mechanisms prevented seniors from interrupting others or challenging the agenda.

Connected to the role of meetings was a culture of planning and evaluation: pre- and postmeeting discussions. The staff set the topics and decided who should discuss each, then they selected which seniors would lead the meeting. These chairs were then "prepped." The leaders and presenters often met in advance, under the guidance of staff, to specify the agenda and timing, reflecting skepticism of spontaneity. On occasion the planning meeting lasted as long as the meeting planned. While this at first seemed to involve much work for little benefit, it was critical to building the relational structure of the organization and allowed staff to exert influence behind the scenes.

Postmeeting (and postevent) evaluations were equally essential. After each meeting, another short meeting evaluated how the main meeting had gone and considered improvements. On several occasions participants remarked half-jokingly that "anything that's worth doing is worth evaluating." But the commitment to evaluation went deeper. As Jane explained, "Let's take a deep breath. We do evaluation so we can learn what we did well and what we could do better." At some of these evaluations the criticism could be sharp, leading Jane to note to an all-White group of leaders, "This is the part we love to do. White people like to criticize. It's good to be critical. We learn from it." But then, perhaps thinking better of where this might lead, she added, "If you hear something and disagree, just keep quiet." In other words, don't argue over criticisms; let everyone say their piece to show respect and to organize better meetings. Criticism that was too harsh could weaken the relational privileging of the organization. These were not Soviet-style self-criticism sessions; they were designed to have the leaders admit what failed as well as to praise what went well. The assessments were largely positive, but there was a sense that one should always concede that something could have been improved. For instance, in one evaluation session, Carrie Stanton, having chaired the meeting, evaluated herself: "I was punctual as a facilitator. That was a good thing that I kept it on time. I felt some movement. We needed some tension." Others congratulated her, but it was important that she found an area of improvement (field notes). Meeting chairs rotated continually. Part of the rationale was that everyone needed to develop the skills to become a leader, but this also prevented any senior from gaining too much authority. Even the Board of Directors operated with co-chairs.

One issue that emerged during my research involved the coordination of meetings. How did meetings connect to the basic structure of the organization? Should the CST function as a single group or as several? In addition to their Movement Politics Group (and the disbanded Racial Justice Leadership Team), the CST depended on two "action" committees: the Housing Committee and one focused on Health Care and Economic Justice. While some overlap existed, there were differences in the makeup of the committees. In general, the Housing Committee was composed of seniors living in subsidized housing and was more racially diverse, including many members with strained finances. The Health Care and Economic Justice Committee, while including a fair number of participants living in affordable housing, had somewhat more affluent members who primarily cared about broader policy issues such as Medicare for All, preserving Social Security, and minimizing inequality. The division between the two groups was made evident when one of the leaders of the Health Care Committee noted, "I don't know the people in Housing. I know the people involved in Economic Justice a lot better" (interview).

Despite some overlap, the groups appealed to different constituencies. At first the two committees held their ninety-minute monthly meetings on different Mondays. Eventually leaders and staff decided these dual meetings were taking too much time and didn't allow members to be aware of the full range of CST activities. (The organization also held quarterly all-member gatherings.) Staff proposed and members accepted that the two meetings be combined: joint meetings. The group would meet together for half an hour, then for the next hour (later seventy-five minutes) the two committees would meet separately, with each attracting about twenty to thirty members.

At the end the two groups would reassemble to share their plans. While this emphasized that the CST was a single organization, it ran into opposition both from those who wanted to attend both meetings, now impossible, and from those who feared discussion would be truncated. Still, the proposal to hold joint meetings was pushed through with the claim that it would be evaluated later. After receiving pushback, the staffer who was most enthusiastic said, "We're running out of time. . . . I think that just saying 'this is a bad idea' doesn't move us anywhere. We want to respect your time. I welcome your comments. I welcome your *constructive* comments." Despite the criticism and without a vote, they moved ahead.

The first joint meetings were, in Davey's words, "somewhat rocky." He clarified: "Today we're trying a new structure. We'll try it out. If it works, we'll continue it, and if not, we'll stop it. We're a democratic organization, and we [seniors] are in control" (field notes). Jane attempted to tamp down the criticism, noting, "Change is always hard, and we went through a process and discussed it all summer. We don't want to be in our silos. . . . By doing these joint meetings we're building solidarity" (field notes). I wondered whether solidarity was being built or corroded. The challenge was to have enough time for each committee to have engaging discussions. Since not all seniors cared much about the topics of the other committee, the sharing of information was limited and routine, and since meetings were shorter, they became used for describing rather than discussing. As one leader noted, "A lot of these seniors, once a month coming to a meeting where you discuss things about health care or housing was just exactly what they wanted. . . . Now coming once a month to these meetings, they're almost virtually useless because they're so short" (interview). Eventually the shared reports were eliminated except for announcements.

Although adjustments were made to this new schedule, after several months it became clear that joint meetings were not working well. In time, after discussion, it was decided that joint meetings would be held only once each quarter, an outcome that satisfied most members and staff. That this—and not policy—was one of most contentious issues suggests the centrality of a meeting culture.

To understand the power of a meeting culture, I treat these events as constituting a performance of belonging. It is not just that meetings are organized, but that they are a stage. Like much theater, they have a distinct ritual aspect. This is evident in the "relational exercises" I described in chapter 1 that attempted to achieve a commitment to comradeship that is deeper than the instrumental and transactional. Some meetings began with a video or a song. (These songs were from the civil rights or old leftist movements. Pete Seeger tunes and gospel hymns were particularly popular.)[9] During meetings, various agenda items were presented, although rarely with vigorous or contentious debate. Finally, as the meeting drew to a close, members were each asked to provide a "feeling word" to describe their response. These were typically positive ("energized," "optimistic," "satisfied"), but they could on occasion be negative ("confused," "tired," "frustrated"). The latter demanded evaluation after adjournment. This process attempted to build strong relational bonds, based on the belief that meetings are where the organization lives. Rather than focusing on political structures or personal complaints, a culture of meetings emphasized the importance of developing local meanings and relations through the act of presence.

Clockwork Rigor

As a longtime professor, perhaps what surprised me most was how Chicago Seniors Together viewed time as a valued commodity, one that influenced the structuring of meetings. For many academics time is negotiated, flexible, and approximate. Although we start meetings more or less on time (often with a five-minute grace period), we rarely slice our meetings into thin segments. It is common for meetings to be longer or shorter than expected.

This temporal fluidity was not evident at the CST, where maintaining the precision of a schedule was considered a mark of respect. Indeed, timing was included as part of the group agreements. As I noted, members were told to "land the plane," meaning "be succinct." To be succinct is to be considerate. Of course what we might term "clockwork" is not unique to the CST; it is known in other social movement organizations,[10] although it seems particularly pronounced among seniors, whose attention and energy often flag. As Davey Gibbs explained to me, "That's a rule of thumb of community organizing. Start on time and end on time" (field notes). Jane Tate claimed that this sensitivity to timing is at the root of the organizational philosophy, "What Saul Alinsky says is that your time is as valuable as these other people in power's time is. . . . Your goal is, I want to start the meeting and I want to end the meeting on time because your time is valuable and my time is valuable." Time becomes a marker of esteem, and in a sense it is monetized as a form of temporal capital. Perhaps this is tied to a fundamentally capitalist view of social organization in which time is money, but it can also be said to constitute temporal justice, in which respect for the rights of others is considered primary. We wished to avoid temporal oppression.

These expectations entailed close attention to time, startling to someone unfamiliar with this form of clockwork. Those seniors who were appointed to chair meetings understood that they would be judged on whether they maintained temporal control and kept the meeting running on time. Once I attended a meeting of the Long-Term Planning Committee. Shortly before the scheduled time the chair declared, "We're going to start in five or six minutes," later updating it to, "We're going to start in thirty seconds" (field notes). While announcing seconds was striking on this occasion, it wasn't unique. Before another meeting there was a ninety-second warning. On a different occasion a speaker was told he had only thirty seconds to make his point because they had to adjourn in one minute. Another time the chair remarked, only half-joking, "We're ten seconds behind schedule." After making his comment he added, tongue in cheek, "We're now twenty seconds behind schedule" (field notes). It was common to note that the meeting was five or ten minutes behind schedule. Once the chair noted that they were "nine minutes over"—true, but rather more precise than I expected. At most meetings someone would mention whether they were ahead of schedule, ending early, or edging toward lateness.

At most meetings agendas were distributed noting the amount of time scheduled for each topic. Consider, for example, the schedule for a Health Care and Economic Justice Committee meeting. Four goals were specified: debrief Moral Monday and get commitments for the next action;, follow up on commitments for house meetings schedule; understand the Fair Tax campaign; and discuss the joint committee meeting structure. The meeting schedule was remarkably detailed:

> 1:00 p.m. Introduction, relational question, and CST action step completed (10 minutes)
> 1:10 p.m. Introduction of a new staff member (5 minutes)
> 1:15 p.m. State Budget and Fair Economy Illinois/Moral Monday (20 minutes total)
> 1:15 p.m. What happened to the Fair Tax? (5 minutes)
> 1:20 p.m. Other state revenue and budget information (5 minutes)
> 1:25 p.m. Debrief of May 9 Moral Monday (5 minutes)
> 1:30 p.m. Fair Economy Illinois Action June 8 (5 minutes)
> 1:35 Health Care and Economic Justice Three-Month Plan (30 minutes total)
> 1:35 House meetings schedule (10 minutes)
> 1:45 CST-led July 18 Moral Monday (15 minutes)
> 2:00 Social Security Action in August (5 minutes)
> 2:05 Description of Joint Committee Meeting Structure (20 minutes)
> 2:25 Announcements
> 2:30 Adjourn

Every topic had an assigned presenter. Some discussions were truncated when the time for the next item had been reached. Each meeting was accompanied by a similar distributed schedule. It was rare that a meeting would end even five minutes after its scheduled close, and when it did, a vote was usually taken to extend the time. To some extent there was a structural reason for this approach. Some seniors used scheduled transportation. However, more significant was the belief that keeping to a schedule demonstrated respect for seniors' capabilities.[11]

Violations could provoke humor or sincere apology. Dr. Ben, who had a well-earned reputation for being verbose, was told he had one minute to tell why he was a member of the CST, a demand that brought laughter. At another meeting a staff member asked for "a minute" to make an announcement. Carrie, chairing the meeting, joked, "One minute, and I'm timing you." Apologies were common as well, particularly when the meeting chair misread the time or didn't check the clock. Richie Douglas was chairing a meeting and didn't realize his wristwatch didn't match the "official" wall clock. Thinking there were five minutes remaining he remarked, "My watch is a little different than the clock on the wall. Let's split the difference and say we have two more minutes." On another occasion Jane looked at the clock and realized it was slow: although the clock said 2:20, it was really 2:25 in a meeting that was to adjourn by 2:30. She apologized, and the rest of the meeting was rushed, despite dealing with an important topic (field notes). These jokes and apologies reflected *temporal respect* despite imperfect clocks, watches, and senior vision.

Clockwork was evident in complaints from members, since keeping to a schedule often meant that taking time for vigorous discussion was impossible. For new members the rules could be off-putting, as in the comment by a longtime member who noted about the "unorganized" 1960s radicals, "There have been occasional visitors to our meetings who want to just speak out whenever and want to push back, but they always leave" (interview). Another senior leader pointed out,

> I think that keeping on a schedule is good. What I don't like, though—and this was one of my beefs with a big organizer from years ago—she was like, you have ten minutes to discuss this and then you go on to the next thing. Sometimes you really have to flesh out and discuss that particular thing, and it takes more than ten minutes. That was when I first became a member of the Housing Committee; I used to complain about it all the time. . . . We could never really flesh out and really discuss each agenda item. (Interview)

These concerns reflected the feeling that "we're so rushed, so cramped," leaving some members frustrated and angry. The dilemma is that meetings must be brief for tired seniors, but they must be long enough for energized discussion. Negotiation is necessary,

> Jane asks our group, working on a vision statement for the organization, "Can you finish in three minutes?" Esther, leading the group, says no. Jane asks, "How much time do you need?" and Esther says five minutes. Jane says, "OK, we've negotiated. I'll take [the time] from something I'll do." The two minutes needed to come from somewhere. (Field notes)

Through the emphasis on time, the temporal structure provides for social control favoring those with authority. The constraints of timing can be raised as needed, shutting down contentious debate. Disagreement was not prized, and having a schedule meant someone had the right to determine what should not be challenged. Jane did this at one point when she referred to the schedule during a discussion she hoped to end: "I want to give a time check. I think we're getting in the weeds a little bit" (field notes). The rhetoric of clockwork can marginalize undesirable topics. This was dramatized at a meeting of the Housing Committee. Carrie Stanton was discussing a proposal that Stephanie Moore, running the meeting, was plainly not interested in. Stephanie remarked, "Carrie, we have to move on," adding, "We have no time for questions." When asked for a feeling word, Carrie said she as "upset." Another member, also shorted, fumed, "We tried to stuff a six-pound bag into a four-pound container." In justification, Stephanie commented, "People's asking questions slows us down." One might argue that these questions are essential to a relational organization, but they disrupt the way leaders think meetings should proceed. That this is a general problem, rather than a response to any particular person, is evident from something similar that occurred when Carrie was chairing a meeting. She explained, "Right now I have to be the bad person and move on . . . I really need to keep you on point because we are three minutes behind" (field notes).

Control could be subtle, as when Richie said, "If speakers go over their time, we'll touch your shoulder, which means you need to wrap up immediately" (field notes). This happened to Dr. Ben, who was giving an impassioned response. The chair, supporting the shut down, noted, "We could go on all day on this."

A temporal culture, sometimes helpful, can be limiting, an ambiguity underlined by a staffer:

> It doesn't feel authentic sometimes. It just feels like we need to get this thing done. It's something that hasn't been totally comfortable for me. . . . I think when we are timing our meetings in this way, that doesn't leave room for discussion. It doesn't do us any good. So scheduling is important. It's not the only thing that's important to consider. It's something you can point to that will cut people off, like certain people from taking up too much space. (Interview)

While social relationships support community organizing, too much sociability—and too much deference—discomfort these relationships. Perhaps this is the inverse of a Quaker meeting in which agreement produces adjournment; here adjournment produces agreement. The belief in the centrality of temporal respect limits how much debate and discussion is possible and provides a lever whereby those with control over the interaction order shape outcomes, justifying clockwork in the name of seniors' attention spans.

The Minuet of Staff and Seniors

One of the key recognitions in organization sociology is the differences between owners and managers. Who "owns" the organization and who has day-to-day control is an issue that dates back nearly a century to the theory of the firm.[12] Social movements are firms of commitment. Managers have interests and expertise that may not be identical to the goals of the owners they supposedly represent. Not all movement groups can afford staff, but examining members and staff in social movements that can has similarities, although they are surely not identical to business enterprises. Staff, after all, are hired to run the organization for members. If members embody the organization, the staff permits this embodiment to happen. Staff must manage a disparate group, but if their management is too obvious or onerous, they are described as "micromanaging." This concern was sometimes raised in a critical way, while in a more positive light the same approach was described as "doing their homework." Staff are not formally "in charge," but because of their knowledge and skills, in important ways they precisely were in charge, and the organization could not run without them. The precise location of boundaries might be a source of contention.

This is a reality in all social movements, but especially in movements of seniors, many of whom lack the energy to engage full time. As a result, granting implicit authority to staff was essential. The question emerged of how far the staff channeled the will of the members and whether they carried out their own designs, manipulating members into doing what they thought best.

As Richie and others noted, the recurring mantra was that the CST is an organization of seniors, for seniors, and run by seniors, but one might ask how this claim applies. While staff considered the members' perspectives, the organization could not be run with the same efficacy if decision-making were left entirely to seniors. Unending democratic discussions might reduce the efficiency of contentious activity, challenging routine circuits of action and never reaching closure. Many social movement organizations have foundered by giving talk priority over action.[13] This was a trap the CST wanted to avoid. As I noted, at many meetings there was little discussion; and as I described in chapter 1, even though the organization appeared to have a consistent political perspective, members privately disagreed on issues such as labor rights, race relations, and health care policy, with some members less progressive than the more politicized staff. The reality that these issues were filtered through the influence of staff and that complaints were hidden allowed the CST to participate in its progressive alliance. In contrast to most senior leaders, the staff were actively embedded within a network of other staff members in the Chicago activist community, including associations less focused on seniors, such as the SEIU union, Fair Economy Illinois, People's Action, or the community group ONE Northside. This gave the staff extensive knowledge that translated into organizational authority.[14] Although members were ostensibly in charge, the staff were expected to lead.[15] In leading the organization staff needed to smooth tensions and to develop member-leaders, but in simultaneously promoting contentious actions they were expected to nurture public tensions as well as providing leadership from their expertise. These multiple expectations could be difficult to reconcile within a community organizing framework, and at times this strained the group culture.

As was true for the membership, there was considerable turnover among the staff, with the exception of the executive director, Jane Tate, who had led the organization for some fifteen years at the time of my research.[16] Apart from Jane, by the end of my thirty months of research, only one staff member remained. Staff positions were not treated as permanent but were seen as a step in a career. Most staff had some organizing experience, and most stayed one to five years. Some left for other opportunities, some left Chicago, and others were not considered right for the position. Further, the responsibilities of staff evolved over the period of my research. When Sheila, the staff member in charge of the Racial Justice Leadership Team, left, her position was not filled. The plan was that all staff would be involved with racial justice, although that focus eventually dissipated. When the organization established its political sister organization, United Chicago Seniors in Action, a staff member was assigned to develop that group.

Although promoting political engagement that one supported while being paid a middle-class wage might seem like an agreeable career, being an organizer was emotionally draining and could challenge a staffer's self-image. As social work scholar Steve Burghardt points out,[17] being an organizer requires awareness of the strains of personal relations, and these relations can include anger, depression, racism, sexism, or (in the case of Chicago Seniors Together) attitudes toward age and ability. Staffers had to work through interpersonal issues and adjust to an organizational culture and a set of interaction routines that were not necessarily their own preferences. Despite their desires, they might fail because of differences with the group's members or with colleagues, or because of a lack of resources. Frustrations and failures were plentiful, and listening to sad stories of those in poverty, victims of abuse, or targets of prejudice could be traumatic. Consider a discussion with a young staff member, Theresa, committed to political activism:

> Sharon [another staffer] held me accountable for making an appointment to see a therapist because processing shouldn't always happen with other people in your life, you know? Like there are things that I can't talk about with [family or friends]. Like every relationship has a different purpose, but to have a therapist [is to have] someone that is solely there to listen to you and help you process. Because what we deal with here, it's hard. I hear heartbreaking stories all the time. That has an effect on you, especially when you see everything else that's happening. [Heartbreaking stories] from members about their lives, from members about their friends' lives, from other organizers. We've had these really deep discussions about what it's like to lose someone, what it's like

to have people in your family with addiction. All these things that we carry with us. Right? And we all somewhat have caretaking tendencies of wanting to make sure that each other is OK, and sometimes we can't always do that for each other, so it's like we have to hold each other accountable to having a backup mechanism. That is definitely like seeking mental health services. . . . I was really stressed out, and Sharon asked if I was talking about that. She was like, "Oh, have you talked about that with anyone?" I have anxiety, and I told her, "I had my first panic attack since I got back to Chicago." She says, "Do you talk to anyone about that?" I say, "No, but I really should." (Interview)

I do not judge individual staff members, but several had reputations as excellent community organizers and others were not retained after their several month trial period. One criterion for admiration was whether a staffer could convert the enthusiasm of senior members into action. Developing community organizing skills takes time, and not everyone learned quickly.

Some of these young activists found it hard to establish directive but supportive relations with seniors. One senior leader commented about her frustration with some staff, "They hire people that are right out of school so they can get them cheap, I guess, but they don't have any experience or maturity, and they really don't understand what it's like to be a senior citizen." One successful staff member, Dan, age twenty-six, confided that he had been afraid he might have more problems in negotiating the age chasm than he found in practice: "I just expected that there would be more misunderstanding or not understanding who I was or what my role was in a senior organization than there has been. . . . I've always worked with young organizers my age" (interview).

Dan was one of the most admired organizers, beloved by these older women, and there was sorrow when he moved out of state. He inspired these seniors. Coming from a background in the disability rights movement, he moved comfortably into housing activism. Further, he appreciated the perspectives of the seniors he worked with. Dan was efficient, worked closely with members, even those perceived as "difficult," complimented them, and devised the Senior Power Assembly, recognized as an organizational triumph. Sharon, the longtime housing organizer, was also widely respected, and her presence along with Dan meant that the organizational focus was on issues of senior housing. In contrast, two staffers proved less effective on the Health Care Committee. As Jane pointed out, "We have just struggled to find the right person for Health Care and Economic Justice. Diane was not the right person. Denise was not the right person. They could be leaders, but they were not organizers. Being an organizer requires some very specific skills." The ability to get seniors to commit to engage in contentious public action and then follow up on those commitments was essential, and these two staffers lacked that skill, allowing seniors to talk about their political complaints but not act on them. Even though the staff was managed by the executive director, believing that "the board shouldn't get in the way of the staff," complaints by core members and by the board were considered.

Rhetorically and in practice, there were warm feelings between staff and leaders. It was expected that the staff would praise and encourage members, attributing success to their hard work, but compliments were directed to staff as well. Senior leaders emphasized to new members what Davey suggested about the relationship between his fellow seniors and the staff: "We run this organization, and they work for us." The question is where and how this is true.

Given that I describe some ways staff manipulated senior leaders to achieve their desired goals—sometimes apart from the goals of members—I emphasize that for the most part members admired the staff and were fond of them. They understood that without the skills staff provided the organization would lack power and their culture would be lacking. There was considerable praise of and affection for Jane Tate despite a few rough moments and some grievances. This goes beyond generic—if sincere—statements such as when Richie noted that "[the staff] are doing a great job, and they have our support" (field notes). More elaborately, Dr. Ben explained, "One of the great things about this organization is the organizers. They have a great skill of working with us inexperienced seniors. It makes me feel unafraid when I realize that I have them behind me" (field notes). Dr. Ben was rarely afraid, but his praise was heartfelt.

Perhaps the most dramatic instance of organizational support occurred when Jane found herself in personal conflict with a grants administrator. The CST hoped to receive renewed funding from one of its major backers who had recently hired a new grants officer. Jane had written what she believed was a straightforward email asking when they might receive the money allocated. As she described the incident, it sounded like a mundane request. But she received an angry response from this new contact, who was upset that she hadn't been thanked and believed the CST board should discuss this affront, implying that funding might not be forthcoming. Jane apologized to the board, although, given her description of the events, that seemed unnecessary. The board members expressed full support for Jane and were critical of her contact. In the process, they revealed how much she was valued.[18]

At many points the belief was raised that staff and members must work together. Jane emphasized this point:

In the best world, I always think leaders should have more power than staff, even though I think the reality is staff always are going to have [more influence]. . . . I mean, you work for an organization; you have a lot more relationships than our leaders do, and you're interacting with a lot of people. . . . A lot more than leaders are. But I've seen our leaders organize themselves when they want to so they can do whatever they want to do. . . . Leaders' voices are the most important voices in this organization, and they should be in control of the decisions. I believe that. Do I think we do that well all the time? No. There are many times I've been disappointed in how that's turned out. But I think when we do it well, they're the best actions. (Interview)

As one younger staffer pointed out, this can be hard:

I asked my supervisor very early on, "What if you're in a meeting asking people about a strategy and they really want to do something that you think isn't a good idea: What do you do?" And she said, "I mean, I'll give my opinion, but it's ultimately up to them, because that's how they'll grow, through making mistakes." I think because I'm afraid of making mistakes myself, I've struggled to necessarily give leaders that freedom. . . . It would be doing them a disservice to just stand back and say "OK, that's what they want" and not challenge them at all. (Interview)

Achieving a balance between expertise and control in an activist group is difficult, as was evident when Jane confessed to the board, "You actually supervise me. It sometimes seems that I'm directing you because I have a big mouth, but you have the obligation to evaluate me. . . . If you have an issue with me, let me know. I know I make a lot of mistakes" (field notes). Challenges perhaps happened less frequently than she claimed, but the point is that they did happen, though rarely. After a board meeting Jane pointed out the number of changes the board had made to her proposed budget, amendments she treated as significant and as indicating board power, even if to outside eyes the proposed and approved budgets seemed similar.

Despite the widespread and optimistic belief that everyone worked fruitfully together, tension was occasionally evident. While, as I noted, some staff were judged not right for their positions, some members were seen as a problem, a topic of staff discussion. At the outset of the research I had hoped to observe staff meetings. (There never was a problem with my attending board meetings or other meetings with senior members.) However, my presence proved contentious. I was invited to a staff meeting at the start of the research and another in the middle of the project, but it wasn't until late in the research, after I had developed close relations with the staff, that I could attend four more staff meetings. These were occasions when staff discussed their frustrations with work, complained about difficult seniors, and debated their colleagues' accountability. The issue of accountability was particularly salient, since it could lead to condemnation of those staffers who had failed to achieve their goals. Ideally this was done to improve the performance of the staff, but it was easy to recognize that the presence of an outsider (and one taking notes) limited their candor and modulated their critiques. Perhaps I was seen as being on the members' side. In time, with staff changes and deeper ethnographic relations, I learned that staff meetings reflected a particular type of status-based critique.[19] The staff also attended training sessions, discussing issues such as popular education, time management, and agitation training, and these meetings created anxiety among them. As one staffer commented, noting the additional work she was assigned, "Meetings don't do great things for my stress level" (field notes). In contrast to the generally positive feeling words at members' meetings, the sentiments at staff meetings were less upbeat, including "flustered," "stressed," and "scattered." For seniors, participating in this tiny public was a pleasure—and if it was not, they could leave—but for staff members it was a job, with consequences—including termination—if they were judged inadequate.

Seniors and Their Juniors

Leaders are essential for any continuing social movement, even if they lack the skills to lead without guidance from professionals. As ethicist Jeffrey Stout points out,

> Elites will always be with us. They rise and fall but are unlikely to disappear.
> The question is how to tame and civilize them, not how to eliminate them.
> Grassroots democratic organizations need leaders and work hard at identifying and cultivating them. The internal structure of such organizations is not anarchic.[20]

Still, leaders must earn the right to lead, and it was the staff who made that determination by selecting those who chaired meetings or spoke at actions.[21] This issue was evident during the discussion at United Chicago Seniors in Action about who had the right to decide on political endorsements. The staff wanted the endorsement process limited to "active members." The identity of these active members was never specified, but it involved those who had served on committees and willingly volunteered and likely would help the candidate endorsed. Perhaps more to the point, leaders were those the staff trusted. Some members worried that this criterion privileged favored leaders, perhaps those with a more professional bearing or more social capital, a problem for movements that hope to overcome class privilege.[22] One skeptic, noting this divide, suggested that the UCSIA "is supposed to be a grassroots organization. . . . There are people who think they are members, but they're not included." This was a rare debate. Jane, hoping to damp down dissent, argued, "I feel we're getting into a discussion that's going nowhere. . . . Not just members, but active members. Even if they are members they have to be active members. . . . If you want to have a strong organization, you have to limit it to active members." But how does one determine who is active? While some leaders supported Jane's position, others wanted to broaden the base. As Davey cautioned, "If we get too narrow, you get an insider deal." Finally they decided that to vote on endorsement members must have volunteered for the organization. Barb Greene argued for five hours of volunteering, but Jane pushed back, and the group decided that a member must have volunteered for ten hours during the past year, although no records were kept of volunteer hours. When the time came to choose a gubernatorial candidate for endorsement a select committee was established, but, as I described in chapter 3, no endorsement was made and there was no vote by active members (field notes).

The question was how the staff could strategically utilize their power to achieve their goals and put the right seniors in place, given diverse backgrounds, abilities, and interests. As one thoughtful staffer explained,

> There are different kinds of leaders. There are leaders that are going to be more the workhorses. They don't really like engaging with a lot of people, or it's hard for them to build relationships, but they want to do work. They want to do tasks, they want to do research, they want to be the workhorses—the steam engine that pushes things through. There are leaders who have relationships; they might not be interested in research or thinking strategy, but they can move people, and that's important. Then there are the people who are the strategists, who like to think of a vision and campaign tactics and campaign strategy. (Interview)

One technique of control was for a staffer to restate what a member had said, emphasizing (and occasionally shading) those points that deserved attention. This strategy occurred often, as in this instance: "I think I've heard three things you want to do. . . . I want to make sure I'm not putting things in people's mouths. Is that what we talked about?" (field notes). Unsurprisingly, no one objected to the rephrasing and the meeting moved on.

Interviewing Theresa, I was startled when she explained, "I think it's my job to manipulate people." She continued, "It's a neutral term. It literally just means to move someone. So it's my job—with their consent, with their partnership in this relationship that we have of organizer and leader—to move them to grow their base, to further their leadership, to deepen their investment in the work" (interview).

Theresa raised a fundamental issue. She was an agent of transformation, even if the seniors weren't fully aware that they were being transformed. This issue of manipulation—of shaping—was central to the relationship between staff and members, whether it was seen as necessary or as deceptive. One senior criticized these staff actions, noting that the staff would say, "Angela, you'd like to do that, wouldn't you?" and she noted, "A lot of times I say yes, but then sometimes I have to say, 'I don't think so, no.' But they can be kind of pushy" (interview).

Another leader made a similar point, also referring to manipulation:

> Not long after I had started at the CST I was talking with my daughter, who's always been kind of a reality check for me, and I said to her, "I don't see much difference between organizing and manipulation." And [my daughter] said, "There probably isn't all that much." That was one of the most difficult things for me, because it's a different atmosphere entirely from a social justice committee in a church, where there's much more of an equality. I find [myself] frequently at CST chafing. (Interview)

Most severe were comments from Gina Pirro, a leader who was frustrated with the lack of input from seniors:

> The staff members make their agenda and basically try to convince the seniors that what they want to do is what the seniors should want to do and what the seniors will do. And there's just not much room for any other outside involvement. [In the past] we would have these very interesting meetings, either Housing or Health Care, where we would really discuss issues and talk about them and why would we want to do something. (Interview)

The problem lies in being simultaneously a grassroots organization and a professional one, operating in two modes of interaction, revealing the conflict between managers and owners or between experts and volunteers. As another key senior reported,

> It says we're a grassroots organization, but a lot of the direction of it does come from staff. I mean, that's just the way it is. So if there's something the staff agrees they want to work on, they move the membership of the committees to [do it], and it's directed by the staff to get people involved and to go that certain way.... A lot of times it's because membership doesn't really know.... The organizers are the ones that work full time, and they're really seeing the big picture. (Interview)

A third senior leader thought that over the years the organization had moved toward control by the staff:

> When I first joined, we were definitely more grassroots than we are today. I think too many things originate with [Jane] and the staff . . . and we're told about it and then we're supposed to implement it. Whereas when I first entered, I felt a lot more started in the committees, went to the board and then the staff, and then we all worked together on how we could implement it. (Interview)

A longtime leader provided examples:

> When we were developing the Health Care Committee, we as a committee were discussing [names for the committee], and we voted on it. And the committee voted that it should be called Health Care, the Committee of Health Care and Well-Being, I think it was. . . . There was a minor movement, and it was backed by one of the staff members to call it Health Care and Economic Justice. So when it came to a vote—that was after it was whittled down to those two prospects—it was a pretty significant difference. The majority went for the well-being rather than economic justice. And so that carried. Then this particular staff member during the following week and before the next committee meeting did what we know so well in Chicago politics [*chuckles*] and started mobilizing the machine and made a lot of calls to individual members on the committee. In theory they tried to persuade them that maybe this was a mistake, that it should be economic justice. . . . It had more traction, this person thought, and well-being would be tied with health. . . . It was a call to readdress that vote or to have a new vote, and the economic justice carried [*chuckles*], even though some of us, including me, stuck by well-being. It's more of a symbolic aspect, but it gives you an idea. . . . The person I was talking to on the phone was saying, "You know, we're supposed to be a grassroots organization, and this just seemed to come from on high." (Interview)

As Nicholas Von Hoffman stated, overly cynically perhaps, about working with Saul Alinsky, "We organized people to determine their destinies except when we determined them."[23] As one senior co-chair pointed out, the staff typically made fundamental decisions and then presented them to leaders to have them "buy in" (field notes). Most members were satisfied with this arrangement, since they didn't have the time, the desire, or the expertise to decide. When they didn't object strongly—as they rarely did—the organization proceeded smoothly.

In planning rallies, the staff often had priority in preparing a detailed agenda. When composing speeches, the staff obtained input from the speaker, then wrote the text, which was then edited, approved, and practiced by the senior member. As Hazel, almost eighty, explained about her speech at a CST rally, "It was Jane, I think, who wrote it up, and then we talked about it and [edited] it" (interview). As someone who was not a public speaker, Hazel was grateful to rely on Jane's experience. Even if the words were not hers alone, she felt the text did represent her perspective.

Leaders and Left Outs

As in all organizations, people bring talents and troubles. The challenge in a grassroots movement is that democracy rules but someone must select leaders from what a member described as "a garden of talents," and gardens contain both flowers and weeds. Organizations founder if the wrong people direct action. A process of ability matching is necessary, based on personality, skills, and behavior,[24] but also on cultural and class compatibility.[25]

Selecting members of the Board of Directors was seemingly a formal process, although often with informal, but consequential, input from the staff as to who might best be "groomed." Considerations of racial, ethnic, gender, occupational,[26] and skill diversity were often explicit bases for selection; cultural capital typically was not mentioned as a criterion, but it could be influential as well.[27] The potential candidate would be approached through one-on-one meetings to "feel the person out." There was a meeting with two members of the Leadership (Nominations) Committee, then a more formal meeting with the full Leadership Committee was arranged. The committee asked the executive director to provide input from the staff. The name of the proposed candidate was raised at a board meeting, and sometimes potential nominees were asked to attend a board meeting to see if they fit and if they felt comfortable with the tasks to be assigned. The final vote, always unanimous, was held at the organization's holiday party.[28] While this was a well-recognized process, less immediately significant leadership choices, such as chairing meetings, were made informally by staff. As Dan put it,

> I understand the intention of turnover of leaders and rotating leadership, but I wonder if that actually lends itself to [the organization's] being more staff led, because no leaders ever get the full breadth of their view, and no leaders are ever given the level of responsibility to really take ownership of a committee, and that it just ends up being the staff that runs it through these proxy committee leaders. . . . Like Sharon and I picked the committee members, the committee leaders. . . . Who do we want this to be? and think, "We want these two people. Let's ask them." . . . I also think that it's important if we think about the committee as a place for training and development, and not as necessarily the place where all decisions are made. (Interview)

As with much interaction, friendships resulted from a linkage of interests and behavioral styles, coupled with similar network locations. Tight relationships depended on a *dyadic culture*. These ties were evident when I attended a staff meeting toward the end of my research. Staff were asked to name the leaders and "potential leaders" they were working with. Each named six to ten seniors they "owned": seniors with whom particular staff members would take the lead. Several seniors were named by two or three staffers. I listened as staff negotiated: "Can I add Delores Hunt to my list? Is that a conflict with anyone?" and "I would be willing to step back because I know she has a good relationship with Sharon." In a few cases there was some negative sentiment, as with one senior of whom Jane Tate said, "I'll attempt that [training]. I don't know if that will work." Once the seniors were divvied up, staff drew spiked circles (termed "spikies") on the erasable wall to depict which staff member would develop a leadership plan with which senior. Once done, they carefully erased the markings so that seniors would not see that they had been chosen—an embarrassing mistake that had been made once before. I don't suggest that this was offensive, since it attempted to ensure that each active senior had a connection with a staffer, but some seniors might have been surprised to hear they were treated like trading cards.

Certain seniors are organizational problems. Groups must control behaviors, embracing virtues while smoothing rough edges. How can generous volunteers be shaped or, when necessary, cooled out? These are delicate matters. One volunteer was not encouraged to return to phone banking because of what staff considered his disruptive tendency to leave overly friendly and persuasive voice-mail messages. On another occasion, after a dispute, a senior leader stormed out and didn't return. In successful movement groups, these interactional breakdowns will be rare. Troublesome individuals could often be incorporated into the soft community of senior activism if they demonstrated skills and commitments. By soft community—a concept based on my previous research on chess worlds[29]—I refer to individuals who demonstrate a commitment to the collective project even if their actions were considered eccentric, disruptive, or disagreeable. They were tolerated despite the interactional challenges they posed, because their devotion overrode their strangeness.

I describe three seniors who participated in Chicago Seniors Together. They all had virtues that allowed them to be members in good standing, but not without friction, although the difficulties were different in each case. One had too much to contribute, one had an agenda distinct from the staff's, and the third had an interactional style that was viewed as troublesome. Each was a valued member, but their reputations were problematic.

CONTROLLING TALK

Dr. Ben Golden was a key member of the organization, age ninety but still spry, widely admired and even beloved. He was a key informant, and I have referred to him throughout this account. As I noted in chapter 2, he has been an advocate for social justice his whole life, a thorn in the side of groups that permit injustice. As a retired physician, he contributed generously to the CST and participated in numerous actions.

The organizational challenge was that Ben freely shared his many opinions. Given the staff's desire to avoid long discussions, Ben's beliefs were often restated by staff, even if these accounts did not fully reflect his position. On one occasion Ben wanted United Chicago Seniors in Action to contribute funds to endorsed candidates as well as supplying volunteers. The staffer leading the meeting said he should bring it up with another committee, effectively ending discussion. Later Ben raised the question whether the organization should have hired a consultant from out of state and not a local person, a seemingly reasonable proposition. Jane seemed annoyed because this required a lengthy discussion and rebuffed him: "It seems that you have questions, Ben, and I will be happy to talk with you after the meeting" (field notes). His concerns were "cooled out." Although Dr. Ben was integral to the organization, and though he had real affection for the staff, his comments were often redirected and his concerns ignored.

CONTROLLING THE AGENDA

Lauren Dornbush was a senior with severe health constraints along with strong opinions about the topics the CST should prioritize. She believed the organization must work on issues senior members felt most strongly about, whether or not they were winnable. One staffer expressed her frustration with Lauren's desire to set the agenda:

> I often felt bossed around by leaders. So I think Lauren Dornbush has talked to me and treated me like I am an instrument for her doing. Or that I'm supposed to basically be doing what she wants because that's what grassroots means. That's not what it means, but that's the way it's been warped. (Interview)

Not all staff would have responded so sharply, but Lauren believed the issues she felt passionately about should top the organization's agenda.

Lauren was an impassioned advocate for single-payer health care (Medicare for All), in part as a result of the struggles of a family member. At first this was not an issue the staff or most members of the CST felt was important, both because it wouldn't directly affect seniors—who had Medicare, after all—and because it was contrary to the Alinsky-inspired belief that movements should choose fights where change was possible. The staff, the board, and the Health Care and Economic Justice Committee were unenthusiastic at first. Lauren kept pushing her agenda, doubtful about more modest goals that she felt missed the point of progressive activism.

In time Lauren's perspective triumphed, particularly because of the enthusiasm members generated and through support by allies. Lauren shaped the group culture and the policy preferences of her fellow members and the staff. By the end of my research, single-payer health care was central to the organizational mission, linked to a belief that medical care was a fundamental right. Lauren repeatedly voiced her belief, and her belief morphed into the members' desire to push for something "big," even if it would be possible only with long-term effort. She recalled proudly,

> We had a workshop. . . . So, we divided up into groups: What were our issues? There were about four or five groups. We divided up. All of us came back with single-payer. Every one of us. Jane was very upset; she did not like that, and she said, "Next time I'm going to assign things." I said, "No, you're not" [*laughs*]. [GAF: "Why do you think she was upset?"] Because it was single-payer. . . . She was upset because we all came back with the same thing. She was anticipating that we were going to come with improving Medicare, expanding Social Security, and all that. She didn't anticipate that. [GAF: "Was her concern because single-payer wasn't seen as a senior issue?"] It's not winnable. You want issues that are winnable, and she did not see that as winnable. What changed Jane was about a year ago when they went to [Racine], . . . and then they went to a church afterward. Jane had a change of heart. . . . But it was not her issue. Whether it was senior or not, that wasn't it; it was not winnable. She said, "It's not going to fly." We had heated discussions about that. I said, "Jane, some things cannot be winnable within three, six, even twelve months. Some of these things are long-range, but we've got to start somewhere." (Interview)[30]

How much was due to a change of heart by the executive director is unclear, but the attitude toward Medicare for All changed during my research, as it did nationally. Because of Lauren's insistence and her unwillingness to accept more modest goals, she shaped the values of the CST members in ways that most of her fellow seniors came to admire.

CONTROLLING CULTURE

For an organization that often claimed that class bias and inequality reflected privilege, putting that belief into practice could be difficult. Carrie Stanton was without question one of the hardest-working seniors in the organization. But she was also a woman who had lived a hard life, including bouts of homelessness and other difficulties, even though she had held a professional position when younger. Many senior members and staff had lived comfortable lives before retirement, but not Carrie. Beyond this, she could be loud, profane, scruffy, and opinionated, even if, unlike Lauren's, her opinions were largely consistent with the organization's priorities. Carrie was the force behind the Senior Housing Bill of Rights and was instrumental in organizing the Senior Power Assembly described in chapter 3. As one of her male colleagues laughingly described her, "She's filled with moxie. . . . If she had balls, she'd be king" (interview).

Still, several of her senior colleagues were not admiring, and the staff could become frustrated with her as well. She did not display the middle-class interactional style of her fellow White women. Being overweight and casually dressed did not endear her to those from professional backgrounds. However, as I noted, no one worked harder when the CST needed volunteers, even if in meetings she could be seen as disruptive. At one point Carrie expressed frustration when her idea was ignored: "I don't get much respect in this room. I say this and it gets pushed aside" (field notes). When staff discussed Carrie's desire for leadership, Lynette said, "I did a leadership meeting with Carrie, and it was a long, slow process. She wanted a building [to organize]. It's important to have her fail. I will work with her." Staff were skeptical about Carrie's ability to organize renters for social action. As Jane pointed out, "She is very competitive in a way that is not helpful" (field notes). Over time, admiration grew, but never without some concern. As Carrie herself recognized,

> When I first came in, I felt I was being led, and we were being told what we could do and what we couldn't do. I don't react well to that. . . . [Serving on the Housing Committee], I wanted to go to CHI [Chicago Housing Initiative, a progressive housing group that is part of CST's alliance] subcommittee meetings, which I was used to doing. It just wasn't as warmly taken. (Interview)

In time Carrie was accepted as a key member, which she attributed to the staff's recognizing that seniors should lead, although they still attempted to control her. Carrie was flattered when asked to chair a meeting and eventually to serve on the board of United Chicago Seniors in Action.

Organizational Politics

In this chapter I address how the structure of Chicago Seniors Together matters for the members' culture and for their interaction order. As tiny publics, social movement organizations inevitably face outward, but to do this they must also be inwardly cohesive. Given that so much can be considered political and contentious, this can be a problem. These groups must develop agreed-on procedures to make decisions and to organize meetings, essential for the creation of community. In this regard the CST struggled in deciding whether to meet as a single community through joint meetings or whether to let subgroups operate independently. The meetings had to fit within the time allotted and be tailored to produce results that staff wanted, minimizing debate or dispute. "Clockwork" contributed to the power dynamics of decision-making.

Following resource mobilization theory,[31] the CST had to obtain sufficient resources to achieve its ends through connections with other institutions and to ensure that those resources were efficiently utilized for activist ends. The range of financial sources was impressive, reflecting the material infrastructure progressive organizations rely on. For the CST this was complicated by the scandal and collapse of an earlier local organization. As a result, Chicago Seniors Together was exquisitely cautious about financial management. This was central to organizational culture, and it served the group well.

In a movement group that relies on both members and organizers, leaders and staff, perhaps the most important reality is the way the two are linked, a complex and sometimes fraught relationship. In theory, members—the seniors—should create policy, but in practice it is not clear that they have the experience, the capacity, the time, or the commitment to do so. Consequently the staff served as managers. They were more political, were sophisticated in activism theory, and had wider networks. Although the two groups had shared goals, the staff determined which leaders were awarded authority, channeling the group culture and modeling appropriate interaction.

In the end—like age, ideology, and memory—organizational relations matter. Chicago Seniors Together could not succeed, or even exist, if it ignored the challenges of being a group whose bonds made progress both difficult and possible.

6

Diversities

A challenge that organizations face—particularly social movement organizations—is how to define their community: its desires, its scope, and its identity. Who are the desired participants? Who is the audience? Who is being served? While culture develops from group membership, membership, in turn, grows from local culture as well as the strategies of outreach and the arenas where outreach occurs. Both the location of actions and the characteristics of members matter, and this is particularly true for groups of seniors, who are often less mobile and more closely tied to long-standing traditions. While not focused on politics, this is a theme of Barbara Myerhoff's moving *Number Our Days*,[1] an account that richly recounts the lifeworlds and locations of older Jews in urban Los Angeles. The demographics and spatial configuration of elderly communities in Chicago are central to understanding the internal dynamics of Chicago Seniors Together as staff and members attempt to provide a space where diversity is treasured.

In this chapter I examine how it matters—and how it doesn't—that Chicago Seniors Together was largely a female-dominated, heteronormative, majority White, anglophone group centered on the wealthier North Side of Chicago, whose members primarily had middle-class occupations before retirement. That demographic reality confronted this progressive organization, engaged in the pragmatics of community organizing but with leaders who wished they could expand throughout the city. Diversity was devoutly desired but not easy to achieve. Discussions often addressed how the organization could become more inclusive, encouraging a chorus of senior voices and with the goal of shaping public policy and local governance.[2]

Among members of Chicago Seniors Together, the issue was framed as whether the group could—or should—become a citywide organization rather

FIGURE 4. The power of old White women

than one centered on the North Side with a pod of members coming from Hyde Park, near the University of Chicago. The poorer, less White South and West Sides were noticeably underrepresented. Many members were dismayed by this, but changing this reality was difficult, and some were skeptical that it was possible. Besides lacking networks of relationships, there was a sense that this was a racialized organization in which some considered whiteness a credential that must be overcome by persons of color.[3] Discussions of outreach, or even possible local chapters, did not gain traction, even though there were efforts to organize residents in senior housing units on the West Side so as to establish a "new base."[4] Even though there was a professed (and sincere) belief in racial justice, much of the activism occurred where many White seniors lived.

Group style affects recruitment and retention. Altering a comfortable culture is difficult and perhaps undesirable. This is particularly true when movements assert that diversity is a virtue yet diversity might produce conflict.[5] Extending a movement's reach,[6] while tempting, may cause internal dissent and disruption.

For an organization that believed deeply in the involvement of all, language was as much a barrier as geography. A decade before my involvement, the organization included a sizable immigrant "Russian" contingent from the former Soviet Union, resulting from a staff member's efforts and the community's concern about affordable senior housing. After she left, and given the differing political and racial perspectives of these members, most drifted away, although at some events Russian translations are still provided for the few who remain. As Davey Gibbs explained, "They got old and are much more conservative" (field notes). South Asians or East Asians were rarely present, although at one event Hindi translation was provided. More salient was an attempt to reach out to the Spanish-language community, significant because of the large population on Chicago's West Side and throughout the city, where Latinx residents make up roughly 30 percent of the city's population and are highly invested in progressive immigration reform. In large meetings Spanish translation was available, although few Latinx participants attended. Recruitment had been largely unsuccessful. Perhaps the translations signaled the organization's desire for inclusive politics, but few of these groups joined. More successful efforts have been for racial inclusion, gender involvement, social class recruitment, and outreach to the aging LGBTQ community.

Class Struggles

In the United States the political left has often found that, while they claim to be fighting for justice for the working class, those they are ostensibly helping have little interest in joining such groups and sometimes are hostile to these benefits. Perhaps this is an instance of what Marx called false consciousness. Not only do many in the working class lack the interest, time, or resources to participate, but many educated professionals find the lure of economic redistribution compelling. Perhaps this is a form of false consciousness as well, whether based in altruism or in folly.

The reality was that despite some class diversity, particularly tied to race, Chicago Seniors Together was largely composed of men and women who in their working lives held middle-class and professional positions—at least the senior leaders I interviewed. I met retired doctors, teachers, professors, lawyers, therapists, bankers, managers, and others in the professional occupations. Although not a highly religious group, many White activists had a Jewish background, and others belonged to liberal denominations such as Unitarianism or to Catholic congregations that embraced liberation theology.[7] One staff member made a point of informing me that the CST founder was a Jewish woman and that many staffers held advanced degrees. However, few if any of these men and women could be described as wealthy in their current circumstances. Despite their backgrounds, many members lived in subsidized senior housing. Although relatively few active members needed

Medicaid,[8] they worried about preserving Social Security, Medicare, and housing subsidies. Still, they had cultural capital of the sort the truly needy lack. A similar pattern was true of organizations such as the Gray Panthers, excluding those who were considered, in the words of founder Maggie Kuhn, "rich old people . . . who do not identify with their peers who are not rich and powerful"[9] but who depend on members' professional skills. For the CST and for the Gray Panthers, one's policy commitments took priority, even though the CST established a tiered dues structure in which inexpensive membership ($15 a year) provided the same benefits as the (slightly) higher-level membership at $30 a year.

One outcome of the 2016 presidential election was evident in the growth of the membership by seniors activated to oppose the Trump presidency. These new supporters, many of them retired women, were more interested in the organization's focus on health care and economic justice than on local housing needs. I previously noted the difference in orientation and background of members of those two committees. As Jane Tate, the executive director, explained,

> The needs of members on the Housing Committee were more immediate. There are people on that committee who need affordable housing. . . . I think they're a little bit more needy. . . . Someone once said that the Housing team . . . their struggles are a lot more intense than sometimes our leaders in Health Care are. (Interview)

Those on the Health Care Committee were more concerned with supporting Medicare for All, and Jane suggested that they sometimes "get caught in the weeds of policy."

Still, despite this, divisions of social class were not a major issue for the organization. They often were invisible, even though those with more cultural capital were advantaged over those without—a frequent issue in social movement organizations.[10] The differences in discursive style were rarely an explicit source of contention, though they did affect who might be selected as leaders because of their articulateness and interpersonal ease. Recruiting the highly disadvantaged into the organization was not a high priority in practice, in spite of the aim to help them by CST activism. One leader noted that the organization did not reach out to the homeless people in Chicago who live under highway overpasses, adding, "There are a lot of seniors under the viaduct." These people would not easily fit the cultural style and decision-making processes that were seen as desirable.

Class-based politics were notable: many felt that, as one well-educated senior pointed out, "People like me consider the police [our] friends" (field notes). The feeling was echoed by the other professionals in the organization and linked to White privilege, even as they recognized they were the fortunate ones.

Cultural taste mattered, and some of the older women had their hair permed, styled, and colored and wore stylish sweaters. Divisions were also evident in nonverbal behavior. Jane Tate noted that "when someone's talking you'll see some of our leaders maybe shake their heads when someone's not as articulate as they might be in a situation. . . . Sometimes people who are in this higher class may see their opinions or their thoughts as more important" (interview). Perhaps this explains some of the reactions to Carrie Stanton, as I described in chapter 5. Members must not display their privilege too explicitly, however. A senior leader who travels extensively and recounted her adventures received "a lot of resentment" for her "trappings of affluence" and for "showing off." One must "restrain one's ego," meaning not discussing one's comfortable finances in any detail. But in general CST members did not consider the economic backgrounds of participants a divide that must be bridged. Some referred to being raised in working-class homes as showing they knew what it meant to be poor. Still, this was a domain in which one staff member said the organization did not need to be concerned about "diversity for diversity's sake." Class represented an irrelevant diversity. Seniors emphasized that "we're a group of equals"; "it seems like an even playing field. . . . I can't personally see a class distinction between the people"; and "it tends to be pretty middle class—I think our class is pretty homogeneous" (interviews). Despite members' having varying resources in retirement, the class structure of the organization was compressed and largely invisible: there were no very wealthy participants, and only a few were desperately poor. In contrast to race, social class diversity was largely ignored as a goal for recruitment. To the extent that class matters, it matters in light of education. As one leader believed, "once you're educated, you're no longer poor" (interview).

Race Matters

In contrast to class, which can be unseen, race is profoundly present. A challenge for Chicago Seniors Together as a group of progressive seniors is that the way Americans think and talk about race has changed and that seniors grew up in a different discursive moment. There was a time, as several members reminded me, when "Negro" was the polite term for people of color, used by members of both races. A reference to "colored people" was an insult. They remembered this time, typically with some pain, but perhaps with some nostalgia, as a time when (for Whites) racial privilege was often not considered. Those I met were all committed to equitable race relations, and early engagement in civil rights protests had led many to activism. Yet what racial justice meant could be contentious, even if they all agreed in a somewhat ambiguous fashion that "Black Lives Matter." Being White activists who believed they were fighting racism potentially exposed them to criticism, given the weight of history.[11] In the current racial climate, a White member might fear that a comment intended to be supportive could be taken as insensitive. Since appropriate language keeps changing, the desire for racial justice had to be handled gingerly. It was often noted—correctly—that Whites had difficulty discussing race. They hoped to respond appropriately, but the rules were foggy and fraught. Few wanted to have their good intentions disdained.

When I began to observe the CST the organization had a Black staff member, Sheila. One of her responsibilities was to organize what was termed the Racial Justice Leadership Team. This group consisted of members, Black and White, who cared about issues of race and racism and wished to address them, even as they affected progressive communities. However, when Sheila left the CST she was not replaced, and after her departure the organization lacked a Black staff member. (It employed several Latinx organizers during this period.)

As I noted, the CST was, in the words of one staffer, "a very White organization," but it did attract a significant number of Black participants, perhaps 20 percent of the total. Some of these were well-respected leaders, but staffers believed that Black members felt "less welcome" (interview). One staffer suggested critically that "the organization needs to decide on its racial identity. As a result, they might scrap their desire to be multiracial and remain a largely North Side organization with a White culture, White organization, White name, and say to communities of color, 'This is who we are. Don't you want to join us?' No. The answer is no" (interview).

From this perspective they could ally with other organizations that were composed of people of color even if they were not multiracial.

The other option, this staffer suggested, was to restructure the organization to make it friendlier to diverse communities. Neither of these options was ideal, and so CST continued as an organization that was antiracist but largely White. As part of its commitment to equal justice and to send a signal of racial inclusion, the CST decided to select co-chairs with one being White and one a person of color—meaning, given the membership, Black. Apparently there had been pushback, with some saying in effect, according to Jane's sarcastic retelling, "Why do we need to do that? We're White people. We're really great." Perhaps the rule was that *at least* one of the co-chairs had to be a person of color, since for a time both were Black.

Many, but not all, members believed there was little interpersonal tension, and I sensed little myself. Leaders emphasized that members "got along," even though African American leaders were more likely to leave their positions before their terms expired. People were deferential. There were no public charges of racism, although there was a concern—shared by many White Americans—that racial controversies might emerge at any moment. One White member suggested that he thought of himself and others as "so-called White." He denied that White was a legitimate racial designation. Another White member participated in the fight for the fifteen-dollar minimum wage, which she described by saying, "That was mostly Black and Brown folk, and I liked to show that they were not alone" (field notes).

Despite this happy vision, issues of racial concern were raised, and there were changes in the group structure during my research. In the current climate of progressive activism, debates about race are inevitably fraught, even if people get along personally. I will discuss three of these issues.

First was the question whether racial engagement should be internally focused, demanding that the organization consider structural racism in its midst as opposed to focusing on actions to combat racism in the city, whether or not this related directly to seniors. Second was whether the organization should attempt to recruit more Black and Latinx members from the South and West Sides of the city. Third was whether the organization should promote a race-blind perspective or treat Blacks as a uniquely challenged category of citizens. In what way did Black lives matter for the organization and for the world?

Internal Critique or External Action

In the early weeks of my research I learned there was a Racial Justice Leadership Team at the CST and chose to attend its meetings regularly. What surprised me was that the primary goal of the group was not to fight against racism in Chicago, but to address issues of racial equity within this progressive organization. The team believed that even if members and staff had good intentions, they needed to confront unexamined racism and promote racial education. I was impressed that the focus was not external others but examining the culture of the group itself "through a racial justice lens." Did their style of interaction solidify racial bias? Would it be better to look within or outward?[12] At the start of my observation, Jane emphasized that people in the progressive community had warned her "in no uncertain terms" that they should not discuss racial dynamics within the organization. But when we spoke she thought it had worked, although perhaps in time she came to appreciate the wisdom of those who had advised her. Criticizing Donald Trump, Paul Ryan, or Rahm Emanuel for being racist was easy; criticizing internal structures and engaged leaders, not so much. I was impressed that the concern was with members of the group itself. The Racial Justice Leadership Team was, in effect, an internal social movement.[13] The goal was to place racial justice on the agenda of every committee meeting. As Sheila explained, "I'll use an old term. We'll infiltrate their meetings. We'll bring our lens into the meeting" (field notes).

During the year I participated in the team, I helped with research—finding published sources—and listened to discussions of unconscious racism and the need to fight against microaggressions. If Blacks and Whites had similar abilities—and similar flaws—was it possible for White members to criticize Black colleagues without being criticized themselves? When would giving compliments be taken as patronizing?[14] These were challenges for good-hearted members. As I became more involved, attending most of the monthly meetings of the Racial Justice Leadership Team, I came to recognize that internal critiques were hard to manage, especially when members considered themselves racially progressive. Support for equal rights was integral to their identity. At various points Sheila and others resented the lack of organizational support, although the team made few specific proposals other than, as Jerry Hackworth, then co-chair of the organization, pointed out, "We ask that every committee spend a little time in each meeting talking about issues of racial justice and report back" (field notes). This racial justice analysis of internal decisions never became the norm.

In time Sheila resigned from her position. As I noted, for the rest of my time as an observer the organization lacked a Black staffer. In considering a replacement for Sheila, Jane spoke about organizational belt tightening. She told the board, "I want to see if that is something we need to hire someone for. . . . There will be a staff member doing that. I want to make that clear" (field notes). After hiring Denise, of South Asian descent, it took several months to reorganize the team. The group never fully re-formed, and the former chair of the team resigned, expressing frustration with what he saw as a lack of interest. He explained that CST is "a hierarchical organization, which is to say, a White organization" (field notes). In making this claim he suggested that the presence of a hierarchy and the desire for consensus were racially coded. As one (White) senior described the local culture of Black organizations, "Theirs is a very different corporate culture. It's much more welcoming. There is more food. There are children." Another White senior admitted,

> You were talking about different organizational cultures. I'm so embedded in the White supremacy way of organization, such as using Robert's Rules of

Order. [My daughter] grew up with the Alinsky model of organization. That model always looked to the organizer and the staff for the answers, and I don't know how to go around it. (Field notes)

Whether using Robert's Rules reflects White supremacy in contrast to having children underfoot is an open question, but a racial division in movement culture was assumed.

A consensus emerged among the team members after Sheila's departure that there was no need to address internal issues of racial privilege, and also that the team in its previous incarnation had failed by not presenting specific proposals. We were talkers, not actors—a heavy criticism. As one team member admitted, "What's the program? What's the goal? I don't know." Another recognized, "If it will continue, we must engage the members, which has been a failure" (field notes).

By the end of my research the emphasis on internal critique had vanished, the committee was essentially disbanded, and the racial focus emphasized Black Lives Matter issues such as police misconduct, an external concern that was less personally relevant to seniors who worried about crime in their neighborhoods. The challenge remained "Can we be closer to being an anti-racist organization?" (field notes). The consensus was that if the CST addresses racial injustice, it should deal with political problems. Jane expressed this explicitly to the board: "I want to push that committee to be more external. We teach through campaign work. It will make people have awareness through a campaign. Let's not just talk that Whites have privilege" (field notes). Or as Richie Douglas, an African American leader, said, "Originally we were looking internally, and now we are looking to go out."

How to do this? Rather than allow members to decide, Denise made a choice. Denise was the lead staffer on racial issues after Sheila left, and she chose to emphasize a movement that was then active in a Black neighborhood on the West Side of Chicago. The "No Cop Academy" movement opposed building a training center for police officers in a predominantly Black neighborhood, believing the money would be better spent on community projects. Mayor Rahm Emanuel and then Chicago's progressive mayor Lori Lightfoot both supported the project over the objections of some members of the community, and money was allocated for the building. The central issue for the CST was whether devoting time and resources to the protest was consistent with the organization's focus on senior issues. This proved controversial, especially when the question was given more attention than how to preserve Social Security. One meeting was especially contentious. Some seniors believed the "No Cop Academy" movement was not relevant to them, and one leader asked if it had been approved by the board (field notes). Denise claimed that one member insisted she would leave the organization if it dealt with racial issues. This claim seemed unlikely in its strong form, but other staff explained that some White members were unconcerned with racial issues. Housing, health care, Social Security, and economic justice were to be the focal issues.

A CITYWIDE ORGANIZATION?

It was often noted that Chicago Seniors Together was a "North Side" organization. The North Side of Chicago was where the organization was birthed and where most members were recruited from. Even though this geographical designation seems neutral, in the context of Chicago it suggested that the CST was a White organization.[15] This reality made it more difficult to retain and recruit Black members as well as to recruit Latinx and Asian members.[16]

In the ideal, expansion was treated as desirable, even necessary, but so was retention. Retention might have been the more immediate problem. How could the CST keep its Black leaders? Over the course of thirty months, I watched many of the leading African Americans, including several co-chairs and officers, leave the organization. Some fretted that the board might become largely White. While this was not true for all African American leaders—Richie Douglas and Angela Knight, for example, were committed activists and integral to the group—there was a rapid turnover of Black leaders, more so than for White leaders. As a consequence, Blacks moved into leadership positions more quickly even though they might not have been as committed or knowledgeable about the organization as those who were long-time supporters. This was made clear when Jane remarked, "You look around; there are a lot of White people around the table." With the White middle-class influx after the 2016 election, the balance became even more one-sided. As noted, at one point the organization held a "Thriving in Color Potluck" for female members of color. Only a few members and their guests showed up, and one, unimpressed, dismissed it as a therapy session, not a serious discussion of political issues.

A question that often emerged was whether the CST should strive to be a "citywide" organization if it was to be truly "antiracist," or whether this was a misuse of its limited resources. Despite its being seen as desirable, it was never clear whether the CST had the capacity to do that kind of organizing outreach, given the size of the staff and the networks of members. One could not simply hope to gain members on the West and South Sides—it would take a strategy. Perhaps this would mean an organization with a different style, in which Black members would feel comfortable and valued. (The Southwest Side, largely Latinx and White ethnic, was rarely mentioned. The Northwest Side is treated as part of the North Side.) As one African American leader commented, "It's going to be hard. We're going to have to go out to the areas where there are seniors and let them know." As optimistic as this view sounds, it didn't happen often, and the organization changed little in its pattern of recruitment.

The issue partially involved time, resources, and transportation, but there was also an emotional divide. Many Chicagoans, both Whites and middle-class African Americans, and especially seniors, find the South and West Sides of the city too dangerous to visit, a perspective validated each weekend with media counts of shootings and deaths. When Jeanne Hyde talked about a modestly attended demonstration, she remarked, "There were people who were afraid to go to the South Side. It showed that we had a lot of work to do" (field notes). While progressive, many of these seniors weigh real and imagined risks. Language also plays a role, since few members are fluent in Spanish and immigration reform is considered secondary as a senior issue. How could they organize when they weren't able to listen? The organizational culture was not conducive to this recruitment.[17] The problem raised on several occasions—surely reasonable—was that "we don't want to spread ourselves too thin." While some attempts were made to organize Latinx senior housing units, the efforts were modest.

RACE-BLIND/RACE MATTERS

It's easy to sympathize with those White seniors, coming of age in the early 1960s, who believe—deeply and passionately—that we should judge people on their character, not on their skin color. This was, after all, Martin Luther King's contention in his address to the 1963 March on Washington. Even if it did not capture the fiery and critical components of King's beliefs, the demand is inspiring. If many are now skeptical, we reveal our cynicism about the possibility of a "beloved community."

Although many progressives today doubt the idea of race blindness, some seniors remained true believers. They were persuaded that they did not "see" race. This stands in sharp contrast with those African Americans—although not all—who saw a continuing pattern of racial affronts. These fears can be intense. One Black member announced after the 2016 election, "We don't know who has a Ku Klux Klan robe in their drawer." Another Black senior mentioned being in a suburb where she and her mother saw a group of young White men standing together. She commented, "Fortunately they didn't do anything to us, but we were afraid." The most extreme case was an African

American woman, being considered for the Board of Directors, who was reported to have said publicly that she thought all Whites were members of the Klan and that they were giving Black youths guns so they could kill each other (field notes). While there was an attempt to differentiate "Black culture and White culture" in the comment's rhetorical tone, the most instructive response was made by a White leader who joked, "Does she support Trump?," suggesting that he found her views bizarre. She was not selected for the board.

A few White members held views that would have been controversial if expressed publicly. Some "Russian" members agreed with the economic demands of the CST but also thought American Blacks were lazy. Most had left the organization or played minor roles. Some Whites suggested that Blacks had been promoted too rapidly, hoping for racial balance, before it was clear how committed they were. A leader cautioned about the danger involved: "We disintegrated into basically grabbing the next Black person that walked by us and seeing if they'd want to be on the board. . . . [Racial balance] is not something that I feel can be overlooked, but it's better [for it] to be overlooked than do it as badly as we did" (interview).

Another member objected to selecting committee chairs based on race rather than on competence or experience. I present these remarks in some detail, since they express what others might have been too cautious to share:

Chicago Seniors has changed so much in the time that I've been there. I wanted to be on the Finance Committee and maybe the board, and I wanted to do more policy work. . . . I was told, "No, you can't because you have to have a couple of years of experience under your belt before we will pick you for these positions." Since then, now they have this Leadership Committee that picks people and if you're picked or not, it has nothing to do with your experience; it mostly has to do with your race. About a year or two years after I started with them, they decided that race was going be one of the primary factors in choosing what they worked on and how they worked on it. They said you couldn't be a sole chairperson . . . it had to be [a co-chair]. One person had to be Black and one person had to be White. I guess they didn't think about others in between.[18] . . . Also, during that time period one of the practically founders—she's a very important person among the members—she interviewed me for being on the board but she told me all about this business where it wasn't going to be on merits anymore; it was just going to be on race. [GAF: She was as explicit as that?] Yes. Oh, very much. And she had fought against it in the board; she was a board member. She said, "Well, if you feel like you can work under these conditions, we'd like to ask you if you want to be on the board." But she herself didn't want to continue working there, and I didn't either because I couldn't understand it. It was so irritating to have people who had no experience jump ahead other people. (Interview)

This informant was candid about her resentment, more explicit than anyone else I came to know. The point is less whether this actually occurred than that this active, progressive senior believed it was true and reported it to explain the perceived racial politics of the organization.[19] Such statements would not have been tolerated in public settings. This was a rare critique, but perhaps it reflected the thoughts of other White members who believed they were denied positions because of their race. Certainly not everyone would agree with these sentiments, and others would emphasize that everyone selected for major positions had a history of organizational activity. Still, whether their comments were justified or reflected racialized resentment, these members claimed to experience what they felt was "White disprivilege" in this activist organization.[20]

Perhaps the biggest obstacle to a progressive view of racial politics was the belief among some older members that Whites should strive to be race-blind, and, as I noted, they claimed passionately that they did not "see" race. One of the few Russians remaining in the organization explained, "We don't have to have the color of the skin as the first question. We have to put the importance of the person first" (field notes). A White leader insisted that she learned this from her mother:

> My mother's best friend was African American. My mother never, ever saw color. That's how I was raised. My best friend, she lives in Atlanta now, she's African American. This year it'll be fifty years. We met in Spanish class in the infamous Chicago summer, in the infamous year, 1968. When I lived in California, my mom and I used to go to her house for Christmas. They came to our house for Passover. I dated African American men. My mother always said to me, "I don't care who you marry. As long as they're good to you, you love them. Just so long as they're not a Sox fan!" (Interview)

Here race is jokingly treated as less significant than sports affiliation. One's generation surely mattered, since an insistence on race blindness had been the default position of progressives before the late 1960s. This was the language—and the belief—they were brought up with in a particular generational context, and, as Sheila noted, trying to change that language could "scare people." Scholars of race recognize that treating one's friends as "raced" is hardly being race-blind, and the speaker didn't mean she couldn't differentiate Black and White faces. What she hoped to get across, however skeptical we might be, is that she—as a White person—treats African Americans the same way she treats those in her own racial category. Given that several of the elderly activists had laid their lives on the line fighting for civil rights during the 1960s—some with Dr. King—their bona fides should be treated with respect.

The claim of race blindness (or color blindness) was not universally accepted. This tension over how to discuss racial bias came to the fore at a session organized by the Racial Justice Leadership Team about Black Lives Matter and the structural racism Blacks experience. Two longtime senior leaders, raised in the 1940s, insisted they were race-blind. Younger seniors and those who were African American asserted in accord with contemporary thinking that to claim to be race-blind is to deny White privilege. One said, "To be color-blind is to be the great White person," and another said, "The first thing you do is to acknowledge." However, one of these older seniors denied this, saying, "I'm going back to my truth. I don't see Black, White, or plaid." The other senior, in suggesting that all people are alike, described an African American nurse: "She was awful to me. . . . I never could see why she was so nasty to me. I even took her to lunch, but I had some White nurses who were awful to me [too]." This transforms what could have been an account about structural racism into a story about idiosyncratic personality. The recognition that some White members refused to assent to the currently accepted view about structural racism, presenting the alternative of mutual goodwill, reverberated throughout my research, with all its rhetorical echoes of past civil rights debates.

Engendered Activism

It is now commonplace to recognize a "gender gap" in politics, with women tending to vote for Democrats and men for Republicans, a reality dating back at least forty years to the 1980 election. This is also evident in activism. Some movements, notably animal rights and local environmentalism, have predominantly female membership.[21] There certainly are many women active in conservative movements, such as pro-life abortion politics and even in the Tea Party movement,[22] but, as in electoral politics, women swing left. For older women, new roles and gendered empowerment are apparent in activism.[23] Some scholars, such as Roger Sanjek, writing about the 1980s Gray Panthers, suggest that men in the movement prefer to talk, while women act. Women emphasize consensus and egalitarian leadership.[24] The Old Left, a male, if not masculinist, movement, was transformed and reimagined as a result of the "Women's Movement" of the 1970s. A similar change occurred with regard to the Raging Grannies in British Columbia, an all-female grouping that defined itself as challenging patriarchy[25] with a belief in the power of empathy and nurturing as a political strategy.[26] In contrast to men, women activists are more likely to engage in nonconfrontational protest, although this was not always their preference and may be changing.[27]

In Chicago Seniors Together, gender politics was noted and sometimes sensitive, although it rarely produced group debate. The culture emphasized the starring role of women, although feminist theory was rarely invoked. Still, the organizational culture fit nicely into the collective identity of the older women who participated.[28] To the extent that these women had a gender consciousness, the CST was seen as supportive.[29]

As I noted, of the dozen staff members at the CST during my period of research, only one, Dan, was male. There was some desire to employ more male staff—and pleasure when Dan was hired—but that never became a demand; most members felt that gender balance among the staff was not an issue worth pursuing.

Further, the gendered structure of the group was not at issue. Because of the increase in membership, it is hard to pin down the gender balance, but viewing attendance at most meetings, the membership of the organization was approximately two-thirds female. Surely this in part reflected the greater longevity of women and a desire for sociability during widowhood, but this likely did not explain the entire difference, since some was linked to the greater progressivism of women in contemporary American politics. This was particularly true in the aftermath of the 2016 election and the heavily attended 2017 Women's March.

Within the organization, some men said they would prefer a more equal gender balance and more male staff members. The female dominance was noted and occasionally commented on. While emphasizing that he saw no gender tension in the CST and that too much male leadership would be undesirable, one male leader explained, "I think we could use a little bit more of a masculine influence in there to round it up as a full organization" (interview). Another man, noting female control, asserted, "Male leadership in the organization is reserved and very conscious of its problems. . . . I think our female leaders value their acceptance in leadership roles and would be very guarded about any males asserting leadership" (interview). At least one senior leader, Jeanne Hyde, worried, "There are so few men in the organization that I think sometimes they might feel [laughs] outnumbered and overlooked" (interview). When a woman was considered for a staff position, a male board member asked how she worked with men, a comment that seemed to startle the executive director.

Significantly, the concern went in the other direction as well. Dan noted that a related issue was raised when he was hired: "One of the leaders that was in my interview . . . I was talking to her about my interview, and she said that one of her concerns . . . was, as a man, was I going to listen to Jane. . . . She had concerns [about] would I be able to work with women basically, which I think is a very fair concern" (interview). While male leaders were accepted and admired—for example, Dr. Ben, Davey, Richie, and Jerry—most leaders were women. In addition, there were occasional critical comments about men as a category, although not about particular male leaders, who were seen as supportive of women's leadership. At least two staffers remarked on their "bad experiences" with men, one involving spousal abuse. Less seriously, the loudest laughter I heard during the entire research was when Dr. Ben mentioned he had been married for forty-seven years and that he viewed marriage as a job, joking that his wife once said, "Buddy, you don't know how many times you were almost fired." The women understood (field notes). Dan, the male staffer, said that he felt that "as a White man, people take me seriously. I don't get treated like a child. . . . The women [staffers] in our organization struggle more with being treated like grandchildren than I do" (interview). In this light, Jane reported at a board meeting as Dan was being hired, "He has a clear understanding of his privilege as a White male. That doesn't mean that he doesn't have to work on it" (field notes).

The issue of gender became salient on only one occasion when some believed men had too much dominance. This was early in my research when new candidates for the Board of Directors were being selected. Because of turnover, most returning members of the board were male, and this was raised as an issue in recruitment, although not in subsequent years when the board had more female members. In a Leadership (Nominations) Committee meeting, after some discussion, Jane remarked, "So here is what I'm hearing people say: 'We really need more women on the board. It's really problematic to have so many males'" (field notes). I couldn't determine how seriously the committee took gender balance, but more women were chosen for the board that year. As I noted, one of the few meetings that was not open to all was an informal gathering open only to women of color, suggesting the desire to ensure that women felt safe and respected.

Perhaps more to the point was the interactional reality that being male was a marked category within the group. Staff and members would refer to things that males did, whereas female behavior was assumed. A mundane, but revealing, example occurred at a meeting where I selected a seat at our U-shaped table. Later a second man arrived and, finding that most seats on the other side of the table were filled, sat on my side. Sharon, a staff member, joked, "The men are all on one side." Jane immediately responded that she was on that side too and that the other seats were taken. She was sensitive to the possibility that these seating choices might be seen as deliberate. On another occasion, I attended a small meeting with only Jane and three other men, since others had canceled. Jane remarked, "We're kind of small today. Jane and the men" (field notes).

This notability of male presence was also evident when Dan was hired. Jane announced at an organizational meeting, "He will start in January." Davey, chairing the meeting, emphasized, so that no one missed the point, "He." On another occasion a female senior commented, "He's very young." Another added, provoking laughter, "And a man." A third said, "We need that." A fourth, referring to Sharon, an unmarried longtime staffer, teased, "Sharon is thinking of him." To which Sharon quickly changed the implication: "He'll allow us to make better coffee." Through this conversation, one sees the salience of gender in an organization that is ostensibly open to all but is dominated by women.

It's not only coffee that matters, but cake too. On two occasions males' cutting a cake, a traditional female responsibility, was commented on, mundane as the chore might otherwise be. At a farewell party for one of the staff, Henry Dowdall, a senior leader, started to cut the cake and, as if to note the gender-inversion quality of his act, announced to the group, "The dude is going to do it" (field notes). At another going-away party it was Dan who had cake-cutting duties, and one of the female seniors joked, "It's so manly that you're cutting the cake." These were light moments, of course, but revealing in their triviality.

Despite these occasional comments, gender balance was not treated as an organizational priority. Indeed, Jane, despite her sensitivity to issues of gender, would routinely refer to "you guys," even in gatherings that were all female. "Guy" was treated not as an "insidious" form of gender bias,[30] but as neutral. In contrast to issues of race, Jane conceded that gender was rarely an explicit source of tension and that she hoped to hire qualified men as staff members when possible, even if, she claimed, men could dominate meetings.

Pronoun Wars

During my observations at Chicago Seniors Together, there was little in the way of sharp internal dispute. Public disagreements were mild and short-lived. Some debates occurred about racial politics and about single-payer health care, but in general members either agreed with progressive orthodoxy or didn't push the point. Perhaps this was the rare community in which a harmonious group culture reigned as seniors were happy to have a place to be, to lead, and to be led. If not satisfied, they could exit without cost. This bolstered an interaction order that shied away from contentious discussions, avoiding the image of grumpy seniors.

By the end of my research this harmony had been overturned on occasion, and the issue on which conflict emerged was revealing in light of the lived experience and selfhood of seniors: the politics of pronouns.

The debate involved LGBTQQIIA+ identity (one gay member, Henry Dowdall, who used this lengthy acronym, spoke of the "Alphabet Soup Community"). During my thirty months of observation I heard nothing that would qualify as homophobic, perhaps because sexuality was invisible as a topic. Henry hoped we would all be "As," or Allies; members agreed that we were. Although I didn't take a survey, I doubt that any member of the group rejected same-sex marriage or employment equity. Even with regard to Trans identity, most of the seniors had an attitude of live and let live, perhaps rolling their eyes and worrying about the pace of social change since their youth or the choices their grandchildren might make. Some might have been dismayed, but they were silent. These were not the issues that set off the battle over pronouns.

As a university faculty member, I was familiar with some students' preference for using "they" as a singular pronoun to reveal their gender fluidity: neither "he" nor "she" fits easily in the context of multiple selves. I confess that when I first learned of this apparent assault on traditional grammar I was guilty of some eye rolling, but I quickly got with the program, and today the option feels legitimate. However, many senior activists admitted that this "pronoun business" was new to them and not appealing. One confessed, "my grandson couldn't believe I didn't know," and some members giggled at the use of the plural pronoun. In an organization that prized cohesion, this linguistic alteration led to a communal altercation.

The issue arose when the CST decided to hire a staffer, Denise, who wished to be referred to as "they." (They presented themselves as female and were biologically female. Because of their name, I've selected a female pseudonym.)[31] In preparation for their hiring, members of the organization were instructed about this preference. So far, so good. There were no complaints, whatever their private feelings. However, beginning with Denise's employment, we were asked to announce *our own* "pronoun preference" at meetings. The group agreements, described in chapter 5, were amended to include, "Respect people's gender pronouns."

For seniors not exposed to the gender politics of the young, discovering that one could be "gender fluid," "nonbinary," or "transgender" and could select a favored pronoun was a novel experience and, for some, disconcerting. This was a group in which jocular "sex talk" was rare, and while one might legitimately speak of a spouse, a partner, or being gay or lesbian, more explicit talk about sexuality was absent, even though some seniors enjoy intimate relations. I don't believe I heard anyone refer to having a "lover." A politics of the erotic characterizes many social movements,[32] and its absence is revealing. Senior activism tends to be platonic in its public display. But the issue went deeper than an unwillingness to discuss sexuality. For these seniors, gender was unambiguous. Like race, it was not subject to negotiation: it was who one was. As one senior declared, "My name defines me. I'm a woman [*laughs*]." The repeated requirement to announce one's gender undercut a stable identity. As a novelty, such a request would have been tolerated, but the continuing demand led to resentment over calling into question what should be visible through physiognomic cues, dress, and naming practices.

The demand to announce one's pronoun at the start of every meeting did not go over well and perhaps contributed to resentment of Denise. Could Denise be respected in their choices while the solidified gender order, taken for granted by seniors, was preserved? Some members, such as Henry, spoke movingly in support of the practice of pronoun naming, telling his colleagues, "We want to respect people. We want people to feel comfortable. I know there is a lot of nervous laughter. This is all about respect. I'm going to make mistakes. You're going to make mistakes." In fact it did not make people comfortable, perhaps not even Denise, who became the center of attention. In Jane's words, "It's been uncomfortable for me, but language is about respect" (field notes). Did it contribute to respect? One of the few truly supportive members noted,

> I do see a little bit of difficulty there during our regular meetings when we're requested to state our gender pronouns. But the whole nation is still trying to figure out their position on that. That's all new for everybody, but they will overcome that once we learn that it's not just the sex of a person. I think everybody still needs a little bit more training on attitudes on gender identification. (Interview)

Many claimed they didn't mind sharing their expected pronouns, even if it seemed unnecessary as a repeated ritual, but a significant number considered routinely announcing their preferred pronouns unnecessary or even offensive, apart from accepting Denise's choice. Even those who professed not to mind were lukewarm in support. Denise might have been better served had their pronoun choice been presented without asking seniors to share what seemed obvious.[33] As I noted, announcing preferred pronouns did not occur just once or twice but was demanded at dozens of meetings, even after Denise had left the organization. The ostensible goal was to make sure "everyone feels comfortable, safe, and heard."[34] Aside from Denise I heard only one member prefer "they, them, their," but he added, "I'm usually with my girlfriend. We do everything together." His "theyness" might have announced his membership in a couple.

As an observer, I found the challenge to an unspoken interaction order revealing. Would this overturn set patterns of relations—the routine circuit of action-especially in an organization where women held much of the power? Further, this was a change that the membership as a whole had not agreed on and that many believed the staff had pushed through without buy-in from senior leaders, raising concern over who controlled the organization.[35]

Some seniors explicitly resisted defining their categorical identities. Critics raised explicit objections such as "I remain opposed to the gender pronoun issue," "I'm not comfortable with that," "I hate pronouns," and "I don't want to say what pronoun I like." Others responded, "she, we," "she, hers, its," "I'm a she or her. Whatever," "You can call me whatever you want," or "Just call me Eric." In this last case Eric was pushed to announce a pronoun, and eventually he did under duress, which he repeated at several meetings. Although his protest could have been ignored, the demands continued. He needed to recognize that he must choose a gender identity, something that would never have been demanded had the issue been race. The reference to "announcing our pronouns" suggested that we have an option in our gender, something many seniors doubted.

The issue of pronouns became a central topic of informal discussion, raised privately outside meetings, with one member asking (and answering), "What do you think about the pronouns? I still have deep reservations about it" (field notes). Others found it "goofy" or "silly" or noted that "it bugs me." Several members, all women, were particularly aggrieved. After several weeks their frustration and anger broke out.

The meeting was run by a young staff intern, Becca, who asked us each provide to our pronouns. [Denise was not present.] Three of the attendees were particularly upset. One ignored the request, but Judith made a point of saying, "I'm just Judith Walsh. I think it's stupid. We're over seventy. We know what we are." Lauren adds, "I am what I am." and The third person who had ignored the request said, "I don't like the gender thing." Henry explained, "I'd say to you that pronouns matter. It's important and a form of respect. I'm willing to discuss that in a civil way. It's like forty years ago when we changed from Mrs. and Miss to Ms." This did not persuade them or reduce tension (field notes).

Even after a year it was hard for many members to justify the need for *announcing* pronouns other than to suggest "respect" or "inclusion." Perhaps most significant, given the politics of the group as a site of collective action, was that one woman said, "I prefer we, our, us." Her point, important for social movement activism, was passed over.

Why should this matter? Several issues combined, including a linkage of identity politics and staff-member power dynamics. The second element was as important as the first. I was not present when the decision was made to demand that members state their pronouns, but it was widely believed by members—even by influential leaders—that the decision came from the staff. Some believed staff members manipulated the senior leaders. Perhaps Jane as executive director made the proposal, then "heard" leaders agree. At no point did I hear a senior leader take ownership of the plan, and for some the dissatisfaction was part of the tension between staff and members that I described in chapter 5. This complaint was raised in several interviews: "I don't really know where this thing on gender came in. It certainly wasn't something that I thought we voted on. . . . I'm not going to do it because Jane tells me to do it. If I do it, it's going to be because I choose to do it." "That's an issue that's been brought up by staff members. . . . We're supposed to be a grassroots organization. It didn't come from membership. A motion has never been made to do that, it has never been voted on or anything like that, and I have a problem with that" (interviews). One staff member admitted, "That certainly didn't come from members" (interview).

In a board meeting Jane, annoyed at the controversy that distracted the group from its activist goals, commented,

> The committee said, "Let's hire Denise and let's start using pronouns." . . . People have said, "This is stupid. This is coming from staff." It's hard to be in a meeting and to be disrespected when people feel like that. I want to challenge you as board members. I want you to say this is coming from the board and the organization. . . . We're saying to the people, "This is right; this is important." It wasn't staff members, it was the board. (Field notes)

Unaware that he'd been named as a sponsor, one board member expressed his own reservations:

> I'm in that group right now that's doing a little pushback. I've never had to give that much thought, and I do know things are changing as the new millennials have come along and things are changing in that respect. [It] just felt uncomfortable to say that I have to identify who I am. Maybe somebody else feels strongly about it, but I shouldn't, just like they feel strong about identifying what they want to be called, but I feel just as strong in not wanting to say how I want to be called. . . . I'm a man, so I would assume you're going to call me my name [*laughs*]. (Interview)

Although in our interview Jane insisted the idea came from members, in retrospect she added:

> I think we probably made a mistake by saying, "Give us your pronouns." That was, I think, our fault. Denise said to me recently, "I think if people don't want to give their pronouns, we shouldn't force them to, but I think for people who want to do their pronouns that we should." And that's what we said. So I think we had a fault in that too, so I get that. But I think what was interesting is [that] instead of anybody coming to me and saying, "I have a huge issue with this. Help me understand it," that was not happening. (Interview)

The internal resistance was ignored or downplayed, and many seniors expressed privately that any direct opposition would only damage their own reputation. I heard no complaints about Denise's own choice of pronouns, even if some people were surprised or confused. (One asked innocently if Denise referred to themselves as "it.") A senior leader confided, "I will never actually understand it, but I do it" (interview). As one critic commented (hypothetically) about a supporter,

> If Henry says that he's not a he or he may come with a wig and a skirt on, I don't care. I'm going to work for his housing; I'm not going to discriminate against him. But I don't need to go through that exercise. It's a waste of time in my view. I probably hurt people's feelings when I say that. Judith is more vocal than I am. . . . She said, "I don't care what your gender is. Be what you want to be. That's your right. I'm not going to discriminate [against] you, but don't have me go through this silly exercise." (Interview)

What was at issue was not so much the time taken as the sudden change in the group culture, style of interaction, and authority structure, all altered without consent and enforced without much persuasion. The level of agreement by members was never clear, but it was taken as a significant challenge to what had been obvious: gender identity. For some this was simply a case of conforming and being agreeable; for others it was being au courant or, as one said, "I'm a senior, but I sure want to stay above the curve. I want to be able to move with the traffic!" (interview). For still others, it shook their sense of reality.

Once Denise left the organization, the exercise became less frequent and less controversial. However, setting aside the awkwardness of its introduction, the contention emphasized that one cannot shake identities and alter practices too far and too fast from shared understandings and unconsidered routines. In time "they" may become as taken for granted as Ms., accepted as a form of identity and inclusiveness and largely unconsidered. The greater issue is whether assumptions of fixed identity will change.

Diversities

Although social movement organizations might conceive of themselves as changing the world to benefit everyone with improved justice and fairness, there are those who benefit and those who do not. Resources are inevitably redistributed as society shifts, whether these are explicitly material resources or symbolic ones such as respect and cultural control. However, in addition to the outcomes, we must consider the authority of those who fight for such changes, a salient point in a divided polity. These identity battles are central to activist agendas, not only for seniors but in all groups.

In this chapter I have analyzed the implications for Chicago Seniors Together of divisions based on class, race, gender, and gender expression. As has become clear, there are dimensions that matter more and those that matter less in formulating a just senior community. For some the salience of one's placement is clear (race or gender), and for others it is obscure or implicit (class, gender expression). Each group has its associated politics and its interactional demands.

For the CST, issues of gender and class—one explicitly recognized and one not—are managed without much conflict or concern. Each member is presumably part of the same community—a community that embraces a demand for all to receive social justice. I found little conflict over the roles of men and women as long as men were perceived as not dominating. Since class privilege was not raised directly, it was assumed that members of the group were, in the words of Martin Luther King, all in the same boat, gazing from a distance at those aboard yachts. The very wealthy were treated as a distant evil or as cartoonish buffoons. The idea of the billionaire was a cultural construct—menacing, but perhaps amusing. All members agreed that billionaires (and sometimes millionaires) had to contribute what was framed as their fair share, contributions they attempted to avoid.

Gender expression was not taken as being a problem as long as it remained personal. Members tolerated others' choices, but they assumed that their own gender preferences were so obvious and stable that they didn't need to be stated. Being forced to express one's preferred pronouns undercut the stability of seniors' gender identity and made some people resentful.

Race in contemporary America is inevitably problematic, even in groups that claim the mantle of antiracism. In saying this I do not suggest that the organization was in turmoil. Several Black members were fully accepted and greatly admired. Whites were not challenged on their personal beliefs. However, in several ways race was a dangerous topic. Should the organization be assumed to be racially enlightened, or is the CST—and are other predominantly White organizations—a proper target for racial criticism? Should a group in which most members are White be permitted to be a racialized (White) organization? The hope is that it should not, but analysis might well find structural bias that potentially undercuts mutual trust. Further, should the organization proactively attempt to recruit and retain a racially diverse membership? When is an organization large enough or resource-rich enough to expand beyond its "natural" geographical base?

Finally, race blindness. What is it? Can it be defined, much less achieved? If the answer depends on not "seeing" skin color, this is clearly impossible, despite the dreams—and claims—of some informants. But even the possibility of ignoring race as a category has been discounted, given the awareness of structural racism: racism without racists.[36] Today most organizations—even corporate or conservative ones—display a multihued array of faces that advertises how open they are, suggesting that the belief in race blindness has been replaced by an explicit commitment to racial inclusion, however imperfect the process.

Ultimately, even though a progressive social movement should be all for one and one for all, such a goal is questionable in a world where we recognize that categories have power in distributing resources, reputation, and respect. Demographic categories matter not in themselves, but because, if divisions can be overcome, they provide structures of interaction, cultural beliefs about the organization of society, and agreements on how change—and whose change—can occur.

The Nexus of Politics

Politics is the art of preventing people from taking part in affairs that properly concern them.

PAUL VALÉRY

If not politically engaged, what purpose do social movement groups serve? They are tiny publics (and sometimes larger ones) that operate within broader political fields, contributing to a civil society that is robust, if occasionally contentious. But this is what democracies require, and it is recognized by scholars who emphasize that social movements strategize and act in light of the opportunities and constraints provided by more extended political structures.[1]

Tiny publics are not islands of agitation: they are found in vast, roiling seas. This perspective is integral to the approach that focuses on how groups of committed actors claim authority in political opportunity structures. However, the nature of this larger field, its functions, and its predictive power can be obscure and subjective. This vagueness points to the structure of political institutions and to the openings for influence they provide.[2] While valuable, this is insufficient for an approach that focuses on how groups create action fields and how relational structures are dynamic, not static.[3]

This perspective takes into account local circumstances and practices of sociality. Small groups must strategize to be noticed; often they are ignored. These tiny publics respond to opportunity structures when they frame them as accessible, as closed, or as oppositional. The challenge for small movements is whether more powerful institutions can be shaped and, if so, which leveraging tactics prove most effective.

While the embrace of policy proposals might appear to be a cognitive process, weighing the advantages and the disadvantages of change, in reality—and in the case I am examining—participants are heavily invested through compassion toward those who are suffering. Social movements are story worlds. Every movement develops a sense of organizational self in order to participate in a political surround. That self must accord with other organizational selves.

To demonstrate the political embeddedness of the CST and its role as an engaged public, I draw on the way its group culture and its interactional style permit forms of political engagement, examining how the organization addresses issues of housing, inequality, and health care and establishes relations with political figures and groups, both supportive and conflictual. During the research, the CST chose to become more explicitly electoral by establishing a "sister organization." This involved creating a linked 501(c)(4) group (United Chicago Seniors in Action) that could engage in partisan politics, since it was not tax-exempt. This left Chicago Seniors Together, as a tax-exempt 501(c)(3) organization, to engage in issue advocacy. Aside from the relationship established between these two groups, they required different funding streams.

I then consider how the election of Donald Trump altered the CST's orientation to activism, refining participants' relations with those who reject their beliefs. Finally, I describe the difficulties the CST faced as a senior activist organization within a relational network of allies that should be sensitive to issues of age, both as policy and as practice, but that often, because of its audiences, routines, and cultures, ignored these concerns, causing problems for collaborative activism. As viewed by seniors, these affronts lessened the effectiveness of a multiage coalition.

Housing and Health

During my observations, Chicago Seniors Together was, in effect, three movements in one. One focused on housing, emphasizing local and even hyperlocal issues. A second focused more on national issues, including health care, economic justice, and preserving and expanding Social Security. The third focused on developing relationships with legislators and, after the creation of United Chicago Seniors in Action, on engagement in the political process, supporting, planning to endorse, and influencing politicians in their electoral campaigns.[4]

HOUSING AS LOCAL WORK

Of the three areas, housing policy—both influencing city policy and improving local senior housing projects—proved the most successful at generating change. It was the domain that involved more members of color and those with fewer resources. The fight for affordable senior housing was a progressive policy demand that could produce positive change in that most decisions were made on the local level where decision makers could be pressured or engaged. Further, it was a demand that was less ideological, even when it faced pushback from developers, property owners, and government agencies.

Housing activism was in line with the mandate of Alinsky-style community organizing. These demands supported the belief that a movement should focus on "winnable" projects. Building managers and landlords made tempting targets.[5] No matter their true motivations, their actions could be framed as prioritizing profit over people. The painful stories of needy residents were personal and powerful. As Jane Tate recognized, "Housing work is very intense for us" (field notes). During my observations the CST achieved several victories. Some organizations, including religious groups, hoped to force seniors to leave their apartments so the owners could rent to different tenants or could gentrify or demolish the building. What had been senior housing might become a mixed-age, mixed-income project with higher rents. In housing units owned by Moody Bible Institute, a conservative Christian college, the CST was able to gain a commitment for a twenty-year extension for affordable senior housing. Jane remarked sarcastically about the Moody leaders, "We care deeply about our seniors. . . . Yeah, yeah. We don't trust Moody. We don't trust anyone until the contract is signed." Another senior housing project that had been affiliated with the more liberal Presbyterian Church was sold to the Chicago Housing Authority. Jane commented that their protests affected the denomination: "Donors stopped giving money, and they changed the name [from Presbyterian Homes]. . . . Getting publicity and making the owner look bad" (field notes). Religious organizations were ripe targets, since moral rhetoric was effective and these organizations needed a positive public image tied to their faith-based principles. These owners were thus vulnerable to pressure from a values-based campaign.

In these local issues the CST pointed to "policy wins," demonstrating that it had power to improve the lives of the needy elderly. As one senior explained, "everything starts with housing." Housing, along with nursing home reform, was the heart and soul of the organization. Narratives about evictions, broken fixtures, promised renovations, dilapidated hallways, and danger from drug sellers and gang members sparked horror. However, beyond their narrative power, given the will and resources these problems could be fixed.

Even when the organization dealt with the Chicago Housing Authority and the City Council, battling over the "Keeping the Promise" ordinance to demand that surpluses be used to improve affordable housing, these problems had a set of local actors with the power to provide solutions. When problems were solved, the CST notched up a victory and gained the gratitude of community residents. The group had numerous organizing projects in senior buildings. At one point in spring 2016, the CST was agitating in seventeen buildings. The goal was to "get buildings" and then to work with interested seniors on residents' councils to demand changes. For these seniors, Chicago Seniors Together demonstrated that they had power.

HEALTH CARE AS A NATIONAL CONCERN

The Health Care and Economic Justice Committee appealed to the middle-class supporters of the CST who cared about broader public policy issues, even though the committee also included members who struggled finan-cially. Although this small organization had no immediate effect on federal welfare policies, it could potentially establish momentum for change within a national coalition.

The advantage that Health Care and Economic Justice has over Housing is that these demands, less achievable in the short term, reach a wider audi-ence. These issues generate well-attended actions and serve—as I discuss later in this chapter—as opportunities to collaborate with a progressive network.

As a result, broad policy issues such as Medicare for All were distinct from most housing demands in which local organizations such as Chicago Seniors Together were perceived as legitimate negotiators. National demands, how-ever, can be conceived as a means to recruit and involve members; the pres-ence of local groups advertises the movement's vision, even if aspirational.

ISSUE POLITICS

The third domain of Chicago Seniors Together involved participation in poli-tics. During this research, I watched the organization reconfigure itself dur-ing spring 2016 by establishing a political 501(c)(4) sister organization, United Chicago Seniors in Action (UCSIA).

When I began the research, the CST maintained connections with sup-portive politicians—progressive Democrats—and with other officeholders who could potentially be helpful. Conservatives could be targets just as long as the pressure focused on issues rather than partisan electoral support. There was never doubt that the members of the CST supported progressive Demo-cratic candidates, although they were careful to separate their issue-oriented advocacy from political endorsement. The fear of being outed by political op-ponents might have been exaggerated, but they took seriously their position as a tax-exempt organization.

Before turning to the creation of United Chicago Seniors in Action, I consider Chicago Seniors Together's often fraught relations with politicians.

The mantra of Alinsky-inspired social movements is "no permanent friends, no permanent enemies." Everything depends on the particular issue. This is perhaps rhetorically too easy, since it would be hard to imagine an issue on which the CST considered President Trump a friend, no matter what his position, and it was recognized that progressive legislators sometimes needed to compromise for strategic reasons.

Still, connecting with politicians over value-based issues is central to demonstrating the organization's influence. In the 2019 city elections, Chicago elected a progressive mayor, Lori Lightfoot, and several progressive aldermen. While certain politicians were admired, the most respected was Congresswoman Jan Schakowsky, whose congressional district included much of the North Side of the city. She was considered a close ally: as one described her, "our most important person." As I wrote, this was evident at the Senior Power Assembly. Several politicians were invited, but only Congresswoman Schakowsky attended. The ostensible goal was to "hold these politicians' feet to the fire," but she spoke without interruption and was loudly applauded.

However, the desire to pressure politicians did not vanish, and it often was directed at Congressman Michael Quigley—whom members of the organization derided as "Wiggly Quigley" or "Squiggly Quigley"—a liberal, pragmatic Democrat representing the less progressive northwest quadrant of the city. Even though Quigley met with representatives of Chicago Seniors Together on several occasions and typically voted for liberal policies, he became a target as they hoped—without success during my research—to have him co-sponsor bills supporting Medicare for All. (He later announced his support, and perhaps the CST can take some credit for his change.) Given the number of its members in his district, the CST pushed him to become a "progressive voice." They demonstrated outside his congressional offices during what was described as "Quigley accountability month." As Jane suggested,

> We need to show him our power before we have another meeting with him. We haven't done enough work in his district to put pressure on him. If you have another demonstration of two or three people, it's not going to work. . . . In six months you want him to sign on to the Conyers [Medicare for All] bill. Five or six people are not going to move him. (Field notes)

Davey Gibbs replied, "We need an action at his office to embarrass him." Then Jane added, "Power is that [he] will vote with us. [He] should want to meet with us because we are important people." The question was, How could they become a public that mattered to politicians? Consideration was given to holding a raucous demonstration outside the Catholic church the congressman attended. Eventually only small protests were held. I attended several in which we marched in a tight circle on a deserted side street outside his office and handed his staffers a list of demands and postcards of support. It was very civilized, but not notably effective in creating tension between the congressman and these few frustrated constituents. The project never generated deep anger. I attended a meeting that seven members were scheduled to attend; six canceled.

Most of CST's connections with politicians were distant. Even Illinois's liberal and powerful Democratic senator, Richard Durbin, was occasionally attacked, with Richie Douglas fuming, "Senator Durbin does not stand up for seniors." The skepticism toward politicians was central to the organizational culture. As Dan warned the members of the Housing Committee, "Do you want to know what [politicians] say or what they really believe?" The two were treated as inherently distinct. Members supposed that politicians lacked fixed beliefs and would change their votes if activists showed their power—the failed plan for the Senior Power Assembly. What mattered for motivating politicians (at least liberal ones) was not their values but gaining the support of their most influential constituents.

The problem from the standpoint of the staff was that seniors were too deferential to politicians, who were considered local celebrities. The staff tried to encourage members to be less respectful, expressing their "inner anger." This was difficult given the emotional habitus of seniors, who could be cranky but rarely irate. Seniors were pushed to reject the claim of one seemingly friendly city official who explained, as reported: "You need to be flexible. [He said], you have my cell phone. You don't need a policy." It seemed like a victory, even though the staff treated it as a defeat. At a staff meeting, Sharon explained about eighty-year-old Hazel Windblatt, "Hazel has a long way to go on being firm." Perhaps this politician was sincere, but the staff was not impressed.

Seniors had to learn, at least according to the staff and the more confrontational members, that apparently sincere words from politicians must be backed by a commitment to act, otherwise they were just being patronized. Sympathy was not wanted.[6] However, even young staff could be cowed at times. Lynnette, an intern, admitted how nervous she was before meeting with a disfavored alderman about progressive housing policies. Jane assured her, "We're not going to let him scare us. I've been involved in meetings with assholes all the time" (field notes). Even a Democratic politician, although one who does not support all of the CST's desired policies, can be typified as an asshole. This was the default image of politicians.

MOVEMENT POLITICS

To this point I have discussed how Chicago Seniors Together engaged with politicians over issues. This approach was necessary as a tax-exempt 501(c)(3) organization. Despite defining itself as having an oppositional consciousness, it carefully followed the government's rules to preserve its status. The tax code suppressed bitter partisan rhetoric.

However, by spring 2016 the staff and some members felt constrained by these rules and, while still obeying the regulations, wanted to become more directly involved in campaigns. The CST desired a role in electoral politics, a plan encouraged by observing allied organizations with a similar structure, a form of organizational isomorphism[7] developed over two years of organizational education. By June 2016, after approval by the CST Board of Directors and support at membership meetings, they established United Chicago Seniors in Action.

The decision was not uncontroversial, even though most members came to support this second, related organization with a different mandate and without tax-exempt status. However, justification was necessary, since the new organization challenged the group's long-standing culture and issue-oriented priorities.

As was often the case, meetings were not structured for back-and-forth discussion. At a meeting to discuss the formation of UCSIA, Richie, as chair, asked, "How many of you want to build senior power? [We dutifully raised our hands, and he did not call for negative votes.] How many of you believe that Chicago Seniors should have a c4? [We all agreed despite private doubts, since there was no opportunity for debate.] We know we will have power when we start working on elections in the fall." At another meeting, leaders engaged in some brief role-playing (jokingly referred to as "the first performance of United Chicago Senior Players"). The first skit showed the limits of the c3 in being unable to persuade a politician, and the second showed the power of the c4 in pressuring that politician to agree when facing a politicized public. When Jane asked, "Which one showed more power?" the answer was obvious. Likewise, a hired consultant explained that other organizations had made the same choice, "A 501(c)(4) is like a tool in a toolbox. . . . The more tools in our toolbox, the more power we can build" (field notes). Who wouldn't want another tool? Here, as elsewhere, power is the group's grail, allowing them to matter. Angela Knight, an African American senior stalwart, explained, "It's important because unless we hold our politicians' [feet] to the fire, they're not going to do anything. If we don't let them know that we want more, we're not going to get it" (interview).

Despite this surface consent, the decision to establish a sister organization was concerning, even if staff direction and member buy-in eventually pushed it through. The opposition raised was not that partisan activity was wrong, but rather that the small organization did not have the capacity to do both advocacy and endorsement: a choice was necessary.[8] Some worried that as a non-tax-exempt organization UCSIA would diminish the CST's fundraising prospects. The hope was that UCSIA money would come from different streams, such as the political arm of supportive labor unions.

Although the staff and leaders eventually were persuasive, concern lasted over both its practicality and its appropriateness. Even after UCSIA's establishment, some members believed the organization lacked sufficient capacity; others thought it diluted the organization's core mission; still others were bothered that endorsing candidates might seem controlling in a democratic organization and might make those who supported different politicians feel uncomfortable and even ostracized. One core member expressed her concern: "Now we can endorse candidates, but we are not a large enough organization for that to make much difference. At the moment, I think that nobody quite knows what to do with it, and we don't quite know how to fund it" (interview).

In time these concerns were overcome, and the UCSIA became accepted as potentially increasing organizational power.

BOUNDARY WORK

In chapter 3 I described how the first attempt at making an endorsement in the gubernatorial election of 2018 failed. This was an effort to gain power by extending what the organization could do. Members of Chicago Seniors Together thought they needed a weapon to influence politicians. Without this, staffers believed it was imperative to avoid anything that might be considered partisan. Yet the boundary was hazy, particularly for those who simply wanted to "do politics" without worrying about the line between advocating for an issue and supporting a candidate. As Richie pointed out, "A lot of people still don't understand. There's a lot of confusion, [even though] there's some overlap" (field notes). Jane was correct in saying, "I can't tell you how many members have wanted us to do things, but we couldn't" (field notes). When Dr. Ben Golden wrote a poem—a poem!—attacking Republican candidates, Jane explained firmly that he could not read it aloud in the office. Only after the meeting could I enjoy his partisan poesy. Given the possibility of surveillance, it was essential to establish "firewalls to protect the c3."

Two related organizations could blur each other's goals. One way the tax-exempt group was protected from possible charges of "contamination," as I noted previously, was that the partisan c4 organization paid somewhat more than necessary to the c3 for staff salaries, hoping to diminish the likelihood that the latter would be audited or have its tax-exempt status removed. As Jane explained it, "We'd rather be cautious by paying a little too much money."

The boundary between the two groups proved hazy, and some members, even leaders, did not feel they understood much about the new organization. One CST leader expressed this concern: "I haven't gotten much feedback from United Chicago Seniors. . . . I think it's a good idea. But, like I said, I haven't really heard any feedback as to how much progress we've made since the starting up of it" (interview).

This confusion was partially a function of the interorganizational divide that was legally required. The "two organizations"—twinned tiny publics— were legally separate, with distinct boards of directors and only a small overlap permitted. Their actions needed to be cleanly separated, even to the extent of wearing different T-shirts (blue for the c3 and yellow for the c4). The funds were kept in separate bank accounts, not commingled. Seniors had to join each organization separately, although they received a discount for joining both. Further, although the CST held joint meetings of the Housing and Health Care committees, the Movement Politics Committee met on a different day, reducing attendance. The staffs were identical, though staffers had to keep careful records of how long they worked on projects for each organization. Rules defined which computer programs could be used for particular projects. Their Voter Activation Network was to be used only for issue-oriented calls. The boundaries were complex and sometimes required legal advice. As a result, they created a list of "c4/c3 Do's and Don'ts." As Jane reminded the staff, fearing their actions might be filmed, "Making even small mistakes can have really big implications. . . . People are trying to stop us" (field notes). As a result, one staffer pointed out ahead of time that an action must not be seen as a "c4" event. "If the media spokesman says anything about endorsement, that could really affect our tax status" (field notes). When the CST wanted to support or oppose candidates, it had to do so implicitly.

This division underlines how movements are constrained and channeled by government regulations. In fighting for progressive values, issues, and candidates, perhaps there is no bright line except that created by government policy. Yet this policy matters because opponents are willing to strike if they discover a violation. Firm procedures preclude such attacks. Even though these errors may be of no great consequence or may have resulted from naive enthusiasm, in a contentious political environment they can have consequences. Partisanship and policies must be kept at arm's length in the movement world, even if not in legislative chambers.

Chasms and Silos

My research extended from September 2015 to February 2018. Although it was not expected—and certainly was not planned—November 2016 provided a dramatic break in how Chicago Seniors Together responded to politics. Although United Chicago Seniors in Action was created before the presidential election of 2016 and led to the possibility of partisan involvement, the election shaped the movement. A community primarily focused on local issues, especially senior housing, now was pressured to respond to the national political scene. Having lived under both Democratic and Republican administrations over the course of decades, these seniors found the Trump administration something new—and it terrified many of them. This was not the swing from moderate liberalism to moderate conservativism that they had experienced before. Some members were afraid it might overturn the core national consensus on Social Security and Medicare. Many with roots in the civil rights struggles feared that racism would characterize this White House through "dog whistles" or bullhorns.

In the weeks after the election, I watched an influx of new members, often middle-class women appalled by the words, attitudes, and policies of the new president. For many, hatred of Trump would not be too strong a description. These joiners were less concerned with housing, despite being generally supportive of CST goals; they wanted a platform to express their animus toward President Trump. They needed an outlet for their emotions by attending a rally or two rather than doing the hard work of community organizing. Over time many fell away, and by 2019 attendance at meetings was not so different from attendance in 2015. An Alinsky-type organization is not about speaking one's mind or chanting slogans but about slogging through hard work. Resist Trump Tuesdays, thrilling in the winter of 2017, lost their charm as they became routine.

Still, movement engagement is a form of emotion work, and hatred for our newly elected leader inflamed—or perhaps infected—the organization, in part because of the unexpected outcome. Shortly after President Trump's victory, Barb Greene reflected, "I'm so angry, but I'm also fearful." Luisa, a staffer, remarked, "I don't have four years or eight years to take action. We're in crisis mode." Others added, "We can't wait to next year" (field notes). Using emotions to create affiliation and immediacy, seniors referred to the policies of Nixon and Reagan in understanding the conservatism of Donald Trump.

Although the list of hostile comments could fill the rest of the chapter, I'll present just a few quotations from interviews with senior activist leaders to give a sense of the intensity of feeling toward the Trump administration while also recalling the fierce opposition to George W. Bush, labeled by conservatives as "Bush Derangement Syndrome."[9] One leader expressed this sentiment by announcing, "I wanted to go through the television and strangle [Trump]." No one considered her reaction abnormal. In my interviews, others had similar reactions, often touching on racial justice, a central, defining value:

> He's such an ass. Do you really want me to say what I think? I think he's the lowest of the low. He's an immoral man. I do think he's a racist.

> He's a racist. I think he's anti-Semitic. He hates. He's a hateful person. I do think there is something mentally wrong with him. If he were to drop dead tomorrow, I wouldn't blink. This man is unconscionable. He's stupid. He has no knowledge of policy, of anything. He cares only about himself. Every characteristic of a narcissist, check off. . . . I can't even look at him. . . . We've never, ever had a president like this.

> The man is incompetent. He's a racist. I loathe him, and I'm ashamed to say that. I mean, I shouldn't hate people. I shouldn't loathe people, but this man is so destructive. I see him as evil.

One activist friend reported flatly, without evidence, that "he comes from a Nazi family." Others played off this extreme imagery: "What are we going to do about living in the United States, living with a fascist in the White House?" Some were afraid of the dictatorial policies they imagined President Trump might enact, as when Jane mused to the board shortly after the Inauguration, "We know people are scared. People are frightened" (field notes). These remarks provided a context in which bipartisan outreach became impossible.

But, as I noted, the 2016 presidential election and its surprising outcome increased involvement, even if that activism faded. One member, after a period of being unwilling to serve on the CST board, now consented, and Jane joked, "That's something you can thank Donald Trump for." After the election, the Movement Politics Committee met with some forty people attending, far above the usual dozen and considerably more energized. As Luisa commented, "We have a lot to discuss, fortunately or unfortunately." Richie added, "I want to say one good thing Trump has done. He has brought us together" (field notes). As another member pointed out, "People are much more fired up. Trump has lit a fire in everybody. Wow. I mean, the energy is so high, like it's never been before he was elected. I can see a difference, definitely a difference in energy" (interview).

Such a sharp sense of grievance and outrage can pose problems, preventing compromise. Given discussions about silos and social fields split by chasms, I wondered how tight their networks were and how closed their culture was. Could members escape their political silos? Would this tiny public cross ideological lines? Would they want to? In fact, many informants had family members with different opinions, including some devoted Trump loyalists. However, with few exceptions my informants did not enjoy political discussions with opponents. The chasm was simply too wide, the emotions too raw. Jeanne Hyde, a committed activist, was nearly unique:

> I have friends who voted for Trump. I'm not too sure how much politics we talk about, you know. I had one friend who thought I wouldn't like her anymore because she voted for Trump [*chuckles*]. I thought, "Oh my gosh, no. I don't care. That's your right to vote for whoever you want to." . . . I get things from Freedom Works. I get enough conservative stuff on my email that balances out what I get that's liberal. I think you ought to know what the enemy is [*laughs*] talking about. I don't watch Fox News, but I do read things that are not what I would call progressive. . . . I think we all want to progress; we don't want to be dinosaurs. But I also think there are things that are worth conserving, and I think sometimes we use those as pejorative words against one another. (Interview)

A few others felt like Richie Douglas: "I like a challenge. I always believe we can agree to disagree. It's always good to know what other people are thinking" (interview). But these views were a distinct minority. More common were those who tried to avoid political discussion or rejected it when it occurred. Consensus was desired; an alternative universe was not.

Many avoiders tried to change the subject when faced with "politically incorrect" relatives or neighbors. One member, notably, described his affection for his conservative brother but recognized a gap between their love and political discussions:

> My brother and I, because of the trajectories of our lives, the paths we took, he . . . has certain definite ideas about labor relations, about religious things as well, where I might differ. But I should be absolutely clear, my brother and I love each other profoundly. If there was a problem I'd be on the train or in the car and over to see him in a heartbeat. So yes, there are people that I have or friends that out of respect, mutual respect, we try to avoid the discussions [*chuckles*], and we stick to what we agree in common. (Interview)

In a similar vein, Stephanie Moore explained that she avoids discussions with her family, "I don't talk politics with them at all, because I wouldn't ever talk to them again." She finds discussing politics with those who disagree depressing and fears it might lead to losing a friend (interview). Esther Harvey had the same experience:

> My best friend, she was going to vote for Trump, and I was really bothered by it, and I had a discussion with her about all the negative things I saw in Trump. I don't know exactly what she ended up doing, but you know that definitely bothered me. I've seen people's friendships fall apart because they don't agree in terms of Trump, and I don't want that to happen to my friendships, so I just avoid the topic. (Interview)

Others take a more sharply critical view of these discussions. Trina Davis, a senior leader, said she avoids contentious arguments because they can quickly become offensive,

> I don't talk about Trump per se, but some of my family is very conservative and they voted for Trump, so I don't discuss politics with them because I don't want to get upset. One of my brothers called me last year about this time, and he started going on and on about stuff, and I just hung up on him. I said, "I can't talk about this anymore." [GAF: There are some people who love to argue.] Well, I sort of like to argue too, but I don't want to be told that the way I think is stupid. (Interview)

In contrast to senior members, often dependent on family relations, staff—perhaps because of their greater ideological commitment, because of their age, or because they live in a tighter bubble—have a more critical perspective on debates with those they disagree with, speaking in ways I never heard from seniors:

> My friends come from my circles, and my circles are pretty justice focused. . . . I wouldn't want to be friends with a Trump supporter, because they don't value the lives of people that are important to me. . . . I definitely live in a silo. That's very true. But also, at this point, if Trump is kind of a White supremacist and whether his followers think they are or not, they kind of are. I don't really want to be friends with them [*laughs*]. And I feel OK about that choice. (Interview)

> [GAF: Do you have conservative or pro-Trump friends?] No. [GAF: Is that by choice?] Yeah. [GAF: People talk about Americans being in silos. Some people will say part of the problem is that conservatives only listen to Fox News and only have conservative friends and progressives only listen to MSNBC and [only] have progressive friends.] We should be able to have some more overlap. But I choose not to be friends with people that support Trump because if they support Trump they support certain ideologies and those ideologies either lead to or directly contribute to the murder of my community. Whether

or not that's them being killed tomorrow or them just never really living good lives in general. (Interview)

These are somewhat extreme positions, and perhaps they are distressing for those who believe that democracy depends on open, free, and diverse communities, but they reveal that those most committed to social movements can, in effect, treasure being in a total institution in which one's position is so morally upstanding that a challenge is offensive. While this does not involve boundaries as strong as Erving Goffman suggests in his theory of total institutions such as mental hospitals or concentration camps,[10] the boundaries limit interaction. For these staffers, ideology and values lead to a powerful and internally consistent perspective. Remaining within one's bubble supports the belief in a just and ethical community, but it is also a luxury for those young people, who can make those choices. Seniors who rely on extended families often cannot do so.

The Network Surround

Every tiny public operates within a social ecology of related publics. This is particularly true of social movements that navigate a world of allies, rivals, and power brokers. Organizations create communities, just as individuals living in proximity do.[11] But this broader field requires integrating multiple cultures and styles of interaction. These may involve negotiations and trade-offs among ostensible allies. If the differences are unrecognized, a failure of coordination may result.[12]

In this section I describe the network of relations through which Chicago Seniors Together operated. Networks permit tiny publics to extend their reach, multiplying their impact by activating others. Like many effective, locally based social movements such as networks of housing advocates, the CST was connected to other groups.[13] As Jeffrey Stout points out with regard to Alinsky-oriented groups, "To be an [Industrial Areas Foundation] group is to be part of a network and to be held accountable not only by individuals participating in the group and by other persons, groups, and institutions with which the group interacts in its own community, but also by the representatives of other groups in the IAF network."[14]

Although allies can drain resources if the group members lack a personal stake in the proposed issues, they have the potential to add legitimacy by incorporating the presence, the experiences, and the voices of those directly affected.[15]

The CST belonged to a web of progressive groups that operates under the umbrella of People's Action, a recently formed national coalition of progressive groups headquartered in Chicago (thirty-seven organizations were listed on their website as of August 2020). Members of the CST attended their founding convention in Washington, DC, and People's Action held a political education workshop for seniors in Chicago. Like the CST, People's Action has a policy arm and a political action arm that engages in partisan activity.[16] Other more local connections existed, such as the Grassroots Collaborative, also based in Chicago with eleven community and labor-based affiliates, such as ONE Northside, an organization the CST had close ties with, and National Nurses United.[17] The CST also had tight relations with the Chicago Housing Initiative (CHI) to which they rented office space and with which they worked on senior housing activism. The CST also belonged to the economic justice coalition Fair Economy Illinois, which provided financial support and whose rallies members were encouraged to attend. Informal ties also existed with the Democratic Socialists of America, although there was no formal affiliation. Beyond this network, the CST hired staff who had held positions in local activist or community service groups such as Access Living (an advocacy group for people with disabilities) or ONE Northside. These groups were seen as providing excellent training for community organizing. The CST also received interns right out of college, supported by Avodah, a Jewish justice organization, and several of these women remained with the organization. Add to this, as I described in chapter 5, the progressive foundations and labor unions that provide funding that permits both the CST and the UCSIA to continue their work. There is a local progressive political infrastructure that Chicago Seniors Together participated in.

These alliances increased the organization's influence and reach. With the participation of multiple groups, demonstrations that might have been small and unnoticed, like Resist Trump Tuesdays, became sizable events covered by the media. Relationships build power, but they also create strains. As Jane pointed out when the board debated becoming a member of the Grassroots Collaborative (and contributing funds), "It will help us build our power. We will belong to a coalition of powerful groups. If it's not powerful, why would we join the group?" (field notes). The framing of "power" justified networking.

Network Tensions

Despite benefits, affiliating with network partners can dilute organizational focus, weakening a tight and well-articulated culture. A band of brothers becomes an orchestra with an uncertain conductor. The pressure to become involved in projects that others have chosen is strong, superseding one's own priorities. The tiny public based on local bonds of comradeship expands, sometimes valuably and sometimes in a way that is counterproductive. Further, coalition involvement often comes with financial obligations, as with the $1,000 contribution necessary for CST to join the Grassroots Collaborative network. As Esther points out,

> Your numbers speak, and so if you have allies it definitely speaks much louder than if we're just trying to do it ourselves; our number turnout wouldn't be as good. I was kind of amazed when we did that [civil disobedience protest] on Michigan [Avenue] at all the different groups that were there in support of that Moral Monday action. So, I think allies are very important. [GAF: Is there a problem because the different groups have different issues?] It's more of an inconvenience in some ways. There's one of the groups that's very much into climate issues, and we're not. We're not opposed to climate issues, but that's not a high priority for us; but we're partnered with that particular group. But I feel like the partnerships are important because it does give us more power. (Interview)

The challenge is how to balance diverse agendas, a challenge richly described by Paul Lichterman in his account of coordinating multiple groups among housing activists in Los Angeles.[18] Lacking a shared commitment, groups that might otherwise be sympathetic can find themselves in parallel, cliquish worlds. Gina Pirro, a skeptical friend, made this point effectively:

> We need to make the pie bigger. [GAF: How can you do that?] That's the one million dollar question. Reaching out to other community-based groups. The way I see an expansion since the 1970s and everyone seems to have their own little cocoon. The Poor People's campaign, that's one group. The Greens are another group. The Women's groups are another group. I wish there was a way for these different progressive groups to get together and work more cooperatively. I have seen cliques within progressive organizations. So the people that are your closest activists are people that you might go out to dinner with. Small, small groups, you know. (Interview)

Turf battles contribute to the strain of networking and creating coalitions. Who owns which issue and which activist? Staff worried about organizations "poaching" active and talented members, a reality when some core members chose to join organizations that focused on their neighborhood or their identity group, as happened with one prominent LGBTQ member. One staffer bemoaned the "turfiness" in Chicago, naming some ostensible allies as examples. Chicago Seniors Together, once a member of ONE Northside, had to carve out its own identity, leading to ongoing resentment. As Sharon, a key housing staffer, originally from California, pointed out,

I've noticed in Chicago there's a lot of turfiness. I think that could be better, but that it's important that we're in allyship, but I think it could probably be better. But that's also something that's always hard. [GAF: Can you give an example?] Just being able to work together on shared vision without . . . how am I trying to say this? I think sometimes we can get lost in the organizational desires of each organization rather than coming together. [GAF: Do we work sufficiently well with ONE Northside or Fair Economy Illinois?] ONE Northside. . . . I think there's also challenges-the way we're supposed to split up turf, for example, sometimes it feels like that's not respected. . . . ONE Northside is not supposed to be organizing in senior buildings, and sometimes that doesn't happen. But ONE Northside is not our enemy. We should be communicating well, but if they're getting more members that's good for us too. . . . Because sometimes there is this sense that we're trying to recruit other people's members. That's a common fear. (Interview)

Turf, a form of interpersonal and organizational real estate, can be a potent source of power, but it can antagonize those who are ostensibly on the same field, battling common opponents.

SENIOR STRAINS

As I noted, the CST belonged to several coalitions, but the challenge as an organization of seniors was how much influence they had in these coalitions *as seniors*. One staffer said these allies pushed them to support causes that the CST was philosophically in agreement with but that were distant from the core of the organization's agenda. For example, one problem in working with the People's Action coalition was that the leaders of the coalition did not originally consider affordable senior housing a major issue. Only after Chicago Seniors Together pushed in frustration was it added to the agenda, and People's Action eventually held a "hearing" on the topic in Washington, DC. As Jane pointed out, with justifiable pride, "Hopefully [the hearing will] raise awareness that affordable housing is a human right. . . . If we weren't there, we wouldn't get the credit for it" (field notes).

A staffer suggested that as far as she was concerned the direction of control in the coalition "really feels top down" from those elites that controlled the network—not ideal for a movement that should be driven by its grass roots. As Davey Gibbs pointed out, "We love our organizers, but this is run by people on the bottom" (field notes). Davey resented that decisions came from the "national office." The CST was told what the actions were to be, and they were supposed to fall in line without local consultation. They were no longer a tiny public, but a small fragment of a vast one. Members learned that the progressive budget the alliance was to present to Congress (the "People and Planet First" budget) was not a "work in progress" as senior member Ralph Phelps expected; rather, "This document is written in stone because this is a coalition budget." CST members played no role in producing it; they were expected just to be loyal followers. This was evident in the formulation of the Community Care proposal, an area where the CST could have made important contributions but lacked the authority to do so. Jane explained, "We need to be in the game and contribute to it. . . . They want us to support the [People's Action] coalition," even without involvement in drafting proposals. Their role was to be supportive, not to create policy. This was a source of irritation for senior members, even if they recognized the value of belonging to a broader movement whose extended power depended on the resources of powerful allies.

This problem was dramatically evident in the March to Springfield, which CST was not centrally involved in planning. Although some CST members attended planning meetings, the march had little to do with senior issues, and some members felt their voices were ignored. Likewise, in planning Resist Trump Tuesdays in collaboration with People's Action and MoveOn.org, each allied group was assigned a specific week. Each would have a policy theme (housing; Medicare; Social Security). Luisa commented, "There was a series of meetings. . . . This is not up for discussion. The decision was made to have a Resist Trump rally every Tuesday for the first hundred days" (field notes). Despite the overarching organizational structure, CST was able to choose its topic, in this case housing justice. As important as linking organizations might be, it removes authority from the local level and ignores the specific movement cultures of each group the coalition comprises. Are seniors, with their distinct needs and interests, a central part of the coalition? Do they make decisions, or do they merely follow orders? This leads to a consideration of the tensions involved in networking and alliances. A frustrated staffer, Denise, pointed out,

> I think it's strained, and it's not perfect at all. I think there's just like a lot more to prove as a senior organization in this way. That's not fair. I'm just thinking about the Fair Economy Illinois meetings that we had for the march to Springfield, and it was just hard to get our leaders to even be able to go to the meetings that they held because they were in the evenings. . . . They don't take us seriously. (Interview)

Given that most of those active in social movements are younger people, often engaged before establishing a family and settling on a career, can seniors be fully incorporated into meetings and actions, given their embodied and temporal needs? Organizations with distinct styles and cultures must be integrated in ways that fit each,[19] which is easier to want than to achieve in practice. These difficulties produced considerable annoyance, which was evident during a two-day training meeting organized by Fair Economy Illinois (FEI). Several CST attendees registered grievances and complained bitterly that seniors were disrespected. Perhaps this was not intentional, but it revealed that seniors were not considered in planning the event. Carrie Stanton, for instance, was given a large banner to hold, even though she used a wheelchair, making her participation difficult. Gina objected that there were no handouts and that the agenda sped by too rapidly. After hearing the complaints, Jane said of the FEI, "They're not really senior friendly. We should be careful not to tell a group that they're senior friendly when they're not" (field notes). As Luisa noted, "It's a constant, convincing our coalition partners to take us seriously. . . . The violations are generational rather than individual" (interview). These complaints were raised on other occasions, both by senior leaders and by staff. As Jeanne Hyde, a longtime senior activist, explained it,

> There's a lot of ageism in those meetings. [GAF: Can you give me an example?] It's mostly just ignoring people who are older. It's not intentional . . . being angry is not going to help. . . . So many people my age have hearing difficulties of one type or another. And so you get in these meetings and the younger people who still hear quite well tend to talk quite softly, and if it's a big room, seniors are kind of excluded, totally unintentionally, but they just have difficulty following the conversation. This is something that Jane has also noticed as occurring and has actually called people out on it. But it's one of the things that if you call someone out on this they would say "Oh, I didn't realize. I'm so sorry" and do it again because it's natural. (Interview)

Sharon, an admired staffer, agreed:

> I think there's a lot of times when planning actions or something like that where we really have to assert seniors' needs as important. You can't just plan a two-mile march without having a place for seniors. . . . If you want to be in a coalition, if you want it to be intergenerational, you can't do a two-mile march. [GAF: Can you think of a specific example?] The march to Springfield, I think even the beginning kickoff was a negotiation. Some of the groups were college students; they were thinking like "Yeah, our members could walk many blocks and that would be fine." And you know, Chicago Seniors Together was like "Well, no, we need to make sure this is accessible." Our members don't like to go and feel like they can't do it. (Interview)

While coalitions multiply the power of movement groups, they must be organized so that each group's members feel they have a voice, even if the leaders have the responsibility for final decisions. This is the challenge of creating a cross-boundary interaction order that extends beyond a local hub and welcomes diversity in practice and not just rhetorically. When participants have different abilities, as is the case with seniors, coalition organizers must adjust to the circumstances of all those who might be present in order to create an inclusive and vital movement of distinct tiny publics.

The Nexus of Politics

The political environment Chicago Seniors Together responded to matters. Movement politics, as Jeff Goodwin and James Jasper have written,[20] is about people joining together within the context of a political opportunity structure. Activists operate through small-group dynamics, considering what can be changed, what can be condemned, and what collaborators can achieve. Politics is not about policy (only), but about the intersection of problems and persons, a point powerfully made by C. Wright Mills in describing the sociological imagination as consisting of a joining of personal troubles and social problems.[21]

Movements that hope to alter policy need politics, both legislative politics, facing elected and appointed officials, and moral politics addressing structural and systemic choices that are value-based in the distribution of resources and opportunities. Activist groups must move those persons and structures that set policies, whether through persuasion or provocation. Confronting politicians, protesting against them and even "bird-dogging" them, disrupting their events, requires the willingness to be an agitator. The question is how these worlds can alter policies in the desired direction.

In Chicago, a Democratic city dominated by politicians who consider themselves liberal or even progressive, Chicago Seniors Together is not confronted by conservative enemies. There is little harsh conflict among rival organizations, but only ferment in the progressive community. The opposition comes from those politicians and officials who avoid changes that activists believe are essential while quietly acquiescing to the desires of the affluent and the influential. Those in power speak honeyed words, but without sweet action. Politics ain't bean-bag in a rough town of big shoulders and sharp elbows. This reality leads to the cynicism that resulted in my informants' opinions about the politician as a social type.

The 2016 election provoked a sharp change in emotion and, for a time, in interaction. For many the outcome was *literally* unimaginable. Suddenly the world had changed, or at least the nation had. Members went to sleep in 2016 and woke up . . . when? 1968? 1957? 1933? The anger raised in the heat of a political campaign did not dissipate. The campaign carried on, particularly because it was so unexpected, coupled with those repulsive aspects of Donald Trump's character. It was less that President Trump's policies were unusual for a conservative than that his moral character produced in his opponents what his MAGA supporters quickly labeled Trump Derangement Syndrome. Did he have the capacity or the desire to be "presidential" and to heal the nation? Most informants said No way!

This reaction generated a commitment to protest, and the CST's membership nearly doubled in a brief period, particularly with an influx of middle-class White women. In time many of these new members stopped attending, but for the moment the organization changed, as events such as Resist Trump Tuesdays were held weekly for several months with The Donald as the focus.

This energy was matched by a deepening civic chasm. Many participants wanted to remain in their bubbles and bunkers. Understandably, most people prefer to discuss politics with people whose views are congenial. In this case many exclude those with other views, even relatives, neighbors, and those soon defriended on social media. Perhaps it was true in the other direction as well, but the winners of the 2016 election seemed more eager to discuss politics with their opponents than were those who were mired in defeat. Winners always do. Progressives hung out with other progressives in their local closets, with whatever destructive effects this might have had on America's civic culture.

In the nexus of engagement, the network where politics occurs shapes involvement. We want to collaborate, but sometimes what we don't see matters greatly. Like so much senior activism, the bodily limitations of the CST members made connecting with allies a challenge. Seniors as a community have policy interests and physical demands. If they are to collaborate, the reality of chronology must be considered. Senior activism with its benefits and its costs must be accepted by those who are more spry but perhaps less flexible. These networks too, however fragile, constitute a political opportunity structure.

8

Our Fair Share

Americans are fighters. We're tough, resourceful, and creative, and if we have the chance
to fight on a level playing field, where everyone pays a *fair share* and everyone has a real
shot, then no one—no one—can stop us.
SENATOR ELIZABETH WARREN

All some folks want is their *fair share* and yours.
ARNOLD GLASOW, businessman and humorist

What about fairness? What's not to like? But what does fairness mean in terms of the division of resources and of responsibilities? How is fairness a political frame for activism? Political actors require compelling slogans, and "fair share" is surely a motivating trope. If we could rely on how political actors frame their demands, we would have a series of happy choices. Fair share sounds more broadly appealing than income redistribution or higher taxes or socialism. That's the point. And, of course, one's political opponents create labels for their own preferences. Who could oppose the dreams of "dreamers," except perhaps those who worry about "illegal aliens" or MS-13 gang members? One can embrace being "pro-choice" or "pro-life." In principle we want to be both. Movements create internal cultures that shape commitments and external cultures that shape responses.

I have presented a granular, deep-dive ethnographic account of one senior citizen progressive organization in order to explore the role of local communities in collective action. From my field observations and interviews drawn from this case I suggest how tiny publics operate, building on their group culture and their interaction order. I have devoted my career to studying the group: the culture within it, the characteristics of those who participate, and the processes that shape their identity. But seniors have some special characteristics. Senior activists are inspired, maintained, and constrained by their life experiences and their bodily infirmities. With their lengthy political histories, sometimes including decades as activists, these seniors draw on past demands and demonstrations. This background provides wisdom, but it can also cause seniors to ignore current perspectives. History can be a spark or a burden. Age can bring embodied freedom or bodily chains.

Recognizing that Chicago Seniors Together is a political community with strong policy preferences, I have attempted to be judicious, to produce an ostensibly "fair" account that neither endorses nor attacks the goals of my friends. Perhaps this is not so fair. It might be said that I care about everything except the justice of their demands. I have not focused on whether these men and women would, as they passionately believe, make the nation a better place or even described in detail the malign conditions that lead to their demands. I address how their beliefs are framed for internal consumption and for presentation in the public square.

My desire to distance myself from arguments about what justice consists of might disappoint both proponents and those partisans who wish to discredit them, but my goal is analysis, not activism. I hope to be sympathetic to their beliefs, supportive of the legitimacy of their actions, but agnostic as to the righteous wisdom of their choices. Many admire Alinsky-style community organizing, others despise it, and still others believe that changes in this style of engagement are needed in a society that has changed markedly—perhaps radically—since Saul Alinsky's day. In addition, Alinsky-style organizing can be borrowed by those on the right; these tactics are not inherently connected to progressive change; they can apply to conservative engagement.[1] Further, after some eighty years, Alinsky-style community organizing is perhaps offensive in its marginalizing of women and minorities and in its suspicion of spontaneity. In my research, the staff of the CST rarely mentioned Saul Alinsky and his form of popular education.

Central to my argument is how an activist social movement organization energizes members through local norms, values, and relations, creating a vibrant tiny public that demands commitment.[2] Of course, each group operates in light of the skills, demands, and limits of its members. In the case of senior activists, their histories, experiences, and limitations shaped the actions they engaged in and how they treated their civic responsibilities.

In this conclusion, I address seven themes that justify an approach that emphasizes the role of local commitments, interaction orders, and group cultures in understanding collective action. I focus on framing beliefs, age and infirmity, action and interaction, preserving memory, organizational culture, category and identity, and political placement. These themes constitute the mosaic of my argument, but when we step back from the tiny, brightly colored ethnographic shards, the larger argument depends on our recognizing the value of a meso-level approach to civil society and collective action. While I admit the value of examining political opportunities, access to resources, or state-level constraints, social movements depend on relationships among those who engage and the framings their past and present provide.

Framing Beliefs

It once was common to argue that social movements depended on people's gathering because of some belief, demand, or grievance. This made sense in that movements must be about *something*. Why else would one sustain the costs of engagement? Although shared values have never been totally ignored, scholars came to prioritize social relations, acquisition of resources, economic positioning, and connections with state authorities as explanations. However, in examining a senior activist organization, while none of these factors should be discounted, ideas matter; and in order to matter they must be framed to provoke action. Framing is not merely an artificial construction; the framing must link to values and beliefs that are tightly held. The question is how ideas are offered and displayed so that they are communally supported and put into action.

The constant refrain of making the rich pay their "fair share"—the title of this book—while ambiguous in its requirements, is such an example. It is influential as a cultural framework, reflecting the shared acceptance of a set of implicit values than can be transformed into policy preferences and attacks on the status quo.

As I bring beliefs back in, I do so through the power of sociality. As an ethnographer, I confront features of movement life that were frequently described as "fighting for our values." Values were the "things" that needed to be fought for. In their presocial form, values can seem ambiguous and amorphous—felt rather than articulated—but they are not so random or vapid that they can stand for just anything. They are linked to an understood group politics and are depicted through collective history. Even if much of what participants believe depends on appealing slogans (Keep the Promise, the Fair Tax, Black Lives Matter), these slogans activate potent political beliefs both within the group, with the fervent hope that they might spread. These goals might be rejected by those enchanted by other slogans. The differences in values and in policies reveal that in a diverse and democratic polity contesting groups adopt competing perspectives with the outcome being the result of a contentious political process, but within the group shared visions are assumed. When these are not evident, stability is threatened.

Age and Infirmity

This is a book about the elderly: a rare ethnography of senior citizens who are politically active. Few field studies explore how age intersects with civic engagement. Because people now have many years of life and of health after retirement, these seniors can choose to become political actors. Their voices must not be ignored, even if their bodies often are.

Senior citizens are a vital demographic category, set apart in many ways from younger people. While many of those who engage in social movement activism are collegians or emerging young adults, not all are. Seniors participate in political debates through their experience, resources, and group interests.

In impelling seniors to demand change, any movement group must consider their embodied fragility. The format of demonstrations that are possible depends on bodily limits. Tactics are tied to the age-specific composition of the movement, whether this involves marches, vigils, or civil disobedience. Organizers must recognize the capabilities of members and—as I have emphasized—realize that the vulnerability of seniors (or of the disabled or of children) often makes them compelling advertisements for the cause. Perhaps acting militantly is less important than advocating through their presence and their claims for a just society that must address their fragility.

The position of seniors in social movements is a strand I weave throughout the tapestry of this book. The deep memories of seniors drape the present in the fabric of past movements, preserving the filaments of activist memory. Temporal threads are a feature of modernity.

Seniors' fragility matters in other ways. I noted the substantial turnover in Chicago Seniors Together even during my thirty months of observation. While some of this was a function of loss of interest or interpersonal friction, health and energy mattered as well. Several of those I knew and admired died during the research, and I grieved in memorial gatherings. Even without death's cold grip, illness circumscribed involvement, and seniors' financial circumstances might alter as well. While each activist had a life story, structures affected their choices.[3] The inequalities some seniors face, linked to their desire to preserve Social Security, affordable housing, medical services, and adequate nursing homes, created conditions in which seniors were able—or unable—to be provocateurs.

Action and Interaction

Every social movement group must determine the types of engagements that staff, leaders, and members find productive and congenial for influencing those outside their domain: targets, authorities, or future allies. The actions chosen carry moral meaning; only some can be imagined as legitimate group projects. This connection constitutes the intersection of action and interaction. Social movements speak of marches, demonstrations, civil disobedience, and rallies as "actions." Sociology, at its core, is the study of action. Yet actions are always situated within set routines, rules, and expectations. This channeling reflects what Erving Goffman spoke of as the interaction order, defining the boundaries and the directions of behavior.[4] In a moral universe, only some actions make social sense.

In chapter 3 I described the "genres" that were organized by the CST. These ranged from civil disobedience that awarded status to those brave souls who were willing to lay on the line their bodies and their civic reputations to other actions that, in their failure, revealed the movement's lack of power. The Senior Power Assembly, attracting nearly three hundred people, mostly seniors, was a major focus of activity for several months and was treated as a signal success, although it has not been repeated. Bringing off an event of such magnitude proved that the CST, despite its modest size and its constant struggle for resources, should not be ignored. The challenge—shared by many social movements—was that it was hard to judge the effectiveness of an action: one had to believe. When activists—seniors and others—chained themselves to the revolving doors at the Chicago Board of Trade for an hour, was the world better after they left? Was this merely a performance, applauded but without impact? It surely revealed the passions and the demands of a tiny public, but could it extend to a larger public or even a patchwork of tiny ones?

This question is widely applicable. Sometimes we can see the linkage, but often movement activities merely serve as background noise in a political surround where this clamor is barely noticed. Still, perhaps the larger impact is not the most important effect. What might be crucial is how actions affect interaction. These engagements create spaces where individuals join together, producing those expected routines that I have termed circuits of action. The joining is what matters. Members recognize these practices as part of what it means to be an organization of moral commitment. We transform *moments of action* into *systems of interaction*. When successful, social movements are circles that are unbroken.

Preserving Memory

Social movements are inevitably aware of past history and the history of their present. This generates collective memory, both for members and for those social movements that surround them. Chicago mayor Rahm Emanuel once said, "You never let a serious crisis go to waste. . . . It's an opportunity to do things you think you could not do before." What he meant by this bon mot is that a crisis focuses people's attention on a previously ignored topic and allows those with an agenda to push a response that might not otherwise have been imagined. Something must be done! A crisis—a memorable moment—demands a response that might not be possible in settled times. We see this in the moments of the pandemic, the killings of African Americans by police, and the attack on the US Capitol. Perhaps nothing much will change, but at least there is an opening for revising social bargains in light of a newly formulated challenge. This becomes increasingly likely if organized groups have the boots and the megaphone to make the case. As a result, social movement groups want to transform a trouble into a crisis. As unsettled times are coded in memory, they require new negotiations.[5]

These events—events that might be interpreted in distinctly different ways—become available to be treated as replicable. Their meaningful past leaks into future possibilities. New problems demand novel solutions. In time these meanings are sedimented into popular memory, whether or not these memories correctly reflect events. Accurate or not, they are powerful forces for change. Fake news can solidify into embraced history.

Given the politics of memory, movement participants are exhorted to tell stories that can be recalled and shape identities. With regard to Chicago Seniors Together, I found this in light of tragic and moving narratives about the ravages of illness, poverty, and homelessness: the holes ripped in the social safety net. Facing a victim makes skepticism or cynicism difficult. While anecdotes are limited in their ability to generalize, their influence as frames of meaning can be substantial.

Seniors can be powerful conveyors of collective memory, since they are, in effect, figures from the past. They have time-traveled and can recount salient moments with authentic claims intact. This proved true for those with lived experience in the early civil rights movement of the 1950s and 1960s. These men and women were revered teachers whose experience was more powerful than textbook accounts.

Ultimately, a social movement is a carrier of memory—a library of alarms—and some have a profound capacity to motivate. Historical events may be obdurate, but they are shaped through the play of politics. To "make America great again," for example, depends on a set of collective memories of the past: of greatness, of decline, and of America. While anyone can make such claims, seniors speak from generational authority—whether or not they speak from truth—giving a movement an authenticity that can renew politics.

Organizational Culture

However much we wish to treat a social movement as grounded in emotion or in faith, it is also an organization or a set of affiliated organizations. Organizations create practices by which they achieve desired ends or, often, fail to achieve them.[6] These institutionalized practices become the routine circuits of action that appear repeatedly, providing the stability that allows for the comfort of expectations.

Social movements do not continually reinvent themselves. Instead, they establish ways of doing things. This includes structures they hope will serve them well. In the case of seniors, timing and sociability matter greatly. Although the organization held few events that were purely social (farewell parties and an occasional potluck), members were encouraged to arrive early for meetings and bring food to share. Among my informants, it was commonly repeated—treated as a mantra—that seniors are attracted by free food. Even if not, they were attracted by the convivial sociality that a rushed meeting agenda could not provide. Chicago Seniors Together constituted itself as a social space as well as a place to express grievances. The more individuals came to know, care for, and trust each other, the less would they remain free riders who avoided the burdens of group labor.

Within many social movements—those that can afford to hire organizers—the role of staff members is crucial as producers and directors of action. Staff are managers; members are, in effect, organizational owners. But who chooses the leaders among the owners? In practice, this is the staff; they have the most extensive contact within the community and the network outside the organization. They recognize talent, but they have agendas as well. In many social movements that include those less committed, staff are the most radical, most desiring to direct action, and least willing to tolerate the watery pleasures of mere discourse. These expert agitators fomenting disruption were viewed with affection and admiration, permitting the organization to embrace their more contentious opinions. This did not prevent members from sometimes feeling they were being manipulated—clay to be molded. While it was often claimed that the CST is an organization of seniors, for seniors, and run by seniors, this could be said—and believed—only because staff made it possible.

Category and Identity

We live in a world of social categories, a world imbued with identity politics. Movements understand this and sometimes rely on it. The foundation of this book is one of these influential categories: age. Being a senior matters, although this age range covers three decades: the combined length of infancy, childhood, adolescence, and young adulthood. It was sometimes remarked that the CST consists of the young old and the old old, although health, mobility, and mental acuity matter more than age. Age is the basis of membership, of culture, and of interest politics.

Other categories matter as well, as they do in many social movements. Class seemed less salient. In part this reflected considerable class homogeneity, certainly more than the organization desired. Many active members—although not all—were seniors who had retired from professional careers, often without substantial personal savings. But in the main these were not the surviving remnants of the working class. They possessed wide cultural capital even if they lacked deep financial capital. But their class positions were similar. This was not a group riven by economic diversity.

Gender itself did not play much of a direct role either. The organization was dominated by women, and there was a belief that women should fill important positions and that men should admit their own gender privilege and act with deference. Men were in general satisfied with this arrangement, and there was little desire to jockey for position. Members assumed that men and women could get along as long as men "knew their place." With a staff almost entirely female, gender was not a major source of contention.

This gendered comfort was so clear that the nearest the organization came to internal conflict was in the response to a staffer who was gender fluid and chose to use the pronoun "they." This grammatical quirk in itself would have posed no problem except that the organization—seemingly encouraged by the staff—insisted that meetings include a new ritual of members' announcing their preferred (and invariably unsurprising) gender pronouns. This proved offensive to some in an age in which gender identification was no longer taken for granted.

Race—as it so often is—was more problematic, even though I observed little interpersonal tension. Still, with members who had navigated considerable change in racial attitudes over long lifetimes, debates between those who believed in race blindness and those who believed in race consciousness could be fraught. For an antiracist organization, at times it became difficult to determine just what racial responsibility meant in practice and how it might influence the group culture and interaction order. While some African Americans played important roles, they did not always set the terms for discourse about race in an organization that might—or might not—be categorized as "White."

Still, being progressive overrode any other categorical division. Politics was the key divide. The group avoided extensive interpersonal divisions because of their shared politics, a smooth reality that allowed actions to be organized with élan.

Political Placement

No book about social movements, even one that focuses on the meso-level dynamics of group culture, can ignore the wider political context. This is particularly true of groups that adopt Alinsky-inspired political organizing. The relationship between the group and politicians and the tensions between the two are critical. Whether the connection with politicians is through friendly meetings or through targeted confrontations, the politician is framed as a figure who must be shaped and pressured. As Saul Alinsky pointed out, there are no permanent friends and no permanent enemies. This may be true in theory, but often in practice some politicians are seen as long-term allies and others as the promoters of unjust policies.

As a rule, politicians as a class were mistrusted, obstacles to be overcome. However, the organization also operated in a political environment. When this ecology was radically reshaped on the national level by the election of Donald Trump—elections do have consequences, sometimes large ones—the organization reassessed and, with its allies, rethought the agenda. As with pushing for Medicare for All, the CST increased its national focus, becoming more willing to engage with broader coalitions to confront an unacceptable president. Whereas their greatest success had been in improving conditions in affordable senior housing and in nursing homes, now that was balanced with protesting national grievances and, perhaps, saving democracy.

This change forced the group to participate in coalitions that did not always recognize the special needs of seniors. Did they really matter? Were seniors merely to be photogenic shock troops, or could they set policy? Too often it seemed to be the former, generating complaints even toward those they largely agreed with. This was another way the categorical role of age and its embodiment had effects. These tensions within coalitions force us to consider how networks negotiate, not only in light of preferred policies but in deciding how actions will be performed. Since diverse categories of members were welcomed, creating a congenial interaction order in which all could participate, this task could be challenging.

A Fair Share for All

Social justice. Will we know it when we see it? Although of course we can agree if we approach it from the same perspective and with a charismatic guide, it may be more proper to treat social justice as an ongoing process, a never-ending debate. But often social movements attempt surety: to provide a firm vision so that policies make sense and members feel confident in their goals. Movements hope to envision a world where social justice carries an uncomplicated meaning and a fair share is unambiguous. Social justice means equality, and a fair share means equality as well. But what does equality mean? These are answers tiny publics must grapple with and then provide for their members as well as transmitting those messages into the consciousness of influential political actors and the unaware public.

As a small-group researcher committed to the local understanding of culture, I chose to observe a single organization, although one with links to its allies. A single case can tell us only so much. By selecting a group of senior citizen activists, I chose activists who were, in most respects, like me. I was within my comfort zone.

However, ethnographies of the elderly have been few, perhaps because few older academics have the energy to observe and observe and observe. Ethnography is my passion, and in this I am not so different from senior activists. This is a project in which I build on concepts that I have developed over the years—group culture, the interaction order, circuits of action, and, especially, tiny publics.

In the end, we may never develop firm criteria for what constitutes an equitable division of resources that provides us each with a fair share or that demands a fair share from everyone. However, we can come to believe that our band is marching toward a bright and just future, picking up adherents along the way. Consider Marx's hazy mantra: From each according to his ability, to each according to his needs. Is that any clearer than from each and to each a fair share? Still, when citizens are committed to shared provisions, everyone at the table will benefit. This is true even if we quibble about how the pie is to be cut and who holds the knife.

Acknowledgments

Every ethnography depends on generosity. I thank the members, leaders, and staff of Chicago Seniors Together who allowed me to share their world as a visitor without previously committing to progressive advocacy. Since I've used pseudonyms throughout, I cannot thank them by name, but I developed close ties with many who shared their beliefs, their time, and their biscotti. I came to admire these men and women who were willing to lay their bodies on the line. I respect their commitment to birthing a better world in which all have a fair share even though they themselves may not long take part.

I appreciate the American voters who by providing a surprising electoral outcome allowed me to witness a change in movement goals and practices. Perhaps "appreciate" is not the ideal wording, given the following four years, but the 2016 election produced important changes in group goals. Beyond those distant voters, I thank many interlocutors who helped shape this manuscript, especially Corey Abramson, Josh Basseches, Max Besbris, Lori Clark, Gemma Edwards, Jun Fang, Tim Hallett, James Jasper, Lauren Langman, Daniel Menchik, Rachel Ramirez, Natalia Ruiz-Junco, Chris Wellin, and Marc Willage for their challenging conversations and helpful comments. I note with admiration the precise transcriptions by Valarie Bentz and Kathleen Wood. The smooth flow of the manuscript owes much to Alice Bennett, who has copyedited more than six hundred manuscripts over the years. If scholarly works are intelligible, she deserves much of the credit. I am also grateful to Elizabeth Branch Dyson and her assistant, Mollie McFee, for shepherding this manuscript to publication. Finally, I thank the Russell Sage Foundation for providing me with a home and a community in the midst of the pandemic.

Notes

Prologue

1. Jeffrey Nash, "Relations in Frozen Places: Observations on Winter Public Order," *Qualitative Sociology* 4, no. 3 (1981): 229–43.

2. Kathleen Blee, *Democracy in the Making: How Activist Groups Form* (New York: Oxford University Press, 2012); James Jasper, Michael Young, and Elke Zuern, *Public Characters: The Politics of Reputation and Blame* (New York: Oxford University Press, 2020).

3. Robert Dingwall, "Atrocity Stories and Professional Relationships," *Sociology of Work and Occupations* 4 (1977): 371–96.

4. Francesca Polletta, *Inventing the Ties That Bind* (Chicago: University of Chicago Press, 2020).

Introduction

1. Ping-Kwong Kam, Chau-Kiu Cheung, Wing-Tai Chan, and Kwan-Kwok Leung, "Mobilized or Civic Minded: Factors Affecting the Political Participation of Senior Citizens," *Research on Aging* 21 (1999): 627–56.

2. Gary Alan Fine, *The Hinge: Civil Society, Group Cultures, and the Power of Local Commitments* (Chicago: University of Chicago Press, 2021).

3. This retirement age was more applicable to middle-class workers and unionized workers than to the poor and those in marginal occupations. I thank Corey Abramson for this insight.

4. This is a technique that people with disabilities have learned well when their limitations make their protests visually powerful. Seeing attacks on the defenseless justifies claims about heartless authority.

5. The structure of these "entitlement" insurance programs, particularly those linked to income contributed, means that this "safety net" is most useful for the middle-class elderly.

6. Frederick Lynch, "Prospects for Senior Power," *Generations* 42, no. 4 (2018–19): 65–72.

7. Nancy Whittier, "Political Generations, Micro-cohorts and the Transformation of Social Movements," *American Sociological Review* 62, no. 5 (1997): 760—78.

8. I use the label "senior citizen" generically, without addressing the fraught debate as to who counts as a citizen.

9. But see Rodrigo Serrat and Feliciano Villar, "Older People's Motivations to Engage in Political Organizations: Evidence from a Catalan Study," *Voluntas* 27 (2016): 1385–1402.

10. In a previously published article, I referred to this organization using the pseudonym Alinsky Senior Coalition. After discussion with the executive director, I changed the pseudonym to avoid a close linkage with the Alinsky model and a masculinist name.

11. Patricia Ewick and Marc Steinberg, *Beyond Betrayal: The Priest Sex Abuse Crisis, the Voice of the Faithful, and the Process of Collective Identity* (Chicago: University of Chicago Press, 2019).

12. Paul Lichterman, *How Civic Action Works: Fighting for Housing in Los Angeles* (Princeton, NJ: Princeton University Press, 2021).

13. Caroline Gatt, *An Ethnography of Global Environmentalism: Becoming Friends of the Earth* (New York: Routledge, 2018).

14. William Westermeyer, *Back to America: Identity, Political Culture and the Tea Party Movement* (Lincoln: University of Nebraska Press, 2019).

15. Kathleen Blee, *Democracy in the Making: How Activist Groups Form* (New York: Oxford University Press, 2012).

16. Gary Alan Fine, "Toward a Peopled Ethnography: Developing Theory from Group Life," *Ethnography* 4 (2003): 41–60.

17. Robert Hudson, "Aging in a Public Space," *Generations* 30, no. 4 (2006–7): 55–57.

18. Dunne/Dooley added, "'Tis a man's game, an' women, childer, cripples an' prohibition-ists 'd do well to keep out iv it."

19. James Jasper, "The Doors That Culture Opened: Parallels between Social Movement Studies and Social Psychology," *Group Process and Intergroup Relations* 20, no. 2 (2017): 285.

20. Charles Kurzman, "Introduction: Meaning-Making in Social Movements," *Anthropology Quarterly* 81 (2008): 5–15.

21. Gary Alan Fine, *Tiny Publics: A Theory of Group Action and Culture* (New York: Russell Sage Foundation, 2012).

22. Miya Narushima, "A Gaggle of Raging Grannies: The Empowerment of Older Canadian Women through Social Activism," *International Journal of Lifelong Education* 23, no. 1 (2004): 23–42; Roger Sanjek, *Gray Panthers* (Philadelphia: University of Pennsylvania Press, 2009).

23. Matthew Desmond, "Relational Ethnography," *Theory and Society* 43, no. 5 (2014): 547–79.

24. Edwin Amenta, *When Movements Matter: The Townsend Plan and the Rise of Social Security* (Princeton, NJ: Princeton University Press, 2008).

25. Roger Sanjek's study *Gray Panthers* provides a detailed account of the group, chronicling the movement as an engaged and partisan insider. Although Sanjek is a well-respected ethnographer, his book is more of a memoir. Another lively account of a social movement describes the Raging Grannies, a group based in British Columbia, but this work makes no claim to be an academic study. See Alison Acker and Betty Brightwell, *Off Our Rockers and into Trouble: The Raging Grannies* (Victoria, BC: TouchWood, 2010). There have been a few academic accounts of the Raging Grannies, such as Dana Sawchuck, "The Raging Grannies: Defying Stereotypes and Embracing Aging through Activism" *Journal of Women and Aging* 21 (2009): 171–85. Sawchuck describes the performative aspects of adopting the feisty grandmother identity. In contrast, Linda Caissie, "The Raging Grannies: Narrative Construction of Gender and Aging," in *Storytelling in Later Life: Issues, Investigations, and Interventions in Narrative Gerontology*, ed. Gary Kenyon, Ernst Bohlmeijer, and William Randall, 126–42 (New York: Oxford University Press, 2013) 135, focuses on how narrative creates the meaning of aging.

26. Donald Reitzes and Dietrich Reitzes, "Metro Seniors in Action: A Case-Study of a City-wide Senior Organization," *Gerontologist* 31 (1991): 256–62.

27. Dick Simpson, *The Good Fight: Life Lessons from a Chicago Progressive* (Emmaus, PA: Golden Alley Press, 2018).

28. Lichterman, *How Civic Action Works*, 26–32.

29. Saul Alinsky, *Rules for Radicals: A Pragmatic Primer for Realistic Radicals* (New York: Vintage, 1971).

30. For a valuable, detailed treatment of the practices and the history of Alinsky-style community organizing, see Aaron Schutz and Mike Miller, eds., *People Power: The Community Organizing Tradition of Saul Alinsky* (Nashville, TN: Vanderbilt University Press, 2015).

31. Since Chicago borders Lake Michigan, there is no East Side.

32. Marian Barnes, Elizabeth Harrison, and Lesley Murray, "Ageing Activists: Who Gets Involved in Older People's Forums?" *Ageing and Society* 32 (2012): 275.

33. Erving Goffman, "The Interaction Order," *American Sociological Review* 48, no. 1 (1983): 1–17.

34. Nina Eliasoph and Paul Lichterman, "Culture in Interaction," *American Journal of Sociology* 108, no. 4 (2003): 735–94.

35. James Jasper, *Getting Your Way: Strategic Dilemmas in the Real World* (Chicago: University of Chicago Press, 2006).

36. Gary Alan Fine, "Public Narration and Group Culture: Discerning Discourse in Social Movements," in *Social Movements and Culture*, ed. Hank Johnston and Bert Klandermans, 127–43 (Minneapolis: University of Minnesota Press, 1995).

37. William Gamson and David Meyer, "Framing Political Opportunity," in *Comparative Perspectives in Social Movements: Political Opportunities, Mobilizing Structures, and Cultural Framings*, ed. Doug McAdam, John McCarthy, and Mayer Zald, 275–90 (New York: Cambridge University Press, 1996), 283.

38. Klaus Eder, "A New Social Movement?," *Telos* 52 (1982): 5–20; Donald Horowitz, "Cultural Movements and Ethnic Change," *Annals of the American Academy of Political and Social Sciences* 433 (1977): 6–18; John Marx and Burkart Holzner, "Ideological Primary Groups in Contemporary Cultural Movements," *Sociological Focus* 8, no. 4 (1975): 311–29.

39. Daniel Silver and Terry Nichols Clark, *Scenescapes: How Qualities of Place Shape Social Life* (Chicago: University of Chicago Press, 2016).

40. Stefan Kühl, "Groups, Organizations, Families, and Movements: The Sociology of Social Systems between Interaction and Society." *Systems Research and Behavioral Science* 37 (2020): 496–519.

41. Bert Klandermans, "Grievance Interpretation and Success Expectations: The Social Construction of Protest," *Social Behaviour* 4 (1989): 113–25.

42. Alberto Melucci, *Nomads of the Present: Social and Individual Needs in Contemporary Society* (Philadelphia: Temple University Press, 1989); Verta Taylor and Nancy Whittier, "Collective Identity in Social Movement Communities: Lesbian Feminist Mobilization," in *Frontiers in Social Movement Theory*, ed. Aldon Morris and Carol Mueller, 104–29 (New Haven, CT: Yale University Press, 1992).

43. Arlie Hochschild, *The Managed Heart* (Berkeley: University of California Press, 1984).

44. Deborah Gould, *Moving Politics: Emotion and ACT UP's Fight against AIDS* (Chicago: University of Chicago Press, 2009), 213.

45. Edward Shils, "The Concept and Function of Ideology," *International Encyclopedia of the Social Sciences* 7 (1968): 70.

46. Fine, *Hinge*.

47. William Gamson, Bruce Fireman, and Steven Rytina, *Encounters with Unjust Authority* (Homewood, IL: Dorsey Press, 1982).

48. Fine, *Tiny Publics*, 14–15, 141.

49. Gary Alan Fine, "Public Narration and Group Culture: Discerning Discourse in Social Movements," in *Social Movements and Culture*, ed. Hank Johnston and Bert Klandermans, 127–43 (Minneapolis: University of Minnesota Press, 1995), 138–41.

50. See Sawchuck, "Raging Grannies."

51. James Jasper, *The Art of Moral Protest: Culture, Biography, and Creativity in Social Movements* (Chicago: University of Chicago Press, 1997).

Chapter One

1. Jane Mansbridge and Aldon Morris, eds., *Oppositional Consciousness: The Subjective Roots of Social Protest* (Chicago: University of Chicago Press, 2001).

2. William Gamson, Bruce Fireman, and Steven Rytina, *Encounters with Unjust Authority* (Homewood, IL: Dorsey Press, 1982).

3. J. L. Johnson, "'Meet Them Where They Are': Attentional Processes in Social Movement Listening," *Symbolic Interaction* 44, no. 2 (2021): 728–47.

4. Ben Jackson, "The Conceptual History of Social Justice," *Political Studies Review* 3 (2005): 356–73.

5. James Jasper, *Getting Your Way: Strategic Dilemmas in the Real World* (Chicago: University of Chicago Press, 2006).

6. Andrew Perrin, *Citizen Speak: The Democratic Imagination in American Life* (Chicago: University of Chicago Press, 2006).

7. Todd Nicholas Fuist, "Towards a Sociology of Imagination," *Theory and Society* 50 (2021): 357–80.

8. Rodrigo Serrat and Feliciano Villar, "Older People's Motivations to Engage in Political Organizations: Evidence from a Catalan Study," *Voluntas* 27 (2016): 1385.

9. David Snow, E. Burke Rochford Jr., Steven Worden, and Robert Benford, "Frame Alignment Processes, Micromobilization, and Movement Participation," *American Sociological Review* 51, no. 4 (1986): 464–81.

10. Marian Barnes, Janet Newman, and Helen Sullivan, "Discursive Arenas: Deliberation and the Constitution of Identity in Public Participation at a Local Level," *Social Movement Studies* 5, no. 3 (2006): 193–207.

11. Paul Lichterman, *How Civic Action Works: Fighting for Housing in Los Angeles* (Princeton, NJ: Princeton University Press, 2021), 6.

12. Marc Eaton, "The Value Activation Process: Developing and Reinforcing Activist Identities in MoveOn.org," unpublished manuscript, 2010.

13. Jacquelien Van Stekelenburg and Bert Klandermans, "The Social Psychology of Protest," *Current Sociology* 61 (2013): 886–905.

14. Gary Alan Fine, *The Hinge: Civil Society, Group Cultures, and the Power of Local Commitments* (Chicago: University of Chicago Press, 2021).

15. Serrat and Villar, "Older People's Motivations," 1395.

16. Kathleen Blee, *Democracy in the Making: How Activist Groups Form* (New York: Oxford University Press, 2012).

17. I thank Chris Wellin for specifying this formulation (personal communication, 2021).

18. David A. Snow, Louis A. Zurcher Jr., and Sheldon Ekland-Olson, "Social Networks and Social Movements: A Microstructural Approach to Differential Recruitment," *American Sociological Review* 45 (1980): 787–801.

19. Doug McAdam, "Recruitment to High-Risk Activism: The Case of Freedom Summer," *American Journal of Sociology* 92 (1986): 64–90.

20. Snow et al., "Frame Alignment Processes."

21. William Gamson, *Talking Politics* (New York: Cambridge University Press, 1992).

22. James Jasper, in *Getting Your Way*, speaks of this as the "extension dilemma." See also Rory McVeigh, Daniel Myers, and David Sikkink, "Corn, Klansmen, and Coolidge: Structure and Framing in Social Movements," *Social Forces* 83, no. 2 (2004): 657.

23. Moira O'Neil, Abigail Heydon, and Nathaniel Kendall-Taylor, "Shaping Professional Discourse," *Generations* 39, no. 3 (2015): 23. See Mike Featherstone and Andrew Wernick, eds., *Images of Aging: Cultural Representations of Later Life* (London: Routledge, 2003).

24. Robert Benford and David Snow, "Framing Processes and Social Movements: An Overview and Assessments," *Annual Review of Sociology* 26 (2000): 623.

25. This does not mean Warren Buffett is paying less tax than his secretary is, only that his overall tax rate was lower, although the principle was sometimes taken in that more dramatic way. One member used Buffett as an example: "The millionaire in Nebraska . . . he says his secretary pays more in taxes than he does. It shouldn't be that way" (interview).

26. See https://www.fairshareonline.org/content/about-fair-share, accessed December 27, 2020.

27. Saul Alinsky, *Reveille for Radicals* (Chicago: University of Chicago Press, 1946), 133.

28. Jeffrey Stout, *Blessed Are the Organized: Grassroots Democracy in America* (Princeton, NJ: Princeton University Press, 2010), 118.

29. Ruth Braunstein, *Prophets and Patriots: Faith in Democracy across the Political Divide* (Berkeley: University of California Press, 2017), 53.

30. Charles Taylor, *Modern Social Imaginaries* (Durham, NC: Duke University Press, 2004).

31. Braunstein, *Prophets and Patriots*, 73.

32. Rachel Ramirez, "The Community Organizing Model of Organizational Leadership: A Value- and Power-Driven Model of Leadership" (MA thesis, Public Policy and Administration, Northwestern University, 2016), 15.

33. Charles Tilly, *Contentious Performances* (Cambridge: Cambridge University Press, 2008).

34. Nathan Crick, ed., *The Rhetoric of Social Movements: Networks, Power, and New Media* (New York: Routledge, 2020).

35. Timur Kuran, *Private Truths, Public Lies: The Social Consequences of Preference Falsification* (Cambridge, MA: Harvard University Press, 1995).

36. Nancy Whittier, "Political Generations, Micro-cohorts, and the Transformation of Social Movements," *American Sociological Review* 62, no. 5 (1997): 760–78.

37. Charles Kiesler, *The Psychology of Commitment: Experiments Linking Behavior to Belief* (San Diego, CA: Academic Press, 1971).

38. Nancy Morrow-Howell, "Volunteering in Later Life: Research Frontiers," *Journal of Gerontology: Social Sciences* 65B, no. 4 (2010): 466.

39. Francesca Polletta, *Inventing the Ties That Bind* (Chicago: University of Chicago Press, 2020).

40. James Jasper, "Emotions and Social Movements: Twenty Years of Theory and Research," *Annual Review of Sociology* 37 (2011): 298.

41. Deborah Gould, *Moving Politics: Emotion and ACT UP's Fight against AIDS* (Chicago: University of Chicago Press, 2009), 213.

42. Gould, *Moving Politics*, 222.

43. Erika Summers-Effler, *Laughing Saints and Righteous Heroes: Emotional Rhythms in Social Movement Groups* (Chicago: University of Chicago Press, 2010).

44. Steve Burghardt, *The Other Side of Organizing: Resolving the Personal Dilemmas and Political Demands of Daily Practice* (Cambridge, MA: Schenkman, 1982).

45. Blee, *Democracy in the Making*.

46. Arlie Hochschild, *The Managed Heart: Commercialization of Human Feeling* (Berkeley: University of California Press, 1984).

47. Susan Hutchinson and Blair Wexler, "Is 'Raging' Good for Health? Older Women's Participation in the Raging Grannies," *Health Care for Women International* 28, no. 1 (2007): 88–118; Miya Narushima, "A Gaggle of Raging Grannies: The Empowerment of Older Canadian Women through Social Activism," *International Journal of Lifelong Education* 23, no. 1 (2004): 23–42.

48. Johnson, "'Meet Them Where They Are.'"

49. Dorothy Holland, Donald Nonini, Catherine Lutz, Lesley Bartlett, Marla Frederick-McGlathery, Thaddeaus Guldbrandsen, and Enrique Murillo Jr., *Local Democracy Under Siege: Activism, Public Interests, and Private Politics* (New York: New York University Press, 2007), 200.

50. Ramirez, "Community Organizing Model."

51. James Jasper, *The Art of Moral Protest* (Chicago: University of Chicago Press, 1997), 362.

52. Jasper, *Art of Moral Protest*, 106.

53. William Gamson, Bruce Fireman, and Steve Rytina, *Encounters with Unjust Authority* (Belmont, CA: Dorsey Press, 1982).

54. Gould, *Moving Politics*.

55. Carol Sterns and Peter Sterns, *Anger: The Struggle for Emotional Control in American History* (Chicago: University of Chicago Press, 1986).

56. Stout, *Blessed Are the Organized*, 64.

57. This seems to be a general problem of emotion work, since emotional displays and their labels recursively influence lived experience.

58. It may be that the display of anger among groups for whom anger should be off-limits (such as African Americans, LGBTQ communities, or seniors) may make that display particularly notable.

59. Seniors are, of course, not the only ones who are deferential to authorities. Students often have similar responses to teachers and administrators. See Deborah Gould, *Moving Politics*, 442–43.

60. Susanne Scheibe, "The Golden Years of Emotion," *Association for Psychological Science* (October 24, 2012), https://www.psychologicalscience.org/observer/the-golden-years-of-emotion, accessed April 8, 2021.

61. John Dewey, *The Public and Its Problems* (Chicago: Swallow Press, 1954).

62. Mancur Olson, *The Logic of Collective Action* (Cambridge. MA: Harvard University Press, 1965); Linda Caissie, "The Raging Grannies: Narrative Construction of Gender and Aging," in *Storytelling in Later Life: Issues, Investigations, and Interventions in Narrative Gerontology*, ed. Gary Kenyon, Ernst Bohlmeijer, and William Randall, 126–42 (New York: Oxford University Press, 2013), 135.

63. Braunstein, *Prophets and Patriots*, 74.

64. Marc Eaton, "Manufacturing Community in an Online Activist Organization: The Rhetoric of MoveOn.org's E-mails," *Information, Communication and Society* 13, no. 2 (2010): 174–92.

65. Fine, *Hinge.*

66. Ernesto Cortés Jr., *Rebuilding Our Institutions* (Skokie, IL: Acta Publications, 2010), 12–13.

67. Stout, *Blessed Are the Organized*, 2.

68. Edward Chambers, *Roots for Radicals: Organizing for Power, Action, and Justice* (New York: Continuum, 2004), 45.

69. Stout, *Blessed Are the Organized*, 148–49.

70. Cortés, *Rebuilding Our Institutions*, 12.

71. Francesca Polletta, *Inventing the Ties That Bind: Imagined Relationships in Moral and Political Life* (Chicago: University of Chicago Press, 2020), 119.

72. Myles Horton and Paulo Freire, *We Make the Road by Walking: Conversations on Education and Social Change* (Philadelphia: Temple University Press, 1990), 211.

73. Erving Goffman, *Relations in Public* (New York: Basic Books, 1971).

74. McVeigh, Myers, and Sikkink, "Corn, Klansmen, and Coolidge."

75. Gemma Edwards, "Close Encounters of the Friendly Kind: Friendship Networks and the Activist Career of Suffrage Campaigners," paper presented at the American Sociological Association meeting, Seattle, WA, 2016.

76. Roger Sanjek, *Gray Panthers* (Philadelphia: University of Pennsylvania Press, 2009), 89.

77. Edwards, "Close Encounters of the Friendly Kind."

78. Jonathan Wynn, "On the Sociology of Occasions," *Sociological Theory* 34, no. 3 (2016): 256–86.

79. Gary Alan Fine, "Small Groups and Culture Creation: The Idioculture of Little League Baseball Teams," *American Sociological Review* 44, no. 5 (1979): 733–45.

80. Amin Ghaziani, "An 'Amorphous Mist'? The Problem of Measurement in the Study of Culture," *Theory and Society* 38 (2009): 581–612.

81. Ann Swidler, "Culture in Action: Symbols and Strategies," *American Sociological Review* 51, no. 2 (1986): 273–86.

82. Gary Alan Fine, *With the Boys: Little League Baseball and Preadolescent Culture* (Chicago: University of Chicago Press, 1987), 125.

83. Ann Mische, *Partisan Publics: Communication and Contention across Brazilian Youth Activist Networks* (Princeton, NJ: Princeton University Press, 2008).

84. Nina Eliasoph and Paul Lichterman, "Culture in Interaction," *American Journal of Sociology* 108, no. 4 (2003): 785–86.

85. Grace Yukich, Brad Fulton, and Richard Wood, "Representative Group Styles: How Ally Immigrant Rights Organizations Promote Immigrant Involvement," *Social Problems* 67, no. 3 (2020): 488–506.

86. James Jasper, Michael Young, and Elke Zuern, *Public Characters: The Politics of Reputation and Blame* (New York: Oxford University Press, 2020).

Chapter Two

1. Corey Abramson, *The End Game: How Inequality Shapes Our Final Years* (Cambridge, MA: Harvard University Press, 2015).

2. Deborah Carr, *Golden Years? Social Inequality in Later Life* (New York: Russell Sage Foundation, 2018).

3. Barbara Myerhoff, *Number Our Days* (New York: Dutton, 1979).

4. Richard Settersten Jr., "Social Sources of Meaning in Later Life," in *Challenges of the Third Age: Meaning and Purpose in Later Life*, ed. Robert Weiss and Scott Bass, 55–79 (New York: Oxford University Press, 2002).

5. Matilda White Riley and John W. Riley Jr., "Age Integration and the Lives of Older People," *Gerontologist* 34 (1994): 110–15.

6. Dale Dannefer, "Aging as Intracohort Differentiation: Accentuation, the Matthew Effect, and the Life Course," *Sociological Forum* 2, no. 2 (1987): 211–36.

7. Rodrigo Serrat and Feliciano Villar, "Older People's Motivations to Engage in Political Organizations: Evidence from a Catalan Study," *Voluntas* 27 (2016): 1387.

8. Nancy Morrow-Howell and Marc Freedman, "Bringing Civic Engagement into Sharper Focus," *Generations* 30, no. 4 (2006–7): 6–9; John Rowe and Robert Kahn, *Successful Aging* (New York: Random House, 1998).

9. Miya Narushima, "A Gaggle of Raging Grannies: The Empowerment of Older Canadian Women through Social Activism," *International Journal of Lifelong Education* 23, no. 1 (2004): 23–42.

10. Arlie Hochschild, *The Unexpected Community: Portrait of an Old Age Subculture* (Englewood Cliffs, NJ: Prentice-Hall, 1973), 60–61.

11. Jackie Fox and Sarah Quinn, "The Meaning of Social Activism to Older Adults in Ireland," *Journal of Occupational Science* 19 (2012): 358–70; Dana Sawchuck, "The Raging Grannies: Defying Stereotypes and Embracing Aging through Activism," *Journal of Women and Aging* 21 (2009): 171–85.

12. Geri Adler, Jennifer Schwartz, and Michael Kuskowski, "An Exploratory Study of Older Adults' Participation in Civic Action," *Clinical Gerontologist* 31, no. 2 (2007): 65–75; Fox and Quinn, "Meaning of Social Activism," 364. Note that generational altruism can work in the other direction, as when young people protest to improve the lives of senior citizens.

13. Andrea Louise Campbell, *How Policies Make Citizens: Senior Political Activism and the American Welfare State* (Princeton, NJ: Princeton University Press, 2003), 14.

14. Robert Binstock, "Older People and Political Engagement: From Avid Voters to 'Cooled-Out Marks,'" *Generations* 30, no. 4 (2006–7): 24–30.

15. Campbell, *How Policies Make Citizens*, 14.

16. Achim Goerres, *The Political Participation of Older People in Europe: The Graying of Our Democracies* (Basingstoke, UK: Palgrave Macmillan, 2009).

17. Ronald Jirovec and John Erich, "The Dynamics of Political Participation among the Urban Elderly," *Journal of Applied Gerontology* 11, no. 2 (1992): 224.

18. Roger Sanjek, *Gray Panthers* (Philadelphia: University of Pennsylvania Press, 2009), 11, 31.

19. Alison Acker and Betty Brightwell, *Off Our Rockers and into Trouble: The Raging Grannies* (Victoria, BC: Touchwood Books, 2004).

20. One informant mentioned that when the CST holds a lunchtime meeting she asks whether a meal will be served or only a "snack."

21. Fox and Quinn, "Meaning of Social Activism," 365.

22. Dana Sawchuck, "The Raging Grannies: Defying Stereotypes and Embracing Aging through Activism," *Journal of Women and Aging* 21 (2009): 171–85.

23. Karen Postle, Peter Wright, and Peter Beresford, "Older People's Participation in Politi-

cal Activity—Making Their Voices Heard: A Potential Support Role for Welfare Professionals in Countering Ageism and Social Exclusion," *Practice: Social Work in Action* 17, no. 3 (2005): 173–89.

24. Robert Butler, *Why Survive? Being Old in America* (New York: Harper and Row, 1975).

25. Serrat and Villar, "Older People's Motivations," 1387.

26. Gary Alan Fine and Michaela Desoucey, "Joking Cultures: Humor Themes as Social Regulation in Group Life," *Humor* 18 (2005): 1–22; Michael Mulkay, *On Humor: Its Nature and Its Place in Modern Society* (Oxford: Blackwell, 1988).

27. James Scott, *Weapons of the Weak: Everyday Forms of Peasant Resistance* (New Haven, CT: Yale University Press, 1985).

28. Howard Becker, *Outsiders* (New York: Free Press, 1963).

29. Erving Goffman, *Asylums* (New York: Anchor, 1961).

30. Gemma Edwards, unpublished manuscript, 2016.

31. Michael Kazin, "Halfway There: Why the Left Wins on Culture and Loses on Economics," *Foreign Affairs* 93, no. 5 (2014): 47.

32. Caroline Gatt, *An Ethnography of Global Environmentalism: Becoming Friends of the Earth* (New York: Routledge, 2018).

33. Anthony Giddens, *The Constitution of Society: Outline of the Theory of Structuration* (Berkeley: University of California Press, 1984).

34. Fox and Quinn, "Meaning of Social Activism," 364.

35. Dorothy Holland, Gretchen Fox, and Vinci Daro, "Social Movements and Collective Identity: A Decentered, Dialogic View," *Anthropological Quarterly* 80 (2008): 95–126.

36. Bert Klandermans, "Identity Politics and Politicized Identities: Identity Processes and the Dynamics of Protest," *Political Psychology* 35 (2014): 1–22.

37. Ruth Braunstein, *Prophets and Patriots: Faith in Democracy across the Political Divide* (Berkeley: University of California Press, 2017); William Westermeyer, *Back to America: Identity Political Culture and the Tea Party Movement* (Lincoln: University of Nebraska Press, 2019), 121.

38. Sarah Mathews, *The Social World of Old Women: Management of Self-Identity* (Beverly Hills, CA: Sage, 1979); Andrea Fontana, *The Last Frontier: The Social Meaning of Growing Old* (Beverly Hills, CA: Sage, 1977).

39. A similar argument applies to youth activism, since an activist identity must be fitted into the demands of one's life stage. At each stage, one must determine what it means to adopt the label "activist." For this, see Thomas Maher, Morgan Johnstonbaugh, and Jennifer Earl, "'One Size Doesn't Fit All': Connecting Views of Activism with Youth Activist Identification," *Mobilization* 25, no. 1 (2020): 27–44. Recognizing this, movements may target their messages to different age cohorts. See Kelly Bergstrand and Monica Whitham, "Targeted Appeals: Online Social Movement Frame Packaging and Tactics Customized for Youth," *Social Movement Studies*, in press.

40. Natalia Ruiz-Junco, "'Losing Neutrality in Your Everyday Life': Framing Experience and Activist Identity Construction in the Spanish Environmental Movement," *Journal of Contemporary Ethnography* 40 (2011): 718, 724.

41. David Snow and Doug McAdam, "Identity Work Processes in the Context of Social Movements: Clarifying the Identity/Movement Nexus," in *Self, Identity, and Social Movements*, ed. Sheldon Stryker, Timothy Owens, and Robert White, 41–67 (Minneapolis: University of Minnesota Press, 2000).

42. Narushima, "Gaggle of Raging Grannies," 29.

43. Marc Eaton, "The Value Activation Process: Developing and Reinforcing Activist Identities in MoveOn.org," unpublished manuscript, 2010.

44. Irene Hardill and Susan Baines, "Active Citizenship in Later Life: Older Volunteers in a Deprived Community in England," *Professional Geographer* 61, no. 1 (2009): 36–45.

45. Nancy Morrow-Howell, "Volunteering in Later Life: Research Frontiers," *Journal of Gerontology: Social Sciences* 65B, no. 4 (2010): 461.

46. Amanda Moore McBride, "Civic Engagement, Older Adults, and Inclusion," *Generations* 30, no. 4 (2006–7): 66–71.

47. Geri Adler, Jennifer Schwartz, and Michael Kuskowski, "An Exploratory Study of Older Adults' Participation in Civic Action," *Clinical Gerontologist* 31, no. 2 (2007): 65–75.

48. Foster-Bey et al., "Volunteering in Later Life," 467.

49. Nancy Morrow-Howell, Jim Hinterlong, Philip Rosario, and Fengyan Tan, "Effects of Volunteering on the Well-Being of Older Adults," *Journal of Gerontology: Social Sciences* 58B (2003):S137.

50. Phyllis Moen, Donna Dempster-McClain, and Robin Williams Jr., "Successful Aging: A Life-Course Perspective on Women's Multiple Roles and Health," *American Journal of Sociology* 97, no. 6 (1992): 1612–38.

51. Morrow-Howell, "Volunteering in Later Life," 464.

52. Fengyan Tan, "Late-Life Volunteering and Trajectories of Physical Health," *Journal of Applied Gerontology* 28, no. 4 (2009): 524.

53. Peggy Thoits and Lyndi Hewitt, "Volunteer Work and Well-Being," *Journal of Health and Social Behavior* 42, no. 2 (2001): 115–31; Nancy Morrow-Howell, "Volunteering in Later Life: Research Frontiers," *Journal of Gerontology: Social Sciences* 65B, no. 4 (2010): 464.

54. Morrow-Howell, "Volunteering in Later Life," 462; Fengyan Tang, "What Resources Are Needed for Volunteerism? A Life Course Perspective," *Journal of Applied Gerontology* 25, no. 5 (2006): 375–90; John Wilson and Marc Musick, "Who Cares? Toward an Integrated Theory of Volunteer Work," *American Sociological Review* 62 (1997): 694–713.

55. Morrow-Howell, "Volunteering in Later Life," 465.

56. Jack Whalen and Richard Flacks, *Beyond the Barricades: The Sixties Generation Grows Up* (Philadelphia: Temple University Press, 1989).

57. James Jasper, *Getting Your Way: Strategic Dilemmas in the Real World* (Chicago: University of Chicago Press, 2006).

58. Sanjek, *Gray Panthers*, 5.

59. Ruth Braunstein, *Prophets and Patriots*.

60. Kyoung-Hee Yu, "Re-conceptualizing Member Participation: Formal Activist Careers in Unions," *Work, Employment, and Society* 28, no. 1 (2014): 58–77.

61. Doug McAdam, "The Biographical Consequences of Activism." *American Sociological Review* 54 (1989): 744–60.

62. Doug McAdam, "Recruitment to High-Risk Activism: The Case of Freedom Summer," *American Journal of Sociology* 92 (1986): 64–90.

63. Alice Goffman, "Go to More Parties? Social Occasions as Home to Unexpected Turning Points in Life Trajectories," *Social Psychology Quarterly* 82, no. 1 (2019): 51–74.

Chapter Three

1. Charles Tilly, *The Contentious French: Four Centuries of Popular Struggle* (Cambridge, MA: Harvard University Press, 1989); Charles Tilly, *The Politics of Collective Violence* (Cambridge: Cambridge University Press, 2003).

2. Sharon Erickson Nepstad, *Religion and War Resistance in the Plowshares Movement* (New York: Cambridge University Press, 2008), 59.

3. William Gamson, Bruce Fireman, and Steven Rytina, *Encounters with Unjust Authority* (Homewood, IL: Dorsey Press, 1982), 59.

4. Sidney Tarrow. *Power in Movement: Social Movements and Contentious Politics* (New York: Cambridge University Press, 1998).

5. William Westermeyer, *Back to America: Identity, Political Culture, and the Tea Party Movement* (Lincoln: University of Nebraska Press, 2019), 61.

6. Jeffrey Stout, *Blessed Are the Organized: Grassroots Democracy in America* (Princeton, NJ: Princeton University Press, 2010), 121.

7. Westermeyer, *Back to America*, 115.

8. Dorothy Holland and Jean Lave, *History in Person: Enduring Struggles, Contentious Practice, Intimate Identities* (Santa Fe, NM: SAR Press, 2001).

9. Dorothy Holland, Donald Nonini, Catherine Lutz, Lesley Bartlett, Marla Frederick-McGlathery, Thaddeus Guldbrandsen, and Enrique Murillo Jr., *Local Democracy Under Siege: Activism, Public Interests, and Private Politics* (New York: New York University Press, 2007), 224.

10. Gregory F. Augustine Pierce, "Publisher's Note," in *The Body Trumps the Brain*, ed. Edward Chambers, 3–5 (Skokie, IL: Acta Publications, 2008), 4.

11. Kim Bobo, Jackie Kendall, and Steve Max, *Organizing for Social Change: Midwest Academy Manual for Activists*, 4th ed. (Santa Ana, CA: Forum Press, 2010), 117–25.

12. Jane Mansbridge and Aldon Morris, eds., *Oppositional Consciousness: The Subjective Roots of Social Protest* (Chicago: University of Chicago Press, 2001).

13. Sanford Horwitt, *Let Them Call Me Rebel: Saul Alinsky—His Life and Legacy* (New York: Vintage, 1992), 548.

14. Benjamin Dulchin, "How a Brooklyn Neighborhood Fought the Free Market, and Won (a Little)," *Race, Poverty and the Environment* 9, no. 1 (2002): 17.

15. William Gamson, *Power and Discontent* (Homewood, IL: Dorsey Press, 1968).

16. My research ended in 2018, before the COVID-19 pandemic struck and CST activities moved to Zoom. One wonders if online meetings will continue after the pandemic recedes.

17. The Brooklyn antigentrification group Fifth Avenue Committee established a Displacement-Free Zone in which they were attempting to prevent the eviction of longtime residents, particularly senior citizens whose stories would inspire sympathy. To make their point, "we held a Valentine's Day theme demonstration in front of a landlord's store with all the protesters dressed in angel costumes, handing out Hershey's Kisses along with the boycott leaflets." Dulchin, "How a Brooklyn Neighborhood Fought the Free Market," 17.

18. Michael Gecan, *Going Public: An Organizer's Guide to Citizen Action* (New York: Anchor, 2008), 45.

19. Like many American cities, Chicago is experiencing considerable gentrification, limiting the options for affordable and safe housing. As public housing high-rises have been demolished, subsidized units have been built elsewhere, but often without considering the needs of seniors in those units. The Senior Housing Bill of Rights attempted to focus attention on the safety and health needs of older residents. With a more progressive city government, these issues have been supported rhetorically, but problems remain, particularly given the isolation caused by the pandemic.

20. Donileen Loseke, *Thinking about Social Problems* 2nd ed. (New Brunswick, NJ: Transaction Books, 2003).

21. Stout, *Blessed Are the Organized*, 45–46.

22. Variables that reflect power include money, mobilizing voters, and the ability to disrupt (James Jasper, personal communication, 2021).

23. J. L. Johnson, "'Meet Them Where They Are': Attentional Processes in Social Movement Listening," *Symbolic Interaction* 44, no. 4 (2021): 728–47.

24. Jonathan Wynn, "On the Sociology of Occasions," *Sociological Theory* 34, 3 (2016): 276–86.

25. Robert Dingwall, "'Atrocity Stories' and Professional Relationships," *Sociology of Work and Occupations* 4 (1977): 371–96.

26. Ruth Braunstein, *Prophets and Patriots: Faith in Democracy across the Political Divide* (Berkeley: University of California Press, 2017).

27. Perhaps my presence as an outsider contributed to this, but, given my lengthy observations, this seemed unlikely after the first few months.

28. Daniel Biss was my state senator, although we had not previously met.

29. At a bank protest, one sympathetic officer commented with a smile, "First Amendment rights. That's what's so great about America" (field notes).

30. Saul Alinsky, *Rules for Radicals: A Pragmatic Primer for Realistic Radicals* (New York: Vintage, 1971), 195; David Walls, *Community Organizing* (Cambridge: Polity, 2015), 76.

31. J. Craig Jenkins and Michael Wallace, "The Generalized Action Potential of Protest Movements: The New Class, Social Trends, and Political Exclusion Explanations," *Sociological Forum* 11, no. 2 (1996): 183–207.

32. Erving Goffman, *Interaction Ritual: Essays on Face-to-Face Behavior* (New York: Pantheon Books, 1967).

33. Johnson, "'Meet Them Where They Are.'"

34. Steven Barkan, "Strategic, Tactical and Organizational Dilemmas of the Protest Movement against Nuclear Power," *Social Problems* 27, no. 1 (1979): 19–37.

35. Rather than spreading analysis of civil disobedience throughout the chapter, some of this discussion includes other instances of civil disobedience during my research.

36. For another example of role-playing before potential arrest (or violence), see Doug McAdam, *Freedom Summer* (New York: Oxford University Press, 1988).

37. Iddo Tavory and Gary Alan Fine, "Disruption and the Theory of the Interaction Order," *Theory and Society* 49 (2020): 365–85.

Chapter Four

1. Eeva Luhtakallio, *Practicing Democracy: Local Activism and Politics in France and Finland* (New York: Palgrave Macmillan, 2012).

2. Paul Ricoeur, *Time and Narrative* (Chicago: University of Chicago Press, 1984).

3. Iddo Tavory and Nina Eliasoph, "Coordinating Futures: Toward a Theory of Anticipation," *American Journal of Sociology* 118 (2013): 908–42.

4. Francesca Polletta, *It Was Like a Fever: Storytelling in Protest and Politics* (Chicago: University of Chicago Press, 2006).

5. Sujatha Fernandes, *Curated Stories: The Uses and Misuses of Storytelling* (New York: Oxford University Press, 2017).

6. Kathleen Blee, *Democracy in the Making: How Activist Groups Form* (New York: Oxford University Press, 2012).

7. William Sewell, "Historical Events as Transformations of Structures: Inventing Revolution at the Bastille," *Theory and Society* 25 (1996): 841–81.

8. Robin Wagner-Pacifici, *What Is an Event?* (Chicago: University of Chicago Press, 2017).

9. Donatella Della Porta, "Eventful Protest, Global Conflicts," *Distinktion: Journal of Social Theory* 9 (2008): 27–56.

10. Michael Farrell, *Collaborative Circles: Friendship Dynamics and Creative Work* (Chicago: University of Chicago Press, 2001); John Parker and Edward Hackett, "Hot Spots and Hot Moments in Scientific Collaborations and Social Movements," *American Sociological Review* 77 (2012): 21—44.

11. Sheldon Stryker, Timothy Owens, and Robert White, eds., *Self, Identity, and Social Movements* (Minneapolis: University of Minnesota Press, 2000); Cristina Fominaya, "Collective Identity in Social Movements: Central Concepts and Debates," *Sociology Compass* 4 (2010): 393–404.

12. Eviatar Zerubavel, *Time Maps: Collective Memory and the Social Shape of the Past* (Chicago: University of Chicago Press, 2003); Andrew Abbott, *Time Matters: On Theory and Method* (Chicago: University of Chicago Press, 2001).

13. Michael Flaherty, *A Watched Pot: How We Experience Time* (New York: NYU Press, 1999).

14. Doug McAdam and William Sewell Jr., "It's About Time: Temporality in the Study of Social Movements and Revolutions," in *Silence and Voice in the Study of Contentious Politics*, ed. Ronald Aminzade, Jack Goldstone, Doug McAdam, Elizabeth Perry, William Sewell Jr., Sidney Tarrow, and Charles Tilly, 89–125 (Cambridge: Cambridge University Press, 2001).

15. Michael Flaherty and Gary Alan Fine, "Present, Past and Future: Conjugating Mead's Perspective of Time," *Time and Society* 10 (2001): 147–61; Zerubavel, *Time Maps*; Tavory and Eliasoph, "Coordinating Futures."

16. David Snow and Robert Bedford, "Master Frames and Cycles of Protest," in *Frontiers in Social Movement Theory,* ed. Aldon Morris and Carol Mueller, 133–55 (New Haven, CT: Yale University Press, 1992); Francesca Polletta and James Jasper, "Collective Memory and Social Movements," *Annual Review of Sociology* 27 (2001): 283–305.

17. Jeffrey Olick and Joyce Robbins, "Social Memory Studies: From 'Collective Memory' to the Historical Sociology of Mnemonic Practices," *Annual Review of Sociology* 24 (1998): 105–40.

18. Lorenzo Zamponi, "Collective Memory and Social Movements," in *Wiley-Blackwell Encyclopedia of Social and Political Movements*, ed. David Snow, Donatella Della Porta, Bert Klandermans, and Doug McAdam, 225–29 (New York: Wiley, 2013).

19. Barry Schwartz, *Abraham Lincoln and the Forge of National Memory* (Chicago: University of Chicago Press, 2000), 19.

20. Zamponi, "Collective Memory and Social Movements."

21. Randall Collins, *Interaction Ritual Chains* (Princeton, NJ: Princeton University Press, 2004).

22. Gary Alan Fine and Randy Stoecker, "Can the Circle Be Unbroken? Small Groups and Social Movements," *Advances in Group Process* 2 (1985): 1–28.

23. Tom McFeat, *Small-Group Cultures* (New York: Pergamon, 1974).

24. Ann Swidler, "Culture in Action: Symbols and Strategies," *American Sociological Review* 51 (1986): 273–86.

25. Tavory and Eliasoph, *Coordinating Futures*.

26. Luke Yates, "Rethinking Prefiguration: Alternatives, Micropolitics and Goals in Social Movements," *Social Movement Studies* 14 (2015): 1–21.

27. Snow and Benford, "Master Frames and Cycles of Protest."

28. Natalia Ruiz-Junco, "'Losing Neutrality in Your Everyday Life': Framing Experience and Activist Identity Construction in the Spanish Environmental Movement," *Journal of Contemporary Ethnography* 40 (2011): 713–33.

29. Elizabeth Pleck, *Celebrating the Family: Ethnicity, Consumer Culture, and Family Rituals* (Cambridge, MA: Harvard University Press, 2000).

30. Jaber Gubrium, "Narrative Events and Biographical Construction in Old Age," in *Storying Later Life: Issues, Investigations, and Interventions in Narrative Gerontology*, ed. Gary Kenyon, Ernst Bohlmeijer, and William Randall, 39–50 (New York: Oxford University Press, 2011).

31. Patricia Ewick and Marc Steinberg, *Beyond Betrayal: The Priest Sex Abuse Crisis, the Voice of the Faithful, and the Process of Collective Identity* (Chicago: University of Chicago Press, 2019), 40.

32. Jeffrey Olick, "Collective Memory: The Two Cultures," *Sociological Theory* 17, no. 3 (1999): 333–48.

33. Todd Nicholas Fuist, "Towards a Sociology of Imagination," *Theory and Society* 50 (2021): 359.

34. Fuist, "Towards a Sociology of Imagination," 359.

35. Tavory and Eliasoph, "Coordinating Futures."

36. Gary Alan Fine, *Authors of the Storm: Meteorologists and the Culture of Prediction* (Chicago: University of Chicago Press, 2007).

37. Ann Mische, *Partisan Publics: Communication and Contention across Brazilian Youth Activist Networks* (Princeton, NJ: Princeton University Press, 2009).

38. Clifford Geertz, *The Interpretation of Cultures* (New York: Basic Books, 1973).

39. Olick and Robbins, "Collective Memory."

40. The death of George Floyd at the hands of the police in Minneapolis and the spread of the novel coronavirus occurred after I finished collecting data, but they served in similar ways in connecting immediate trauma to historical events.

41. Francesca Polletta, *Freedom Is an Endless Meeting: Democracy in American Social Movements* (Chicago: University of Chicago Press, 2002); Joseph Davis, "Narrative and Social Movements: The Power of Stories," in *Stories of Change: Narrative and Social Movements*, ed. Joseph Davis, 3–29 (Albany: SUNY Press, 2002).

42. Mark Warren, *Fire in the Heart: How White Activists Embrace Racial Justice* (New York: Oxford University Press, 2010).

43. Alice Goffman, "Go to More Parties? Social Occasions as Home to Unexpected Turning Points in Life Trajectories," *Social Psychology Quarterly* 82, no. 1 (2019): 51–74.

44. Fred Davis, *Yearning for Yesterday: A Sociology of Nostalgia* (New York: Free Press, 1979).

45. Francesca Polletta, "Plotting Protest: Mobilizing Stories in the 1960 Student Sit-Ins," in *Stories of Change: Narrative and Social Movements*, ed. Joseph Davis, 31–51 (Albany: SUNY Press, 2002).

46. Gary Alan Fine, "Public Narration and Group Culture: Discerning Discourse in Social Movements," in *Social Movements and Culture*, ed. Hank Johnston and Bert Klandermans, 127–43 (Minneapolis: University of Minnesota Press, 1995); Davis, *Yearning for Yesterday*.

47. Ruth Braunstein, *Prophets and Patriots: Faith in Democracy across the Political Divide* (Berkeley: University of California Press, 2017), 72.

48. Polletta, *Freedom*.

49. Scott Hunt and Robert Benford, "Identity Talk in the Peace and Justice Movement,"

Journal of Contemporary Ethnography 22, no. 4 (1994): 488–517; Ruiz-Junco, "'Losing Neutrality in Your Everyday Life,'" 716.

50. Sandra Stahl, *Literary Folkloristics and the Personal Narrative* (Bloomington: Indiana University Press, 1989).

51. Fernandes, *Curated Stories*, 3. See also Jonah Sachs, *Winning the Story Wars* (Cambridge, MA: Harvard Business Review Press, 2012).

52. Orrin Klapp, *Inflation of Symbols: Loss of Values in American Culture* (New York: Routledge, 1991).

53. Nina Eliasoph, *Avoiding Politics: How Americans Produce Apathy in Everyday Life* (New York: Cambridge University Press, 1998).

54. Elizabeth Bennett, Alissa Cordner, Peter Taylor Klein, Stephanie Savell, and Gianpaolo Baiocchi, "Disavowing Politics: Civic Engagement in an Era of Political Skepticism," *American Journal of Sociology* 114 (2013): 518–48; Paul Lichterman, *The Search for Political Community: American Activists Reinventing Community* (New York: Cambridge University Press, 2010).

55. Doug McAdam, *Freedom Summer* (New York: Oxford University Press, 1988).

56. Alberto Melucci, *Nomads of the Present: Social Movements and Individual Needs in Contemporary Society* (Philadelphia: Temple University Press, 1989).

57. C. Wright Mills, *The Sociological Imagination* (New York: Oxford University Press, 1959).

58. Ewick and Steinberg, *Beyond Betrayal*.

59. Gary Alan Fine, "The Storied Group: Social Movements as Bundles of Narratives," in *Stories of Change: Narrative and Social Movements*, ed. Joseph Davis, 229–45 (Albany: SUNY Press, 2002); Polletta, *It Was Like a Fever*.

60. Joanne Martin, *Culture in Organizations: Three Perspectives* (New York: Oxford University Press, 1992).

61. Marshall Ganz, *Why David Sometimes Wins: Leadership, Organization, and Strategy in the California Farm Workers Movement* (New York: Oxford University Press, 2009).

62. Francesca Polletta, *Inventing Ties That Bind: Imagined Relationships in Moral and Political Life* (Chicago: University of Chicago Press, 2020), 119.

63. Joel Best, *Damned Lies and Statistics: Untangling Numbers from the Media, Politicians, and Activists* (Berkeley: University of California Press, 2001).

64. Hayden White, *The Content of the Form* (Baltimore: Johns Hopkins University Press, 1990).

65. Polletta, *Inventing the Ties That Bind*, 132–36.

66. Francesca Polletta, Tania DoCarmo, Kelly Marie Ward, and Jessica Callahan, "Personal Storytelling in Professionalized Social Movements," *Mobilization* 26, no. 1 (2021): 65–86.

67. Candace Clark, "Sympathy Biography and Sympathy Margin," *American Journal of Sociology* 93, no. 2 (1987): 290–321.

68. Bess Rothenberg, "Movement Advocates as Battered Women's Storytellers: From Varied Experiences, One Message," in *Stories of Change: Narrative and Social Movements*, ed. Joseph Davis, 203–25 (Albany: SUNY Press, 2002).

69. Todd Gitlin, *The Whole World Is Watching: Mass Media in the Making and Unmaking of the New Left* (Berkeley: University of California Press, 1980).

70. William Gamson and David Meyer, "Framing Political Opportunity," in *Comparative Perspectives in Social Movements: Political Opportunities, Mobilizing Structures, and Cultural Framings*, ed. Doug McAdam, John McCarthy, and Mayer Zald, 275–90 (New York: Cambridge University Press, 1996), 288.

71. Polletta, *Inventing the Ties That Bind*; White, *Content of the Form*.

72. James Jasper, "The Doors That Culture Opened: Parallels between Social Movement Studies and Social Psychology," *Group Processes and Intergroup Relations* 20 (2017): 285-302.

73. Mills, *Sociological Imagination*.

Chapter Five

1. Jeffrey Stout, *Blessed Are the Organized: Grassroots Democracy in America* (Princeton, NJ: Princeton University Press, 2010), 137.

2. David Walls, *Community Organizing* (Cambridge: Polity, 2015), 55.

3. James Jasper, "The Doors That Culture Opened: Parallels between Social Movement Studies and Social Psychology," *Group Process and Intergroup Relations* 20, no. 2 (2017): 295.

4. Dan Ryan, *Organizations Past: Communities of Organizations as Settings for Change* (Philadelphia: Temple University Press, 2015).

5. Donald Reitzes and Dietrich Reitzes, "Metro Seniors in Action: A Case Study of a City-wide Senior Organization," *Gerontologist* 31, no. 2 (1992): 256-62.

6. During part of the research the organization employed an African American woman and a South Asian woman.

7. Christoph Haug, "Organizing Spaces: Meeting Arenas as a Social Movement Infrastructure between Organization, Network, and Institution," *Organization Studies* 34, no. 5-6 (2013): 705-32; Helen Schwartzman, *The Meeting: Gatherings in Organizations and Communities* (New York: Plenum Press, 1989).

8. At no point in the research did the organization serve alcoholic beverages for members.

9. Music has often been found to be central to the bonding found in social movements. See Ron Eyerman and Andrew Jamison, *Music and Social Movements: Mobilizing Traditions in the Twentieth Century* (New York: Cambridge University Press, 1998).

10. Joshua Basseches, "Changing the World One Agenda Item at a Time: How a National Network of Political Organizations Reconciles Idealism with Pragmatism," unpublished manuscript, 23.

11. The staff meetings did not reveal such reverence for timing. Several meetings started fifteen minutes late, beginning when the staff had a break in their work. The meetings would end when all matters had been discussed.

12. Adolf A. Berle Jr. and Gardiner Means, *The Modern Corporation and Private Property* (New York: Macmillan, 1932).

13. Kathleen Blee, *Democracy in the Making: How Activist Groups Form* (New York: Oxford University Press, 2012).

14. Ece Kaynak and Stephen Barley, "Shaping the Political Environment: An Ethnography of Public Affairs Professionals at Work," *Work and Occupations* 46 (2019): 265-306.

15. Rachel Leonor Ramirez, "The Community Organizing Model of Organizational Leadership: A Value and Power-Driven Model of Leadership" (MA thesis, Public Policy and Administration, Northwestern University, 2016), 10.

16. She has since retired, shortly after turning sixty.

17. Steve Burghardt, *The Other Side of Organizing: Resolving the Personal Dilemmas and Political Demands of Daily Practice* (Cambridge, MA: Schenkman Books, 1982).

18. Fortunately, the CST had positive connections with local members of this granting agency, and in time the dispute was resolved. However, relations between Chicago Seniors and granters were essential to organizational survival.

19. Even so, I was not invited to the staff retreat and potluck at a staffer's home.

20. Stout, *Blessed Are the Organized*, 94.

21. Stout, *Blessed Are the Organized*, 2–3.

22. Betsy Leondar-Wright, *Missing Class: Strengthening Social Movement Groups by Seeing Class Cultures* (Ithaca, NY: ILR Press, 2014).

23. Nicholas Von Hoffman, *Radical: A Portrait of Saul Alinsky* (New York: Nation Books, 2010), 57.

24. See Andrew Szilagyi Jr. and David Schweiger, "Matching Managers to Strategies: A Review and Suggested Framework," *Academy of Management Review* 9, no. 4 (1984): 626–37.

25. Lauren Rivera, *Pedigree: How Elite Students Get Elite Jobs* (Princeton, NJ: Princeton University Press, 2016).

26. Religious figures, particularly Catholic nuns, were desired, consistent with the Alinsky desire to align with churches.

27. Leondar-Wright, *Missing Class*.

28. Board members could serve two consecutive two-year terms, then they had to take a break before being invited back to the board. This was an attempt to include a diversity of talents and broaden the base of participation.

29. Gary Alan Fine, *Players and Pawns: How Chess Builds Community and Culture* (Chicago: University of Chicago Press, 2015).

30. This was Lauren's memory; Jane, the executive director, did not recall the meeting.

31. John McCarthy and Mayer Zald, "Resource Mobilization and Social Movements: A Partial Theory," *American Journal of Sociology* 82, no. 6 (1977): 1212–41.

Chapter Six

1. Barbara Myerhoff, *Number Our Days: A Triumph of Continuity and Culture among Jewish Old People in an Urban Ghetto* (New York: Dutton, 1979).

2. Andrea Petriwskyj, Jeni Warburton, Jo-Anne Everingham, and Michael Cuthill, "Diversity and Inclusion in Local Governance: An Australian Study of Seniors' Participation," *Journal of Aging Studies* 26 (2012): 182–91.

3. Victor Ray, "A Theory of Racialized Organizations," *American Sociological Review* 84, no. 1 (2019): 26–53.

4. Jane Tate suggested that one-third of the participants at the Senior Power Assembly were from the West Side, but if this was so, most did not attend other events.

5. Grace Yukich, Brad Fulton, and Richard Wood, "Representative Group Styles: How Ally Immigrant Rights Organizations Promote Immigrant Involvement," *Social Problems* 67 (2020): 488–506.

6. James Jasper, *Getting Your Way: Strategic Dilemmas in the Real World* (Chicago: University of Chicago Press, 2006).

7. Large meetings, such as the Senior Power Assembly, were often held in churches of various (liberal) denominations and in synagogues. Some Catholic churches were known for their progressive politics as well.

8. At one meeting with about fifty in attendance, only three raised their hands when asked if anyone was on Medicaid (field notes).

9. Roger Sanjek, *Gray Panthers* (Philadelphia: University of Pennsylvania Press, 2009), 52.

10. Betsy Leondar-Wright, *Missing Class: Strengthening Social Movement Groups by Seeing Class Cultures* (Ithaca, NY: ILR Press, 2014).

11. Mark Warren, *Fire in the Heart: How White Activists Embrace Racial Justice* (New York: Oxford University Press, 2010).

12. This question of internal/external focus is a form of the "Janus dilemma" described by Jasper, *Getting Your Way*.

13. Mikaila Arthur, "Social Movements in Organizations," *Sociology Compass* 2, no. 3 (2008): 1014—30.

14. This sensitivity was evident when the White leader of the team spoke of a Black member who was leaving. He commented, "Lena brought a lot to us in her time with us." Sheila, mishearing "time," asked, "Did you say her kind?" (field notes).

15. This is not geographically exact, since there are mixed-race neighborhoods on the South Side (Hyde Park, Bridgeport) and on the North Side (Uptown, Rogers Park), but Chicagoans use North, West, and South Side as easy racial designations.

16. There was little interest in reaching out to the Asian community. One day in a phone bank, a White member became frustrated with the number of Asians on his call list who could not speak English. He joked, "There are so many Chings and Changs. We need someone who can speak Chinese." I was not aware of any Asian member of the organization.

17. Yukich, Fulton, and Wood, "Representative Group Styles."

18. Possibly the speaker is referring to mixed-race members or perhaps to Latinx members.

19. Finding out the "truth" of the narrative was impossible, especially given my commitment to anonymity of interviews.

20. One might find that this grievance was itself a form of unacknowledged privilege, reaffirmed by resentment. Those who felt aggrieved might argue that "race-blind" choices would provide them with more opportunities.

21. Personal communication, James Jasper, 2021.

22. William Westermeyer, *Back to America: Identity, Political Culture, and the Tea Party Movement* (Lincoln: University of Nebraska Press, 2019).

23. J. Diane Garner, "Feminism and Feminist Gerontology," in *Fundamentals of Feminist Gerontology*, ed. J. Diane Garner, 3–12 (New York: Haworth Press, 1999); Linda Caissie, "The Raging Grannies: Narrative Construction of Gender and Aging," in *Storying Later Life: Issues, Investigations, and Interventions in Narrative Gerontology*, ed. Gary Kenyon, Ernst Bohlmeijer, and William Randall, 126–42 (New York: Oxford University Press, 2013), 129.

24. Sanjek, *Gray Panthers*, 108.

25. Alison Acker and Betty Brightwell, *Off Our Rockers and into Trouble: The Raging Grannies* (Victoria, BC: Touchwood Books, 2004), 2.

26. Caissie, *Raging Grannies*, 135.

27. Kyle Dodson, "Gendered Activism: A Cross-National View on Gender Differences in Protest Activity," *Social Currents* 2, no. 4 (2015): 377–92.

28. In contrast to more culturally radical older women, there was no discussion of women as "witches" or "crones." None of the women revealed a Wiccan sensibility. The politics may have been progressive, but the cultural commitments were not.

29. Lee Ann Banaszak, "Women's Movements and Women in Movements: Influencing American Democracy from the 'Outside'?" in *Political Women and American Democracy*, ed. Christina Wolbrecht, Karen Beckwith, and Lisa Baldez, 79–95 (New York: Cambridge University Press, 2008), 87.

30. Sherryl Kleinman, "Why Sexist Language Matters," *Qualitative Sociology* 25, no. 2 (2002): 299–304.

31. Denise's tenure with the organization was not long, perhaps in part—but not entirely—because of the issue of gender pronouns. More relevant was that their strongest concerns were not about senior issues, and they never received the full support of senior leaders.

32. Deborah Gould, *Moving Politics: Emotion and ACT UP's Fight against AIDS* (Chicago: University of Chicago Press, 2009), 192-96.

33. Given that Denise had applied for a job working with seniors in community organizing, I wondered whether they might have tolerated being referred to as "she" in the workplace. In their presence one would typically use not the third-person pronoun but rather the conventional second-person "you."

34. By 2020 the CST had hired a staffer who used the "they" pronoun, which may have contributed to the continuation of announcing pronouns.

35. Jane Tate reported that she had talked with members about this pronoun issue; she said some members suggested holding a training session and having members introduce themselves with their preferred pronouns (personal communication, 2021). Although this is possible and some members did support the exercise, I heard no member take credit for the ritual. Perhaps the exercise created a safety zone, or perhaps it emphasized that Denise was different. Adjustments were made over time, as members were not forced to participate even though there was social pressure to do so.

36. Eduardo Bonilla-Silva, *Racism without Racists: Color-Blind Racism and the Persistence of Racial Inequality in America,* 5th ed. (Lanham, MD: Rowman and Littlefield, 2018).

Chapter Seven

1. This is an extensive literature, but see, for example, Doug McAdam, Sidney Tarrow, and Charles Tilly, *Dynamics of Contention* (Cambridge: Cambridge University Press, 2001).

2. Charles Kurzman, "Structural Opportunity and Perceived Opportunity in Social-Movement Theory," *American Sociological Review* 61 (1996): 151-70.

3. William Gamson and David Meyer, "Framing Political Opportunity," in *Comparative Perspectives in Social Movements: Political Opportunities, Mobilizing Structures, and Cultural Framings*, ed. Doug McAdam, John McCarthy, and Mayer Zald, 275-90 (New York: Cambridge University Press, 1996), 275.

4. Before my research, the CST was involved in a movement for nursing home reform that was successful enough that it was no longer an issue during my observation.

5. Benjamin Dulchin, "How a Brooklyn Neighborhood Fought the Free Market, and Won (a Little)," *Race, Poverty and the Environment* 9, no. 1 (2002): 17.

6. I thank Natalia Ruiz-Junco for this formulation.

7. Paul DiMaggio and Walter Powell, "The Iron Cage Revisited: Institutional Isomorphism and Collective Rationality in Organizational Fields," *American Sociological Review* 48, no. 2 (1983): 147-60.

8. James Jasper speaks of this as the "basket dilemma." See James Jasper, *Getting Your Way: Strategic Dilemmas in the Real World* (Chicago: University of Chicago Press, 2006).

9. Hatred is bipartisan, and there was intense distaste for both Richard Nixon and Bill Clinton. See Gary Alan Fine and Emily Eisenberg, "Tricky Dick and Slick Willie: Despised Presidents and Generational Imprinting," *American Behavioral Scientist* 46 (2002): 553-65.

10. Erving Goffman, *Asylums: Essays on the Social Situation of Mental Patients and Other Inmates* (Garden City, NY: Anchor, 1961).

11. Dan Ryan, *Organizations Past: Communities of Organizations as Settings for Change* (Philadelphia: Temple University Press, 2015).

12. Paul Lichterman, *How Civic Action Works: Fighting for Housing in Los Angeles* (Princeton, NJ: Princeton University Press, 2021).

13. Lichterman, *How Civic Action Works*.

14. Jeffrey Stout, *Blessed Are the Organized: Grassroots Democracy in America* (Princeton, NJ: Princeton University Press, 2010), 132.

15. Grace Yukich, Brad Fulton, and Richard Wood, "Representative Group Styles: How Ally Immigrant Rights Organizations Promote Immigrant Involvement," *Social Problems* 67, no. 3 (2020): 488–506.

16. A second progressive action coalition exists in Chicago, United Working Families, but this is not a group the CST participated with. That group had a stronger base on Chicago's West Side. I was told that People's Action and United Working Families are not in alliance, and that they have "different styles."

17. Some local neighborhoods have their own activist groups, such as KOCO, the Kenwood Oakwood Community Organization.

18. Lichterman, *How Civic Action Works*.

19. Lichterman, *How Civic Action Works*, 63.

20. Jeff Goodwin and James Jasper, "Emotions and Social Movements," in *Handbook of the Sociology of Emotions*, ed. Jan Stets and Jonathan Turner, 611–35 (New York: Springer, 2006).

21. C. Wright Mills, *The Sociological Imagination* (New York: Oxford University Press, 1959).

Chapter Eight

1. David Kahane, *Rules for Radical Conservatives: Beating the Left at Its Own Game to Take Back America* (New York: Ballantine, 2010).

2. Gary Alan Fine, *Tiny Publics: Civil Society, Group Cultures, and the Power of Local Commitments* (Chicago: University of Chicago Press, 2021).

3. Corey Abramson, *The End Game: How Inequality Shapes Our Final Years* (Cambridge, MA: Harvard University Press, 2015).

4. Erving Goffman, "The Interaction Order," *American Sociological Review* 48 (1983): 1–17.

5. Ann Swidler, "Culture in Action: Symbols and Strategies," *American Sociological Review* 51 (1986): 273–86.

6. Kathleen Blee, *Democracy in the Making: How Activist Groups Form* (New York: Oxford University Press, 2012).